S0-DQV-013

PEMDAS

Parentheses first, then **Exponents**, then **Multiplication** and **Division** (left to right), and lastly **Addition** and **Subtraction** (left to right).

Median and Mode

The median is the **value that falls in the middle of the set**.

The mode is the **value that appears most often**.

Counting the Possibilities

If there are **m ways** one event can happen and **n ways** a second event can happen, then there are **$m \times n$ ways** for the 2 events to happen.

ESSENTIAL FORMULAS

Average Rate Formula

Average A per B $= \dfrac{\text{Total } A}{\text{Total } B}$

Average Speed $= \dfrac{\text{Total distance}}{\text{Total time}}$

Average Formula

Average $= \dfrac{\text{Sum of the terms}}{\text{Number of terms}}$

Probability Formula

Probability $= \dfrac{\text{Favorable Outcomes}}{\text{Total Possible Outcomes}}$

Percent Formula

Part $=$ Percent $\times$ Whole

Multiplying and Dividing Powers

To multiply powers with the same base, **add the exponents and keep the same base**.

To divide powers with the same base, **subtract the exponents and keep the same base**.

Raising Powers to Powers

To raise a power to a power, **multiply the exponents**.

Negative Exponent and Rational Exponent

$x^{-n} = \dfrac{1}{x^n}$ $x^{\frac{1}{n}} = \sqrt[n]{x}$

FUNCTIONS

Direct and Inverse Variation

In direct variation, $y = kx$, where k is a nonzero constant. In inverse variation, $xy = k$, where k is a constant.

Domain and Range of a Function

The domain of a function is the set of values for which the function is defined.

Determining Absolute Value

The absolute value of a number is the distance of the number from zero on the number line.

Multiplying Binomials—FOIL

To multiply binomials, use **FOIL**. First multiply the **F**irst terms. Next the **O**uter terms. Then the **I**nner terms. And finally the **L**ast terms. Then add and combine like terms.

Factoring the Difference of Squares

$a^2 - b^2 = (a - b)(a + b)$

Factoring the Square of a Binomial

$a^2 + 2ab + b^2 = (a + b)^2$ $a^2 - 2ab + b^2 = (a - b)^2$

Quadratic Equation

$ax^2 + bx + c = 0$

Solving an Inequality

When you **multiply or divide both sides by a negative number**, you must **reverse the sign**.

Finding the Distance Between Two Points

$d = \sqrt{(x_1 - x_2)^2 + (y_1 - y_2)^2}$

Using Two Points to Find the Slope

Slope $= \dfrac{\text{Change in } y}{\text{Change in } x} = \dfrac{\text{Rise}}{\text{Run}}$

Using an Equation to Find the Slope (slope-intercept)

$y = mx + b$

Finding the Midpoint

If the endpoints are (x_1, y_1) and (x_2, y_2), the midpoint is.

$\left(\dfrac{(x_1 + x_2)}{2}, \dfrac{(y_1 + y_2)}{2} \right)$

Intersecting Lines

When two lines intersect, **adjacent angles are supplementary and vertical angles are equal**.

GEOMETRY

Interior and Exterior Angles of a Triangle

The 3 angles of any triangle **add up to 180 degrees**.

The 3 exterior angles of a triangle add up to **360 degrees**.

Area of a Triangle

Area of Triangle $= \dfrac{1}{2}$(base)(height)

Pythagorean Theorem

For all right triangles: $(\text{leg}_1)^2 + (\text{leg}_2)^2 = (\text{hypotenuse})^2$

Special Right Triangles

The 3-4-5 Triangle
The 30-60-90 Triangle
The 5-12-13 Triangle
The 45-45-90 Triangle

Area of a Rectangle

Area of Rectangle $=$ length $\times$ width

Area of a Parallelogram

Area of Parallelogram $=$ base $\times$ height

Area of a Square

Area of Square $=$ (Side)^2

Interior Angles of a Polygon

The sum of the measures of the interior angles of a polygon $= (n - 2) \times 180$, where n is the number of sides.

Circumference of a Circle

Circumference $= 2\pi r$

Length of an Arc

If n is the degree measure of the arc's central angle, then the formula is:

Length of an Arc $= 1\left(\dfrac{n}{360}\right)(2\pi r)$

Area of a Circle

Area of a Circle $= \pi r^2$

Area of a Sector

If n is the degree measure of the sector's central angle, then the formula is:

Area of a Sector $= 1\left(\dfrac{n}{360}\right)(\pi r)^2$

Surface Area of a Rectangular Solid

Surface Area $= 2lw + 2wh + 2lh$

Volume of a Rectangular Solid

Volume of a Rectangular Solid $= lwh$
Volume of a Cube $= \ell 3$

Volume of a Cylinder

Volume of a Cylinder $= \pi r^2 h$

SAT Verbal Skills

Kaplan's 5-Step Method for Reading Comprehension

Step 1: Read the question stem.

Step 2: Locate the needed material.

Step 3: Predict the answer.

Step 4: Scan the answer choices.

Step 5: Select your answer.

Kaplan's 4-Step Method for Sentence Completions

Step 1: Read for clue words.

Step 2: Predict the answer.

Step 3: Select the best match.

Step 4: Read your selection in the sentence.

Kaplan's 4-Step Method for the Essay

Step 1: **T** HINK about the topic.

Step 2: **O** RGANIZE your paragraphs.

Step 3: **W** RITE your essay.

Step 4: **F** IX any mistakes.

PRINCIPLES

Reading

Principle 1: Focus on the author.

Principle 2: Don't sweat the details.

Principle 3: Read the first 1/3 closely.

Principle 4: Make a roadmap.

Principle 5: Stop to sum up.

Writing

Principle 1: Eliminate choices that distort the meaning.

Principle 2: Eliminate choices that contain internal errors.

Principle 3: Short answers are right more often than long ones.

Principle 4: If you think it might be verbose or irrelevant, it probably is.

Kaplan's 3-Step Method for Usage Questions

Step 1: Read the sentence, listening for an error.

Step 2: Identify the error, if you didn't hear it.

Step 3: Check the other choices to confirm your answer, if necessary.

Kaplan's 4-Step Method for Sentence Corrections

Step 1: Read the sentence, listening for an error.

Step 2: Identify the error, if you didn't hear it.

Step 3: Predict a correction.

Step 4: Check the choices for a match that doesn't introduce a new error.

WORD ROOT LIST

If you don't have much time to spend on vocabulary, word roots can get you through the most commonly tested SAT words. Here are some samples:

A, AN—not, without
• amoral, anarchy

AC, ACR—sharp, sour
• acute, acrid

AMBI, AMPHI—both
• ambiguous, amphibious

AMBL, AMBUL—walk
• amble, ambulatory

AUD—hear
• audio

BENE, BEN—good
• benefactor, benign

BIO—life
• biology

CARN—flesh
• carnage

CEDE, CESS—yield, go
• cessation, secede

CO, COM, CON—with, together
• cogent, compliant, consensus

CURR, CURS—run
• current, precurso

DE—down, out, apart
• debilitate, deride

DEMO, DEM—people
• democrat, demagogue

DUC, DUCT—lead
• induce, conduct

EGO—self
• egoist

EN, EM—in, into
• enter, embroil

EU—well, good
• euphemism

FAL, FALS—deceive
• infallible, false

FORE—before
• forecast

FRAG, FRAC—break
• fragment, fracture

GRAPH, GRAM—writing
• biography, grammar

GRAT—pleasing
• gratitude

HELIO, HELI—sun
• heliocentric, perihelion

HOL—whole
• holocaust

INTRA, INTR—within
• intravenous, intrinsic

JECT, JET—throw
• trajectory, jettison

JUD—judge
• judicious

LAT—side
• lateral

LING, LANG—tongue
• lingo, language

MACRO—great
• macrocosm

MAL—bad
• maladroit

MEM, MIN—remember
• memento, reminisce

MIT, MISS—send
• transmit, missive

NAU, NAV—ship, sailor
• nautical, circumnavigate

NEO—new
• neoclassical

OB—against
• obsequious

OMNI—all
• omnipotent

PAC—peace
• pacifist

PHON—sound
• phonograph

POT—drink
• potable

QUAD, QUAR, QUAT—four
• quadrant, quarantine, quaternary

QUIE—quiet
• acquiesce

RETRO—backward
• retrospective

RID, RIS—laugh
• ridiculous, derision

SED, SID—sit
• sedentary, residence

SEN—old
• senior

SYN, SYM—together
• synthesis, symbiosis

TACIT, TIC—silent
• tacit, reticent

TERM—end
• terminal

TORT—twist
• distort

TOX—poison
• toxic

UNI, UN—one
• unify, unanimous

URB—city
• urban

VAC—empty
• evacuate

VOLV, VOLUT—turn, roll
• revolve, convoluted

VOR—eat
• voracious

Kaplan's 5-Step Method for Paragraph Corrections

Step 1: Read the text for tone and overall idea.

Step 2: Read the question.

Step 3: Reread the relevant text and consider its context.

Step 4: Predict the correction.

Step 5: Check the choices for a match that doesn't add a new error.

THE 18 MOST-TESTED WRITING ERRORS

1. A pronoun must agree with its antecedent in person and number.

2. Verbs should use the simplest tense that conveys the meaning.

3. Items in a list or comparison should be in parallel form.

4. Know your idioms.

5. Know correct word choice.

6. A sentence needs a subject and verb in an independent clause.

7. Use the right transition words.

8. Modifiers should be as near as possible to the words they modify.

9. A verb must agree with its subject in person and number.

10. Don't use a clause where a phrase will do or a phrase where a word will do.

11. In comparisons, make sure items are parallel, the right things are compared, and the comparison is structured correctly.

12. Know the forms of irregular verbs.

13. Generally avoid the passive voice.

14. Avoid ambiguity.

15. Nouns in a sentence must agree.

16. Adjectives modify nouns or pronouns; adverbs modify verbs or modifiers.

17. The comparative is used to compare two items, the superlative to compare more than two.

18. The case of a pronoun is determined by its role in the sentence.

Kaplan Publishing
Published by SIMON & SCHUSTER
Rockefeller Center
1230 Avenue of the Americas
New York, NY 10010

Executive Editor: Jennifer Farthing
Project Editors: Eileen McDonnell and Charli Engelhorn
Production Manager: Michael Shevlin
Page Layout: Jan Gladish
Cover Design: Cheung Tai

Manufactured in the United States of America.
Published simultaneously in Canada.

10 9 8 7 6 5 4 3 2 1

September 2005

ISBN-13: 978-0-7432-8755-5
ISBN-10:   0-7432-8755-X

For bulk sales contact your local Borders store and ask to speak to the Corporate Sales Representative.

Test Prep and Admissions

SAT®

Diagnostic Test and Practice Questions

Second Edition

A BORDERS EXCLUSIVE

By the Staff of Kaplan Test Prep and Admissions

Simon & Schuster

NEW YORK · LONDON · SYDNEY · TORONTO

RELATED KAPLAN TITLES FOR COLLEGE-BOUND STUDENTS

SAT Critical Reading Flashcards
SAT Writing Flashcards

Table of Contents

How to Use This Book

You are planning to take the SAT, and you don't have much time. Where to begin? The first step is to assess your strengths and weaknesses, so you can focus your study time. This book helps you do just that.

Here's how to use the *SAT Diagnostic:*

STEP ONE: TAKE THE DIAGNOSTIC SAT TEST

Take the full-length practice test—timed—as a test run for the real thing. The explanations for every question are included at the end so you can understand your mistakes.

STEP TWO: IDENTIFY YOUR STRENGTHS AND WEAKNESSES

Check your answers to the diagnostic test, and note how many you got right and how many you got wrong. Look for patterns. Did Sentence Completion questions trip you up? Did you ace the Reading Comprehension questions? Try not to limit your review only to the questions you got wrong. Instead, read all the explanations, to reinforce key concepts and sharpen your skills. If necessary, go back to the questions to better understand the material and concepts on which you will be tested.

STEP THREE: CREATE A CUSTOMIZED STUDY PLAN

Based on your performance on the diagnostic test and the amount of time you have available to study before the SAT, you can use the content in Section One to create a customized study plan. Think about the material you need to focus on. Then, realistically determine how much time you have to devote to SAT study. Use the information and tools in this section to build your plan. Then stick to it—your study plan works only if you follow it!

STEP FOUR: REVIEW TO REINFORCE AND BUILD SKILLS

Section Two provides you with targeted quizzes to help you conquer the content you need to know to score high on the SAT. Based on your study plan, take the quizzes here to help prepare you for test day.

About the SAT

The SAT is a standardized test that helps college and university admissions officers assess the qualifications of students applying to their schools. Though many factors play a role in admissions decisions, the SAT is one of the most important aspects of your college application. Acceptance into your college of choice is becoming more and more competitive, and juniors and seniors are taking control and doing more to make their application more desirable. A high SAT score can help do just that.

The first thing to know about the SAT is that it is 3 hours 45 minutes long and consists of 10 sections. These sections can appear in any order and measure vocabulary and reasoning skills, basic and advanced math skills, and grammar and writing skills.

They are broken down as follows:
- Two 25-minute Critical Reading sections
- One 20-minute Critical Reading section
- Two 25-minute Math sections
- One 20-minute Math section
- One 25-minute Writing section: Essay
- One 25-minute Writing section: Multiple choice
- One 10-minute Writing section: Multiple choice
- One 25-minute Experimental section

The Experimental section can look like any of the 25-minute multiple-choice subject sections and is not scored. However, you will not be able to determine which section is experimental, so it is not worth your effort to guess.

The Critical Reading section consists of Sentence Completion questions and Reading Comprehension questions. Sentence Completion questions test your ability to see how the parts of a sentence relate and will have one or two words missing from a sentence. Reading Comprehension questions relate to either short or long passages and will test your ability to draw conclusions based on the context of the passage(s).

The Math section uses multiple-choice questions and student-produced responses (Grid-ins) to test basic and advanced math concepts, including concepts from Algebra II. There are 10 Grid-in questions on the SAT, and for this question type, you will write your answers in a special grid rather than choose from given choices.

The Writing section includes a student-produced Essay and three types of multiple-choice questions. Your essay will be written using a question prompt that is based on one or two given quotations. The three multiple-choice question types are Usage, Sentence Correction, and Paragraph Correction, and you will be tested on your ability to choose the appropriate error from a sentence, fix or re-word part of sentence, and to correct or combine sentences to fix a paragraph, respectively.

Scaled scores range between 200 and 800 for each section, making the overall scaled score between 600 and 2400.

For complete registration information about the SAT, go to collegeboard.com.

Section One:

SAT Personalized Study Plan

CHAPTER ONE

Diagnostic Test

Diagnostic Test
Answer Sheet

Remove (or photocopy) the answer sheet and use it to complete the practice test.
See the answer key following the test when finished.

Start with number 1 for each section. If a section has fewer questions than answer spaces, leave the extra spaces blank.

SECTION

1

Section One is the writing section's essay component.
Lined pages on which you will write your essay can be found in that section.

SECTION

2

1. Ⓐ Ⓑ Ⓒ Ⓓ Ⓔ	11. Ⓐ Ⓑ Ⓒ Ⓓ Ⓔ	21. Ⓐ Ⓑ Ⓒ Ⓓ Ⓔ	31. Ⓐ Ⓑ Ⓒ Ⓓ Ⓔ
2. Ⓐ Ⓑ Ⓒ Ⓓ Ⓔ	12. Ⓐ Ⓑ Ⓒ Ⓓ Ⓔ	22. Ⓐ Ⓑ Ⓒ Ⓓ Ⓔ	32. Ⓐ Ⓑ Ⓒ Ⓓ Ⓔ
3. Ⓐ Ⓑ Ⓒ Ⓓ Ⓔ	13. Ⓐ Ⓑ Ⓒ Ⓓ Ⓔ	23. Ⓐ Ⓑ Ⓒ Ⓓ Ⓔ	33. Ⓐ Ⓑ Ⓒ Ⓓ Ⓔ
4. Ⓐ Ⓑ Ⓒ Ⓓ Ⓔ	14. Ⓐ Ⓑ Ⓒ Ⓓ Ⓔ	24. Ⓐ Ⓑ Ⓒ Ⓓ Ⓔ	34. Ⓐ Ⓑ Ⓒ Ⓓ Ⓔ
5. Ⓐ Ⓑ Ⓒ Ⓓ Ⓔ	15. Ⓐ Ⓑ Ⓒ Ⓓ Ⓔ	25. Ⓐ Ⓑ Ⓒ Ⓓ Ⓔ	35. Ⓐ Ⓑ Ⓒ Ⓓ Ⓔ
6. Ⓐ Ⓑ Ⓒ Ⓓ Ⓔ	16. Ⓐ Ⓑ Ⓒ Ⓓ Ⓔ	26. Ⓐ Ⓑ Ⓒ Ⓓ Ⓔ	36. Ⓐ Ⓑ Ⓒ Ⓓ Ⓔ
7. Ⓐ Ⓑ Ⓒ Ⓓ Ⓔ	17. Ⓐ Ⓑ Ⓒ Ⓓ Ⓔ	27. Ⓐ Ⓑ Ⓒ Ⓓ Ⓔ	37. Ⓐ Ⓑ Ⓒ Ⓓ Ⓔ
8. Ⓐ Ⓑ Ⓒ Ⓓ Ⓔ	18. Ⓐ Ⓑ Ⓒ Ⓓ Ⓔ	28. Ⓐ Ⓑ Ⓒ Ⓓ Ⓔ	38. Ⓐ Ⓑ Ⓒ Ⓓ Ⓔ
9. Ⓐ Ⓑ Ⓒ Ⓓ Ⓔ	19. Ⓐ Ⓑ Ⓒ Ⓓ Ⓔ	29. Ⓐ Ⓑ Ⓒ Ⓓ Ⓔ	39. Ⓐ Ⓑ Ⓒ Ⓓ Ⓔ
10. Ⓐ Ⓑ Ⓒ Ⓓ Ⓔ	20. Ⓐ Ⓑ Ⓒ Ⓓ Ⓔ	30. Ⓐ Ⓑ Ⓒ Ⓓ Ⓔ	40. Ⓐ Ⓑ Ⓒ Ⓓ Ⓔ

☐ # right in Section 2

☐ # wrong in Section 2

SECTION

3

1. Ⓐ Ⓑ Ⓒ Ⓓ Ⓔ	11. Ⓐ Ⓑ Ⓒ Ⓓ Ⓔ	21. Ⓐ Ⓑ Ⓒ Ⓓ Ⓔ	31. Ⓐ Ⓑ Ⓒ Ⓓ Ⓔ
2. Ⓐ Ⓑ Ⓒ Ⓓ Ⓔ	12. Ⓐ Ⓑ Ⓒ Ⓓ Ⓔ	22. Ⓐ Ⓑ Ⓒ Ⓓ Ⓔ	32. Ⓐ Ⓑ Ⓒ Ⓓ Ⓔ
3. Ⓐ Ⓑ Ⓒ Ⓓ Ⓔ	13. Ⓐ Ⓑ Ⓒ Ⓓ Ⓔ	23. Ⓐ Ⓑ Ⓒ Ⓓ Ⓔ	33. Ⓐ Ⓑ Ⓒ Ⓓ Ⓔ
4. Ⓐ Ⓑ Ⓒ Ⓓ Ⓔ	14. Ⓐ Ⓑ Ⓒ Ⓓ Ⓔ	24. Ⓐ Ⓑ Ⓒ Ⓓ Ⓔ	34. Ⓐ Ⓑ Ⓒ Ⓓ Ⓔ
5. Ⓐ Ⓑ Ⓒ Ⓓ Ⓔ	15. Ⓐ Ⓑ Ⓒ Ⓓ Ⓔ	25. Ⓐ Ⓑ Ⓒ Ⓓ Ⓔ	35. Ⓐ Ⓑ Ⓒ Ⓓ Ⓔ
6. Ⓐ Ⓑ Ⓒ Ⓓ Ⓔ	16. Ⓐ Ⓑ Ⓒ Ⓓ Ⓔ	26. Ⓐ Ⓑ Ⓒ Ⓓ Ⓔ	36. Ⓐ Ⓑ Ⓒ Ⓓ Ⓔ
7. Ⓐ Ⓑ Ⓒ Ⓓ Ⓔ	17. Ⓐ Ⓑ Ⓒ Ⓓ Ⓔ	27. Ⓐ Ⓑ Ⓒ Ⓓ Ⓔ	37. Ⓐ Ⓑ Ⓒ Ⓓ Ⓔ
8. Ⓐ Ⓑ Ⓒ Ⓓ Ⓔ	18. Ⓐ Ⓑ Ⓒ Ⓓ Ⓔ	28. Ⓐ Ⓑ Ⓒ Ⓓ Ⓔ	38. Ⓐ Ⓑ Ⓒ Ⓓ Ⓔ
9. Ⓐ Ⓑ Ⓒ Ⓓ Ⓔ	19. Ⓐ Ⓑ Ⓒ Ⓓ Ⓔ	29. Ⓐ Ⓑ Ⓒ Ⓓ Ⓔ	39. Ⓐ Ⓑ Ⓒ Ⓓ Ⓔ
10. Ⓐ Ⓑ Ⓒ Ⓓ Ⓔ	20. Ⓐ Ⓑ Ⓒ Ⓓ Ⓔ	30. Ⓐ Ⓑ Ⓒ Ⓓ Ⓔ	40. Ⓐ Ⓑ Ⓒ Ⓓ Ⓔ

☐ # right in Section 3

☐ # wrong in Section 3

Remove (or photocopy) this answer sheet and use it to complete the practice test.

Start with number 1 for each section. If a section has fewer questions than answer spaces, leave the extra spaces blank.

SECTION

4

1. Ⓐ Ⓑ Ⓒ Ⓓ Ⓔ	11. Ⓐ Ⓑ Ⓒ Ⓓ Ⓔ	21. Ⓐ Ⓑ Ⓒ Ⓓ Ⓔ	31. Ⓐ Ⓑ Ⓒ Ⓓ Ⓔ
2. Ⓐ Ⓑ Ⓒ Ⓓ Ⓔ	12. Ⓐ Ⓑ Ⓒ Ⓓ Ⓔ	22. Ⓐ Ⓑ Ⓒ Ⓓ Ⓔ	32. Ⓐ Ⓑ Ⓒ Ⓓ Ⓔ
3. Ⓐ Ⓑ Ⓒ Ⓓ Ⓔ	13. Ⓐ Ⓑ Ⓒ Ⓓ Ⓔ	23. Ⓐ Ⓑ Ⓒ Ⓓ Ⓔ	33. Ⓐ Ⓑ Ⓒ Ⓓ Ⓔ
4. Ⓐ Ⓑ Ⓒ Ⓓ Ⓔ	14. Ⓐ Ⓑ Ⓒ Ⓓ Ⓔ	24. Ⓐ Ⓑ Ⓒ Ⓓ Ⓔ	34. Ⓐ Ⓑ Ⓒ Ⓓ Ⓔ
5. Ⓐ Ⓑ Ⓒ Ⓓ Ⓔ	15. Ⓐ Ⓑ Ⓒ Ⓓ Ⓔ	25. Ⓐ Ⓑ Ⓒ Ⓓ Ⓔ	35. Ⓐ Ⓑ Ⓒ Ⓓ Ⓔ
6. Ⓐ Ⓑ Ⓒ Ⓓ Ⓔ	16. Ⓐ Ⓑ Ⓒ Ⓓ Ⓔ	26. Ⓐ Ⓑ Ⓒ Ⓓ Ⓔ	36. Ⓐ Ⓑ Ⓒ Ⓓ Ⓔ
7. Ⓐ Ⓑ Ⓒ Ⓓ Ⓔ	17. Ⓐ Ⓑ Ⓒ Ⓓ Ⓔ	27. Ⓐ Ⓑ Ⓒ Ⓓ Ⓔ	37. Ⓐ Ⓑ Ⓒ Ⓓ Ⓔ
8. Ⓐ Ⓑ Ⓒ Ⓓ Ⓔ	18. Ⓐ Ⓑ Ⓒ Ⓓ Ⓔ	28. Ⓐ Ⓑ Ⓒ Ⓓ Ⓔ	38. Ⓐ Ⓑ Ⓒ Ⓓ Ⓔ
▶9. Ⓐ Ⓑ Ⓒ Ⓓ Ⓔ	19. Ⓐ Ⓑ Ⓒ Ⓓ Ⓔ	29. Ⓐ Ⓑ Ⓒ Ⓓ Ⓔ	39. Ⓐ Ⓑ Ⓒ Ⓓ Ⓔ
10. Ⓐ Ⓑ Ⓒ Ⓓ Ⓔ	20. Ⓐ Ⓑ Ⓒ Ⓓ Ⓔ	30. Ⓐ Ⓑ Ⓒ Ⓓ Ⓔ	40. Ⓐ Ⓑ Ⓒ Ⓓ Ⓔ

☐ # right in Section 4

☐ # wrong in Section 4

If section 4 of your test book contains math questions that are not multiple choice, continue to item 9 below. Otherwise, continue to item 9 above.

9. 10. 11. 12. 13.

14. 15. 16. 17. 18.

SECTION

5

1. Ⓐ Ⓑ Ⓒ Ⓓ Ⓔ	11. Ⓐ Ⓑ Ⓒ Ⓓ Ⓔ	21. Ⓐ Ⓑ Ⓒ Ⓓ Ⓔ	31. Ⓐ Ⓑ Ⓒ Ⓓ Ⓔ
2. Ⓐ Ⓑ Ⓒ Ⓓ Ⓔ	12. Ⓐ Ⓑ Ⓒ Ⓓ Ⓔ	22. Ⓐ Ⓑ Ⓒ Ⓓ Ⓔ	32. Ⓐ Ⓑ Ⓒ Ⓓ Ⓔ
3. Ⓐ Ⓑ Ⓒ Ⓓ Ⓔ	13. Ⓐ Ⓑ Ⓒ Ⓓ Ⓔ	23. Ⓐ Ⓑ Ⓒ Ⓓ Ⓔ	33. Ⓐ Ⓑ Ⓒ Ⓓ Ⓔ
4. Ⓐ Ⓑ Ⓒ Ⓓ Ⓔ	14. Ⓐ Ⓑ Ⓒ Ⓓ Ⓔ	24. Ⓐ Ⓑ Ⓒ Ⓓ Ⓔ	34. Ⓐ Ⓑ Ⓒ Ⓓ Ⓔ
5. Ⓐ Ⓑ Ⓒ Ⓓ Ⓔ	15. Ⓐ Ⓑ Ⓒ Ⓓ Ⓔ	25. Ⓐ Ⓑ Ⓒ Ⓓ Ⓔ	35. Ⓐ Ⓑ Ⓒ Ⓓ Ⓔ
6. Ⓐ Ⓑ Ⓒ Ⓓ Ⓔ	16. Ⓐ Ⓑ Ⓒ Ⓓ Ⓔ	26. Ⓐ Ⓑ Ⓒ Ⓓ Ⓔ	36. Ⓐ Ⓑ Ⓒ Ⓓ Ⓔ
7. Ⓐ Ⓑ Ⓒ Ⓓ Ⓔ	17. Ⓐ Ⓑ Ⓒ Ⓓ Ⓔ	27. Ⓐ Ⓑ Ⓒ Ⓓ Ⓔ	37. Ⓐ Ⓑ Ⓒ Ⓓ Ⓔ
8. Ⓐ Ⓑ Ⓒ Ⓓ Ⓔ	18. Ⓐ Ⓑ Ⓒ Ⓓ Ⓔ	28. Ⓐ Ⓑ Ⓒ Ⓓ Ⓔ	38. Ⓐ Ⓑ Ⓒ Ⓓ Ⓔ
9. Ⓐ Ⓑ Ⓒ Ⓓ Ⓔ	19. Ⓐ Ⓑ Ⓒ Ⓓ Ⓔ	29. Ⓐ Ⓑ Ⓒ Ⓓ Ⓔ	39. Ⓐ Ⓑ Ⓒ Ⓓ Ⓔ
10. Ⓐ Ⓑ Ⓒ Ⓓ Ⓔ	20. Ⓐ Ⓑ Ⓒ Ⓓ Ⓔ	30. Ⓐ Ⓑ Ⓒ Ⓓ Ⓔ	40. Ⓐ Ⓑ Ⓒ Ⓓ Ⓔ

☐ # right in Section 5

☐ # wrong in Section 5

KAPLAN

Remove (or photocopy) this answer sheet and use it to complete the practice test.

Start with number 1 for each section. If a section has fewer questions than answer spaces, leave the extra spaces blank.

SECTION

6

1. Ⓐ Ⓑ Ⓒ Ⓓ Ⓔ　11. Ⓐ Ⓑ Ⓒ Ⓓ Ⓔ　21. Ⓐ Ⓑ Ⓒ Ⓓ Ⓔ　31. Ⓐ Ⓑ Ⓒ Ⓓ Ⓔ
2. Ⓐ Ⓑ Ⓒ Ⓓ Ⓔ　12. Ⓐ Ⓑ Ⓒ Ⓓ Ⓔ　22. Ⓐ Ⓑ Ⓒ Ⓓ Ⓔ　32. Ⓐ Ⓑ Ⓒ Ⓓ Ⓔ
3. Ⓐ Ⓑ Ⓒ Ⓓ Ⓔ　13. Ⓐ Ⓑ Ⓒ Ⓓ Ⓔ　23. Ⓐ Ⓑ Ⓒ Ⓓ Ⓔ　33. Ⓐ Ⓑ Ⓒ Ⓓ Ⓔ
4. Ⓐ Ⓑ Ⓒ Ⓓ Ⓔ　14. Ⓐ Ⓑ Ⓒ Ⓓ Ⓔ　24. Ⓐ Ⓑ Ⓒ Ⓓ Ⓔ　34. Ⓐ Ⓑ Ⓒ Ⓓ Ⓔ　# right in Section 6
5. Ⓐ Ⓑ Ⓒ Ⓓ Ⓔ　15. Ⓐ Ⓑ Ⓒ Ⓓ Ⓔ　25. Ⓐ Ⓑ Ⓒ Ⓓ Ⓔ　35. Ⓐ Ⓑ Ⓒ Ⓓ Ⓔ
6. Ⓐ Ⓑ Ⓒ Ⓓ Ⓔ　16. Ⓐ Ⓑ Ⓒ Ⓓ Ⓔ　26. Ⓐ Ⓑ Ⓒ Ⓓ Ⓔ　36. Ⓐ Ⓑ Ⓒ Ⓓ Ⓔ
7. Ⓐ Ⓑ Ⓒ Ⓓ Ⓔ　17. Ⓐ Ⓑ Ⓒ Ⓓ Ⓔ　27. Ⓐ Ⓑ Ⓒ Ⓓ Ⓔ　37. Ⓐ Ⓑ Ⓒ Ⓓ Ⓔ
8. Ⓐ Ⓑ Ⓒ Ⓓ Ⓔ　18. Ⓐ Ⓑ Ⓒ Ⓓ Ⓔ　28. Ⓐ Ⓑ Ⓒ Ⓓ Ⓔ　38. Ⓐ Ⓑ Ⓒ Ⓓ Ⓔ　# wrong in Section 6
9. Ⓐ Ⓑ Ⓒ Ⓓ Ⓔ　19. Ⓐ Ⓑ Ⓒ Ⓓ Ⓔ　29. Ⓐ Ⓑ Ⓒ Ⓓ Ⓔ　39. Ⓐ Ⓑ Ⓒ Ⓓ Ⓔ
10. Ⓐ Ⓑ Ⓒ Ⓓ Ⓔ　20. Ⓐ Ⓑ Ⓒ Ⓓ Ⓔ　30. Ⓐ Ⓑ Ⓒ Ⓓ Ⓔ　40. Ⓐ Ⓑ Ⓒ Ⓓ Ⓔ

SECTION

7

1. Ⓐ Ⓑ Ⓒ Ⓓ Ⓔ　11. Ⓐ Ⓑ Ⓒ Ⓓ Ⓔ　21. Ⓐ Ⓑ Ⓒ Ⓓ Ⓔ　31. Ⓐ Ⓑ Ⓒ Ⓓ Ⓔ
2. Ⓐ Ⓑ Ⓒ Ⓓ Ⓔ　12. Ⓐ Ⓑ Ⓒ Ⓓ Ⓔ　22. Ⓐ Ⓑ Ⓒ Ⓓ Ⓔ　32. Ⓐ Ⓑ Ⓒ Ⓓ Ⓔ
3. Ⓐ Ⓑ Ⓒ Ⓓ Ⓔ　13. Ⓐ Ⓑ Ⓒ Ⓓ Ⓔ　23. Ⓐ Ⓑ Ⓒ Ⓓ Ⓔ　33. Ⓐ Ⓑ Ⓒ Ⓓ Ⓔ
4. Ⓐ Ⓑ Ⓒ Ⓓ Ⓔ　14. Ⓐ Ⓑ Ⓒ Ⓓ Ⓔ　24. Ⓐ Ⓑ Ⓒ Ⓓ Ⓔ　34. Ⓐ Ⓑ Ⓒ Ⓓ Ⓔ　# right in Section 7
5. Ⓐ Ⓑ Ⓒ Ⓓ Ⓔ　15. Ⓐ Ⓑ Ⓒ Ⓓ Ⓔ　25. Ⓐ Ⓑ Ⓒ Ⓓ Ⓔ　35. Ⓐ Ⓑ Ⓒ Ⓓ Ⓔ
6. Ⓐ Ⓑ Ⓒ Ⓓ Ⓔ　16. Ⓐ Ⓑ Ⓒ Ⓓ Ⓔ　26. Ⓐ Ⓑ Ⓒ Ⓓ Ⓔ　36. Ⓐ Ⓑ Ⓒ Ⓓ Ⓔ
7. Ⓐ Ⓑ Ⓒ Ⓓ Ⓔ　17. Ⓐ Ⓑ Ⓒ Ⓓ Ⓔ　27. Ⓐ Ⓑ Ⓒ Ⓓ Ⓔ　37. Ⓐ Ⓑ Ⓒ Ⓓ Ⓔ
8. Ⓐ Ⓑ Ⓒ Ⓓ Ⓔ　18. Ⓐ Ⓑ Ⓒ Ⓓ Ⓔ　28. Ⓐ Ⓑ Ⓒ Ⓓ Ⓔ　38. Ⓐ Ⓑ Ⓒ Ⓓ Ⓔ　# wrong in Section 7
9. Ⓐ Ⓑ Ⓒ Ⓓ Ⓔ　19. Ⓐ Ⓑ Ⓒ Ⓓ Ⓔ　29. Ⓐ Ⓑ Ⓒ Ⓓ Ⓔ　39. Ⓐ Ⓑ Ⓒ Ⓓ Ⓔ
10. Ⓐ Ⓑ Ⓒ Ⓓ Ⓔ　20. Ⓐ Ⓑ Ⓒ Ⓓ Ⓔ　30. Ⓐ Ⓑ Ⓒ Ⓓ Ⓔ　40. Ⓐ Ⓑ Ⓒ Ⓓ Ⓔ

SECTION

8

1. Ⓐ Ⓑ Ⓒ Ⓓ Ⓔ　11. Ⓐ Ⓑ Ⓒ Ⓓ Ⓔ　21. Ⓐ Ⓑ Ⓒ Ⓓ Ⓔ　31. Ⓐ Ⓑ Ⓒ Ⓓ Ⓔ
2. Ⓐ Ⓑ Ⓒ Ⓓ Ⓔ　12. Ⓐ Ⓑ Ⓒ Ⓓ Ⓔ　22. Ⓐ Ⓑ Ⓒ Ⓓ Ⓔ　32. Ⓐ Ⓑ Ⓒ Ⓓ Ⓔ
3. Ⓐ Ⓑ Ⓒ Ⓓ Ⓔ　13. Ⓐ Ⓑ Ⓒ Ⓓ Ⓔ　23. Ⓐ Ⓑ Ⓒ Ⓓ Ⓔ　33. Ⓐ Ⓑ Ⓒ Ⓓ Ⓔ
4. Ⓐ Ⓑ Ⓒ Ⓓ Ⓔ　14. Ⓐ Ⓑ Ⓒ Ⓓ Ⓔ　24. Ⓐ Ⓑ Ⓒ Ⓓ Ⓔ　34. Ⓐ Ⓑ Ⓒ Ⓓ Ⓔ　# right in Section 8
5. Ⓐ Ⓑ Ⓒ Ⓓ Ⓔ　15. Ⓐ Ⓑ Ⓒ Ⓓ Ⓔ　25. Ⓐ Ⓑ Ⓒ Ⓓ Ⓔ　35. Ⓐ Ⓑ Ⓒ Ⓓ Ⓔ
6. Ⓐ Ⓑ Ⓒ Ⓓ Ⓔ　16. Ⓐ Ⓑ Ⓒ Ⓓ Ⓔ　26. Ⓐ Ⓑ Ⓒ Ⓓ Ⓔ　36. Ⓐ Ⓑ Ⓒ Ⓓ Ⓔ
7. Ⓐ Ⓑ Ⓒ Ⓓ Ⓔ　17. Ⓐ Ⓑ Ⓒ Ⓓ Ⓔ　27. Ⓐ Ⓑ Ⓒ Ⓓ Ⓔ　37. Ⓐ Ⓑ Ⓒ Ⓓ Ⓔ
8. Ⓐ Ⓑ Ⓒ Ⓓ Ⓔ　18. Ⓐ Ⓑ Ⓒ Ⓓ Ⓔ　28. Ⓐ Ⓑ Ⓒ Ⓓ Ⓔ　38. Ⓐ Ⓑ Ⓒ Ⓓ Ⓔ　# wrong in Section 8
9. Ⓐ Ⓑ Ⓒ Ⓓ Ⓔ　19. Ⓐ Ⓑ Ⓒ Ⓓ Ⓔ　29. Ⓐ Ⓑ Ⓒ Ⓓ Ⓔ　39. Ⓐ Ⓑ Ⓒ Ⓓ Ⓔ
10. Ⓐ Ⓑ Ⓒ Ⓓ Ⓔ　20. Ⓐ Ⓑ Ⓒ Ⓓ Ⓔ　30. Ⓐ Ⓑ Ⓒ Ⓓ Ⓔ　40. Ⓐ Ⓑ Ⓒ Ⓓ Ⓔ

Remove (or photocopy) this answer sheet and use it to complete the practice test.

Start with number 1 for each section. If a section has fewer questions than answer spaces, leave the extra spaces blank.

SECTION 9

1. Ⓐ Ⓑ Ⓒ Ⓓ Ⓔ
2. Ⓐ Ⓑ Ⓒ Ⓓ Ⓔ
3. Ⓐ Ⓑ Ⓒ Ⓓ Ⓔ
4. Ⓐ Ⓑ Ⓒ Ⓓ Ⓔ
5. Ⓐ Ⓑ Ⓒ Ⓓ Ⓔ
6. Ⓐ Ⓑ Ⓒ Ⓓ Ⓔ
7. Ⓐ Ⓑ Ⓒ Ⓓ Ⓔ
8. Ⓐ Ⓑ Ⓒ Ⓓ Ⓔ
9. Ⓐ Ⓑ Ⓒ Ⓓ Ⓔ
10. Ⓐ Ⓑ Ⓒ Ⓓ Ⓔ

11. Ⓐ Ⓑ Ⓒ Ⓓ Ⓔ
12. Ⓐ Ⓑ Ⓒ Ⓓ Ⓔ
13. Ⓐ Ⓑ Ⓒ Ⓓ Ⓔ
14. Ⓐ Ⓑ Ⓒ Ⓓ Ⓔ
15. Ⓐ Ⓑ Ⓒ Ⓓ Ⓔ
16. Ⓐ Ⓑ Ⓒ Ⓓ Ⓔ
17. Ⓐ Ⓑ Ⓒ Ⓓ Ⓔ
18. Ⓐ Ⓑ Ⓒ Ⓓ Ⓔ
19. Ⓐ Ⓑ Ⓒ Ⓓ Ⓔ
20. Ⓐ Ⓑ Ⓒ Ⓓ Ⓔ

21. Ⓐ Ⓑ Ⓒ Ⓓ Ⓔ
22. Ⓐ Ⓑ Ⓒ Ⓓ Ⓔ
23. Ⓐ Ⓑ Ⓒ Ⓓ Ⓔ
24. Ⓐ Ⓑ Ⓒ Ⓓ Ⓔ
25. Ⓐ Ⓑ Ⓒ Ⓓ Ⓔ
26. Ⓐ Ⓑ Ⓒ Ⓓ Ⓔ
27. Ⓐ Ⓑ Ⓒ Ⓓ Ⓔ
28. Ⓐ Ⓑ Ⓒ Ⓓ Ⓔ
29. Ⓐ Ⓑ Ⓒ Ⓓ Ⓔ
30. Ⓐ Ⓑ Ⓒ Ⓓ Ⓔ

31. Ⓐ Ⓑ Ⓒ Ⓓ Ⓔ
32. Ⓐ Ⓑ Ⓒ Ⓓ Ⓔ
33. Ⓐ Ⓑ Ⓒ Ⓓ Ⓔ
34. Ⓐ Ⓑ Ⓒ Ⓓ Ⓔ
35. Ⓐ Ⓑ Ⓒ Ⓓ Ⓔ
36. Ⓐ Ⓑ Ⓒ Ⓓ Ⓔ
37. Ⓐ Ⓑ Ⓒ Ⓓ Ⓔ
38. Ⓐ Ⓑ Ⓒ Ⓓ Ⓔ
39. Ⓐ Ⓑ Ⓒ Ⓓ Ⓔ
40. Ⓐ Ⓑ Ⓒ Ⓓ Ⓔ

right in Section 9

wrong in Section 9

The essay gives you an opportunity to show how effectively you can develop and express ideas. You should, therefore, take care to develop your point of view, present your ideas logically and clearly, and use language precisely.

Your essay must be written on the lines provided on the following pages—you will receive no other paper on which to write. You will have enough space if you write on every line, avoid wide margins, and keep your handwriting to a reasonable size. Remember that people who are not familiar with your handwriting will read what you write. Try to write or print so that what you are writing is legible to those readers.

You have twenty-five minutes to write an essay on the topic assigned below. DO NOT WRITE ON ANOTHER TOPIC. AN OFF-TOPIC ESSAY WILL RECEIVE A SCORE OF ZERO.

Think carefully about the issue presented in the following excerpt and the assignment below.

"When you reach an obstacle, turn it into an opportunity. You have the choice. You can overcome and be a winner, or you can allow it to overcome you, and be a loser. It is far better to be exhausted from success than to be rested from failure."

Mary Kay Ash

Assignment: What is your view of the idea that every obstacle can be turned into an opportunity? Plan and write an essay in which you develop your point of view on this issue. Support your position with reasoning and examples taken from your reading, studies, experience, or observations.

DO NOT WRITE YOUR ESSAY IN YOUR TEST BOOK.
You will receive credit only for what you write on your answer sheet.

GO ON TO THE NEXT PAGE

KAPLAN

SECTION 2
Time—25 Minutes
20 Questions

Directions: For this section, sove each problem and decide which is the best of the choices given. Fill in the corresponding oval on the answer sheet. You may use any available space for scratchwork.

Notes:

(1) Calculator use is permitted.

(2) All numbers used are real numbers.

(3) Figures are provided for some problems. All figures are drawn to scale and lie in a plane UNLESS otherwise indicated.

(4) Unless otherwise specified, the domain of any function f is assumed to be the set of all real numbers x for which $f(x)$ is a real number.

Information

 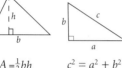

$A = \frac{1}{2}bh$ $c^2 = a^2 + b^2$ Special Right Triangles $A = \pi r^2$ $C = 2\pi r$ $V = \ell wh$ $V = \pi r^2 h$ $A = \ell w$

The sum of the degree measures of the angles in a triangle is 180.
The number of degrees of arc in a circle is 360.
A straight angle has a degree measure of 180.

---

1   If $b \neq 0$ and $ab = \dfrac{b}{4}$, then $a =$

(A) $\dfrac{1}{8}$

(B) $\dfrac{1}{4}$

(C) $\dfrac{1}{2}$

(D) 1

(E) 4

handwritten: $a = \dfrac{1}{4}$

2   It takes a bus anywhere from 7 minutes to 10 minutes to travel from Town A to Town B. It takes the bus anywhere from 16 minutes to 24 minutes to travel from Town B to Town C. What are the least and greatest total travel times for a bus that travels from Town A to Town B and then from Town B to Town C? (Disregard the time the bus could be standing still in Town B.)

(A) 7 minutes and 24 minutes
(B) 10 minutes and 24 minutes
(C) 23 minutes and 26 minutes
(D) 23 minutes and 34 minutes
(E) 26 minutes and 40 minutes

handwritten:
$A \rightarrow B$ 7-10 $7+16 = 23$
$B \rightarrow C$ 16-24 $10 + 24 = 34$

GO ON TO THE NEXT PAGE

3 By what number must the number 3.475817 be multiplied in order to obtain the number 34,758.17?

(A)   100
(B)   1,000
(C)   10,000
(D)   100,000
(E) 1,000,000

10,000

5 If the manager of a store adds 50 lamps to its current inventory, the resulting total number of lamps is the same as three-halves of the current inventory. If the manager wanted to increase the current inventory by 40%, what would his new inventory of lamps be?

(A) 150
(B) 140
(C) 100
(D) 75
(E) 40

$50 + c = \dfrac{3}{2} c$

$\dfrac{1}{2} c = 50$

$c = 100$

$\dfrac{140}{100} \cdot 100 = 140$

4

Number of students	Grade
18	97
13	78
18	67
7	54
5	46

For a university class of 61 students, the table above shows the number of students receiving each grade on the mid-term exam. What is the median of those 61 scores?

(A) 97   → middle
(B) 78
(C) 67
(D) 54
(E) 46

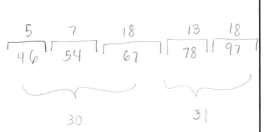

6

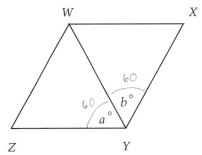

In the figure above, $WX = XY = YZ = ZW = WY$. What is the value of $a + b$?

(A) 60
(B) 100
(C) 105
(D) 120
(E) 135

120

GO ON TO THE NEXT PAGE

7 How much greater than the value of $3x - 7$ is the value of $3x + 5$?

(A) 12
(B) 10
(C) 7
(D) 5
(E) 2

$(3x + 5) - (3x - 7) = 12$

9 Which of the following statements expresses the statement "When z is decreased by 3, the result is twice the square of the sum of y and 4"?

(A) $z - 3 = 2(y + 4)^2$
(B) $z - 3 = 2(y^2 + 4^2)$
(C) $z = 2(y + 4)^2 - 3$
(D) $z - 3 = 2(y^2 + 4)$
(E) $z + 3 = 2(y + 4)^2$

$z - 3 = 2(y + 4)^2$

8 The Environment Club receives a certain amount of money from the school to host a teach-in. They budget 40% for a guest speaker, 25% for books, 20% for use of the auditorium, and the remainder for lunch. If the club plans to spend $90 on lunch for the participants, how much do they plan to spend on the guest speaker?

(A) $40
(B) $90
(C) $120
(D) $240
(E) $600

$$\begin{array}{c} 40 \\ 25 \\ 20 \\ \hline 85 \end{array}$$

15% lunch

$\dfrac{15}{100} x = 90$

$x = 90 \cdot \dfrac{100}{15}$

$\dfrac{40}{100} \cdot 600 = 240 \quad = 600$

10 Line ℓ passes through the point $(-1, 2)$. Which of the following CANNOT be the equation of line ℓ?

(A) $y = 1 - x$
(B) $y = x + 1$
(C) $x = -1$
(D) $y = x + 3$
(E) $y = 2$

11 For all numbers c and d, the symbol # is defined by $c \# d = (c + 1)(d - 1)$. What is the value of $(5 \# 2) \# (6 \# 4)$?

(A)   35
(B)   72
(C)   108
(D)   110
(E)   140

$(5+1)(2-1) \quad \# \quad (6+1)(4-1)$

$(6)(1) \quad \# \quad (7)(3)$

$6 \quad \# \quad 21$

$(6+1)(21-1)$

$(7)(20) = 140$

13 If the length of one side of a triangle is 5, which of the following could be the perimeter of the triangle?

(A)   11
(B)   10
(C)   9
(D)   8
(E)   7

12 If p is an integer greater than 1, such that p divided by 4 yields a remainder of 0, which of the following could be a prime number?

(A) $\dfrac{p}{4}$

(B) $2\sqrt{p}$

(C) $\dfrac{p}{3}$

(D) p

(E) $2p$

$p > 1$

$\dfrac{p}{4} = x$

14 The ratio of the areas of three circles is $1 : 4 : 8$, and the radius of the smallest circle is a positive integer. If the sum of the lengths of the diameters of the three circles is x, which of the following is a possible value of x?

(A)   12
(B) $8 + 4\sqrt{3}$
(C)   15
(D) $12 + 4\sqrt{2}$
(E) $18 + 12\sqrt{2}$

$1 : 4 : 8$

$A = \pi r^2$

$4(2+\sqrt{3})$

$4(3+\sqrt{2})$ $r_1 = 1$ $A = \pi$

$r_2 = 2$ $A = 4\pi$

$3(6 + 4\sqrt{2})$ $r_3 = 2\sqrt{2}$ $A = 8\pi$

$2(1) + 2(2) + 2(2\sqrt{2}) = x$

$2 + 4 + 4\sqrt{2} = x$

$6 + 4\sqrt{2} = x$

15 For any odd integer x, where $x < 0$, how many negative, even integers are greater than x?

(A) $-x - 2$

(B) $\dfrac{-x}{2}$

(C) $\dfrac{-x - 1}{2}$

(D) $x + 4$

(E) $\dfrac{-x - 2}{2}$

Handwritten work:

$x = -7$

$\left.\begin{array}{c} -6 \\ -4 \\ -2 \end{array}\right\} 3$

$x = -5$

$\left.\begin{array}{c} -4 \\ -2 \end{array}\right\} 2$

$x = -9$

$\left.\begin{array}{c} -8 \\ -6 \\ -4 \\ -2 \end{array}\right\} 4$

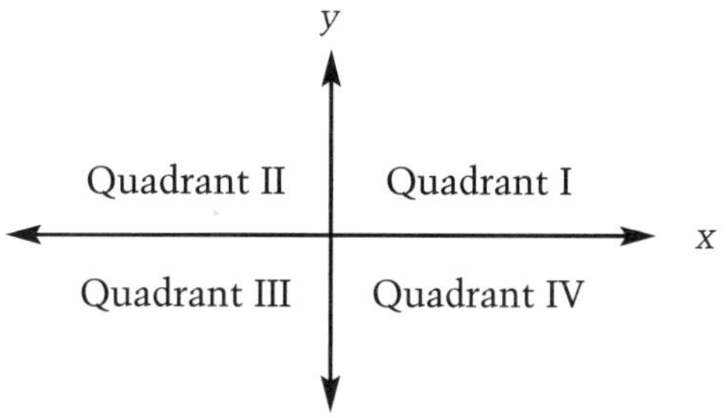

17 If the product of the x-coordinate and y-coordinate of a point is 20, in which quadrant must that point lie?

(A) I

(B) II

(C) III

(D) IV

(E) It cannot be determined from the information given.

16 A particular slot machine has three rotating wheels, called wheels A, B, and C. Each wheel displays the following pictures: a rose, a pen, a waterfall, an apple, a candle, a dollar sign, and an emerald. The machine awards a cash prize to a player whenever wheels A and B land on the same picture and wheel C lands on a candle. Assuming that for each wheel there is an equal probability of landing on each picture, what is the probability that the player will win a cash prize?

(A) $\dfrac{1}{343}$

(B) $\dfrac{1}{49}$

(C) $\dfrac{1}{21}$

(D) $\dfrac{1}{7}$

(E) $\dfrac{3}{7}$

Handwritten work:

7 pics

$\dfrac{7}{7} \cdot \dfrac{1}{7} \cdot \dfrac{1}{7} = \dfrac{1}{49}$

18 If $z > 0$, $x = z^2 + 3y$, and $y - 1 = z^2$, what is z in terms of x?

(A) $\sqrt{\dfrac{x}{2}}$

(B) $\sqrt{\dfrac{3 + x}{2}}$

(C) $\sqrt{\dfrac{3 - x}{2}}$

(D) $\sqrt{\dfrac{x + 3}{4}}$

(E) $\sqrt{\dfrac{x - 3}{4}}$

Handwritten work:

$z^2 = y - 1$

$y = z^2 + 1$

$x = z^2 + 3(z^2 + 1)$

$x = z^2 + 3z^2 + 3$

$x = 4z^2 + 3$

$\dfrac{x - 3}{4} = z^2$

$z = \pm\sqrt{\dfrac{x - 3}{4}}$

GO ON TO THE NEXT PAGE

19

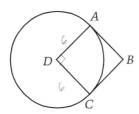

In the figure above, *D* is the center of the circle, and the perimeter of square *ABCD* is 24. What is the area of the entire figure?

(A) $36 + 18\pi$
(B) $18 + 27\pi$
(C) $36 + 27\pi$
(D) $27 + 36\pi$
(E) $36 + 54\pi$

Handwritten work:

$4\overline{)24}$ → 6

$36\pi + (36 - 9\pi)$

$27\pi + 36$

circle $\pi(6)^2 = 36\pi$

edge · $6^2 - \left(\dfrac{\pi(6)^2}{4}\right)$

$= 36 - 9\pi$

20 Brand *A* drink contains 30 percent orange juice by volume. Brand *B* drink contains 40 percent orange juice by volume. Which of the following expressions gives the percent of orange juice in a mixture of *x* gallons of brand *A* drink, *y* gallons of brand *B* drink, and *z* gallons of water?

(A) $\dfrac{x+y}{x+y+z}\%$

(B) $\dfrac{40y}{x+y+z}\%$

(C) $\dfrac{30x+40y}{x+y}\%$

(D) $\dfrac{30x+40y}{x+y+z}\%$

(E) $\dfrac{30x+40y+z}{x+y+z}\%$

Handwritten work:

x gallons A

y gallons B

z gallons water

$\left(\dfrac{30}{100}\right)x + \left(\dfrac{40}{100}\right)y + (0)z$

$\overline{}$

$x + y + z$

→ $\dfrac{30x+40y}{x+y+z}\%$

IF YOU FINISH BEFORE TIME IS CALLED, YOU MAY CHECK YOUR WORK ON THIS SECTION ONLY. DO NOT TURN TO ANY OTHER SECTION IN THE TEST.

STOP

SECTION 3
Time—25 Minutes
24 Questions

Directions: For each question in this section, select the best answer from among the choices given and fill in the corresponding oval on the answer sheet.

Each sentence below has one or two blanks, each blank indicating that something has been omitted. Beneath the sentence are five words or sets of words labeled A through E. Choose the word or set of words that, when inserted in the sentence, <u>best</u> fits the meaning of the sentence as a whole.

EXAMPLE:

Today's small, portable computers contrast markedly with the earliest electronic computers, which were -------.

(A) effective   (B) invented   (C) useful
   (D) destructive   (E) enormous

ANSWER:

Ⓐ Ⓑ Ⓒ Ⓓ ●

---

1 University professors are frequently ------- to utilize multimedia materials in their class presentations; however, many ------- the expertise in new educational technology to be able to use such materials effectively.

(A) encouraged .. lack
(B) inspired .. enjoy
(C) determined .. require
(D) forced .. elect
(E) trusted .. embrace

2 Despite the poet's best efforts to ------- the symbolism in her latest work, it nonetheless remained -------.

(A) corrupt .. obscure
(B) simplify .. lustrous
(C) illuminate .. explicit
(D) clarify .. opaque
(E) cleanse .. enigmatic

3 However ------- the speech may have sounded to the audience, it was in fact the product of a great deal of rehearsal.

(A) imprecise (B) relentless (C) premeditated
  (D) practiced (E) impromptu

4 Acknowledging the ------- of their recent consensus, the partners struggled to uphold their ------- agreement.

(A) fragility .. tenuous
(B) persistence .. paltry
(C) durability .. stalwart
(D) estimation .. delicate
(E) omission .. tractable

5 The ------- nature of the security guard is evidenced by his ill-temper and penchant for quarreling with entrants to the building.

(A) cantankerous (B) engaging (C) urbane
  (D) perspicacious (E) cautious

GO ON TO THE NEXT PAGE

KAPLAN

The passages below are followed by questions based on their content; questions following a pair of related passages may also be based on the relationship between the paired passages. Answer the questions on the basis of what is <u>stated</u> or <u>implied</u> in the passages and in any introductory material that may be provided.

Questions 6–7 are based on the following passage.

Ever since the movie *Jaws*, sharks have been feared and reviled as menaces of the sea. Can you picture, then, a shark swimming close to the
Line surface of the ocean, its mouth wide open, looking
(5) for all the world like it's "catching rays"? The basking shark, named for its propensity to bask (or laze about) in the sun, does just that. Don't be fooled, though; like all sharks, the basking shark can be dangerous to human beings. In fact, there
(10) are reports of harpooned basking sharks attacking the boat in which the harpooner is riding. In addition, the basking shark's skin contains dermal denticles that have seriously wounded divers and scientists who have come in contact with the
(15) sharks.

6 The second sentence ("Can. . .rays") is meant to convey

(A) a comical picture of an animal that is usually regarded as menacing
(B) that sharks are not dangerous, despite their portrayal in *Jaws*
(C) an in-depth look at the habits of the basking shark
(D) the reason why basking sharks have attacked boats
(E) why sharks are menaces of the sea

7 A "dermal denticle" (lines 12–13) is most likely

(A) one of the basking shark's teeth
(B) a dangerous part of the basking shark's skin
(C) something that protects the basking shark from the sun
(D) a conduit for the basking shark's food
(E) the only way a basking shark can defend itself

Questions 8–9 are based on the following passage.

While some playwrights are known for writing essays defending their own work or criticizing the work of competing writers,
Line Arthur Miller's essays are simply about theater.
(5) While we may discover politics and favoritism when we comb through Miller's essays looking for such things, in doing so, we may risk missing the point of the works—Miller wants only for us to benefit from his years of
(10) experience. Even his earliest essays read as virtual how-to manuals for new playwrights and directors. These works ring with clarity and forthrightness, and are filled with thoughtful and often provocative opinions. These essays
(15) teach us what the theater is, what it might be, and how to make it so.

8 In line 11, "virtual" most nearly means

(A) organic
(B) electronic
(C) moral
(D) near
(E) cybernetic

9 The author of the passage suggests that Miller's essays differ from other playwrights' essays in that

(A) Miller's essays are more recent than those of other playwrights
(B) Miller wrote more essays than most other playwrights
(C) Miller's essays have had more influence than anyone else's
(D) Miller's essays are not self-serving
(E) Miller wrote essays about American theater

GO ON TO THE NEXT PAGE

Questions 10–18 are based on the following passage.

The passage below is written by an Australian conservation scientist and activist.

The koala, or *Phascolarctos cinereus*, has, for decades, been Australia's most recognizable symbol and a global emblem of endangered species and
Line conservation efforts. The unsuccessful fight to keep
(5) koalas from the endangered list—the animal was added to the U.S. list in May 2000—has in the last few years become more complex: while koala populations are on the brink of extinction in Australia's north, they are undergoing a population
(10) boom in the south where the animals are killing trees by over-browsing in their habitats. Habitat destruction and the degradation that has resulted from over-browsing have aggravated a number of factors that have placed susceptible koala
(15) populations at risk of extinction. At the same time, conservationists point out that the population boom in the south is vital to preserve the species as a whole in Australia.

The greatest current threat to koala populations in
(20) the north is the destruction of approximately 80 percent of their habitat. Degradation of eucalyptus habitats decreases the abundance of eucalyptus trees, forcing koalas to travel great distances in search of food. Koalas, known for their slothfulness caused by
(25) a low metabolic rate, do not obtain sufficient nutrients from eucalyptus leaves to enable this long-distance foraging. Degradation is further aggravated by habitat fragmentation, whereby suitable patches of eucalyptus are separated by great distances.
(30) Fragmentation increases the amount of open space koalas are forced to cross in search of foraging opportunities. This is a particular problem in urban areas, where dog attacks and accidents with cars are major causes of koala mortality.

(35) Conservationists also point to the danger mistletoe presents to healthy eucalyptus habitats for koalas. Mistletoe is a parasite that uses eucalyptus for water and mineral nutrients. Prior to European settlement, wildfires kept mistletoe in check by
(40) burning the parasitic plant without dramatically affecting its eucalyptus host. Fire suppression by humans, however, has caused an increase in the abundance of mistletoe, enabling this parasite to destroy numerous eucalyptus trees. Many ecologists
(45) note that the danger to koala populations posed by unchecked mistletoe, while real, is far less grave than that caused by outright habitat destruction.

Genetic variance has also become a notable concern for koala populations in southern Australia.
(50) Unlike populations in the north, the southern population was established by a single genetic strain that came from French Island in the Australian state of Victoria. Genetic studies among this population have revealed a low genetic variance, which has
(55) negative implications for the fitness, and even survival, of the species. Widespread habitat fragmentation separates populations of koalas already low in genetic variance. Mating among small numbers of koalas with low genetic variance leads to
(60) inbreeding, leading to offspring that are incapable of reproducing, causing further population decline.

Conservationists propose two methods of alleviating the problem of low genetic variance. First, both the public and private spheres should be
(65) encouraged to create land corridors—long strips of eucalyptus habitat between fragmented populations to reduce the chances of genetic inbreeding. As habitats become increasingly fragmented due to urban development, these corridors will be important
(70) means of gene flow among isolated populations. Additionally, moving koalas from over- to under-populated areas would not only help to save the forests that are currently over-browsed but also introduce new genes into a population whose genetic
(75) variety has been decimated.

Conservation scientists are also concerned with identifying those habitats that can best sustain koala populations. They note that further study should be conducted to explain why koalas prefer certain
(80) forests to others that are seemingly identical, since this question is particularly important in determining which regions of Australia should be preserved for the koala. While it was once believed that the koala's preferences for certain trees was
(85) based on the tree's species, new studies have found that the preference is based more on the quantity of nutrients available in a forest. Leaves of eucalyptus trees with access to abundant nutrients can better afford to lose leaves than can trees whose
(90) environments provide them with meager resources. Also, eucalyptus trees in nutrient-rich environments produce leaves with lower toxin levels, which koalas prefer. Many scientists now believe that further studies should be done to identify the forests with

GO ON TO THE NEXT PAGE

KAPLAN

(95) the highest nutrient availability so that these
forests can be strongly considered for koala habitat.
   Sadly, the greatest threat koalas face is the
destruction of their habitat by human beings.
Logging and development practices that result in
(100) forest clearing should be prevented whenever
possible. Conservation efforts should focus on
saving the koala habitats that remain in Australia
to sustain existing populations. When commercial
interests are in conflict with those of the koala,
(105) planners can implement simple but effective
measures such as reducing speed limits and
building roads that bypass the animals' habitat.

10 The primary purpose of this passage is to

(A) examine the dietary habits of koalas
(B) prove the importance of koalas to the
     Australian ecosystem
(C) refute the argument that habitat
     fragmentation does not harm koala
     populations
(D) analyze the importance of eucalyptus trees for
     koala populations
(E) discuss threats facing koala populations and
     possible solutions

11 The author notes that the efforts to fight the
extinction of the koala have recently "become
more complex" (line 7) because

(A) the animals' habitats are increasingly
     fragmented
(B) the koalas in the northern portion of the
     country have a very low genetic variance
(C) it is difficult to determine which groups of
     eucalyptus trees will produce the lowest
     levels of toxins
(D) humans pose an increasing threat through
     land development
(E) some areas of the country now have large
     populations of the animal, posing a new set
     of problems

12 All of the following are discussed as threats to
koala populations EXCEPT

(A) dogs
(B) habitat fragmentation
(C) decreasing eucalyptus trees
(D) urban development
(E) disease

13 The author would most likely support all of the
following EXCEPT

(A) restricting urban development in conservation
     areas
(B) researching eucalyptus habitats to determine
     which has the richest nutrients
(C) banning the movement of the southern koala
     population to the north
(D) encouraging individuals near koala habitats to
     keep dogs on leashes or behind fences
(E) allotting public land to build corridors
     between habitats

14 Which of the following, if true, would undermine
the author's claim that koala populations are
under threat of extinction?

(A) Degradation of eucalyptus will only accelerate
     in the coming years.
(B) Habitats in the southern region of Australia
     are more fragmented and degraded than
     those in the northern region.
(C) Koalas only feed on eucalyptus leaves.
(D) Australian citizens oppose the use of public
     lands for conservation efforts.
(E) There is greater genetic variance in the south
     than in the north.

15 In line 77, the word "sustain" most likely means

(A) defend
(B) suffer
(C) encounter
(D) maintain
(E) endure

16 In lines 91–93, the author implies that a eucalyptus
leaf with high toxin levels is

(A) made by trees living in environments without
     enough nutrients
(B) of high nutrient value
(C) preferred by koalas for food
(D) providing insufficient nutrients to a koala
(E) the cause for koala's endangered species status

17 In the sixth paragraph (lines 93–96), the author argues that research should be designed to

(A) analyze the means by which to increase nutrient availability

(B) discover the reason that koalas prefer only eucalyptus leaves

(C) decide how much land should be allotted toward conservation efforts

(D) discover alternate habitats for koalas

(E) determine which areas of eucalyptus are richest in nutrients

18 It can be inferred from the passage that the author believes that koalas are

(A) the most vital species to Australian ecosystems

(B) doomed to become extinct

(C) in need of more conservation efforts to preserve the species

(D) not under a grave risk of extinction

(E) not worthy of being Australia's symbol for conservation efforts

Questions 19–24 are based on the following passage.

This passage is from a book about neurobiology and linguistics written in the 1990s. It examines theories about whether all human languages share a common underlying structure.

Noam Chomsky's influential theory of Universal Grammar postulates that all humans have an innate, genetic understanding of certain grammatical
Line "rules," which are universal across all languages and
(5) absolutely not affected by environment. We are all born, Chomsky says, with a knowledge of "deep structure," basic linguistic constructions that allow us, if not to understand all languages, at least to understand how they are put together. From there,
(10) we have only to learn how the options are set in our particular language in order to create an unlimited number of "correct" utterances.

For example, he suggests that structure dependency—a rule that says that sentences are
(15) defined by phrase structure, not linear structure—is inherent to all languages, with minor variations. (Thus, the meaning of a sentence is really dependent on the meaning of its phrases, rather than each individual word.) In addition, the head parameter
(20) rule stipulates that each phrase contains a "head" (main) word, and all languages have it in essentially the same position within the phrase. Chomsky's famous sentence "Colorless green ideas sleep furiously" exemplifies this theory of Universal
(25) Grammar—while the sentence itself is meaningless, it is easily recognizable as a grammatical sentence that fits a basic, but higher level of organization. "Furiously sleep ideas green colorless," on the other hand, is obviously not grammatical, and it is difficult
(30) to discern any kind of meaning in it. For other evidence to support this theory, Chomsky points to our relative ease in translating one language to another; again, while we may not necessarily recognize individual words in an unfamiliar
(35) language, we can certainly recognize and engage with sentences that are grammatical.

This evidence is still fairly theoretical, receiving play mostly in the linguistic sphere. Most researchers seem more concerned with attempting to
(40) draw universal parallels across languages than searching for biological evidence of such phenomena. We might ask: Where exactly are these Universal Grammar constraints located? How and when are they altered by natural evolutionary processes—or do
(45) they remain relatively unaltered and nonmutated from generation to generation? As language evolves over time, does Universal Grammar also evolve or stay relatively stable? Other scientists say that Universal Grammar is not nearly as ordered and
(50) absolute as Chomsky and other linguists make it out to be and suggest that the Universal Grammar

theory is the result of our flawed human tendency to impose order where there is none. Still others suggest that by completely ignoring the role of
(55) environment in language development, Chomsky completely discredits the possible important effect our surroundings could have on language development.

A few researchers are beginning to suggest that,
(60) rather than focusing on explaining linguistic similarities among various languages, we instead acknowledge the evolutionary roots of language, and look specifically for neurobiological explanations. Claiming that the humanistic exploration of
(65) Universal Grammar is too abstract, they recommend that we instead view language (and grammar) as a function of the brain. Because language is so unbelievably complex, offering several definitions and associations contained within a single word, any
(70) single connection between, say, two languages causes those myriad associations to become oversimplified and sterile. For example, simply pointing out the position of a sentence's subject in Turkish versus that same subject position in English
(75) as an illustration of the existence of Universal Grammar merely acknowledges that single linguistic association without taking into account any social circumstances that may cause the mind to modify that grammar. In short, say these scientists, not
(80) until we create a better marriage between biology and linguistics—and a better understanding of the human brain—can we even begin to address the complexities of human language development.

19 Structure dependency and the head parameter rule (lines 13–22) are provided as examples of observable facts that

(A) linguists cannot find a complete explanation for
(B) suggest the existence of Universal Grammar across all human languages
(C) refute the theory of Universal Grammar
(D) biologists believe are exceptions to the rule of Universal Grammar
(E) scientists think are part of typical nongrammatical sentences

20 The primary function of the information provided in the second paragraph is to

(A) provide evidence for the theory of Universal Grammar
(B) dispute the theory of Universal Grammar
(C) explain why the theory of Universal Grammar is accepted by most linguists
(D) explain the role of head parameters in language
(E) suggest that Universal Grammar oversimplifies the mechanics of language

21 The word "play" in line 38 most nearly means

(A) fun
(B) performance
(C) imitation
(D) gambling
(E) exposure

22 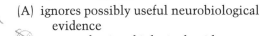 In the last paragraph, the author suggests that some biologists believe an emphasis on linguistics as an explanation for language development

(A) ignores possibly useful neurobiological evidence
(B) overemphasizes biological evidence
(C) eliminates any need for study of social circumstances affecting language development
(D) requires linguists to completely ignore existing biological evidence
(E) oversimplifies the evolutionary role of language

23 The statement in lines 67–72 ("Because language... oversimplified and sterile") suggests that

(A) biological evidence for the existence of Universal Grammar does not exist
(B) biologists have begun gathering genetic evidence to refute the existence of Universal Grammar
(C) simple linguistic connections are enough to prove the existence of Universal Grammar
(D) linguistic methods for proving the existence of Universal Grammar work for some languages, but not others
(E) linguistic explanations cannot account for the complexity of all human languages

24 The author uses the term "marriage" (line 80) to refer to

(A) a flawless combination of linguistics and biology
(B) a romantic relationship between biologists and linguists
(C) a legal union between neurobiologists and Universal Grammar linguists
(D) an intellectual union between biology and linguistics
(E) a long-term unification between science and social science

IF YOU FINISH BEFORE TIME IS CALLED, YOU MAY CHECK YOUR WORK ON THIS SECTION ONLY. DO NOT TURN TO ANY OTHER SECTION IN THE TEST.

STOP

SECTION 4
Time—25 Minutes
18 Questions

Directions: This section contains two kinds of questions. You have 25 minutes to complete both types. For questions 1–8, solve each problem and decide which is the best of the choices given. Fill in the corresponding oval on the answer sheet. You may use any available space for scratchwork.

Notes:

(1) Calculator use is permitted.

(2) All numbers used are real numbers.

(3) Figures are provided for some problems. All figures are drawn to scale and lie in a plane UNLESS otherwise indicated.

(4) Unless otherwise specified, the domain of any function f is assumed to be the set of all real numbers x for which $f(x)$ is a real number.

Information

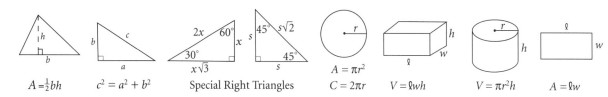

$A = \frac{1}{2}bh$ $\qquad$ $c^2 = a^2 + b^2$ $\qquad$ Special Right Triangles $\qquad$ $A = \pi r^2$ $\qquad$ $C = 2\pi r$ $\qquad$ $V = \ell wh$ $\qquad$ $V = \pi r^2 h$ $\qquad$ $A = \ell w$

The sum of the degree measures of the angles in a triangle is 180.
The number of degrees of arc in a circle is 360.
A straight angle has a degree measure of 180.

1 If $\sqrt{ab} = 3$, $b = c^3$, and $c = 3$, what is the value of $\dfrac{1}{a}$?

(A) $\dfrac{1}{3}$

(B) 1

(C) 3

(D) 9

(E) 27

Handwritten work:
$c = 3$
$b = 3^3 = 27$
$\sqrt{ab} = 3$
$(\sqrt{a \cdot 27})^2 (3)^2$
$27a = 9$
$a = \frac{1}{3}$
$\frac{1}{a} = 3$

2

Note: Figure not drawn to scale

In the figure above, if $h = 20$, $g = 4h$, and $f = 2g$, what is the value of j?

(A) 60
(B) 80
(C) 90
(D) 100
(E) 260

Handwritten work:
360
-260
100

160
80
20
260

GO ON TO THE NEXT PAGE

KAPLAN

3 If $x < 0 < y < 1$, which of the following CANNOT be true?

I. $xy = -\dfrac{1}{4}$

II. $\dfrac{x}{y} = -1$

III. $x + y > 1$

(A) I only
(B) II only
(C) III only
(D) I and II only
(E) I, II, and III

Handwritten:
$-2 \cdot \frac{1}{2} = -1$
$\frac{-\frac{1}{2}}{\frac{1}{2}} = -1$
$-2 \cdot \frac{1}{8} = -\frac{1}{4}$

4 If a and b are positive integers and the ratio of $a + 1$ to $a + 2$ is the same as the ratio of $b + 3$ to $b + 4$, which of the following must be true?

I. $a = 4$
II. $b = 2$
III. $a - b = 2$

(A) I only
(B) II only
(C) III only
(D) I and II only
(E) I, II, and III

Handwritten:
I. $a = 4$ II. $b = 2$ } not required!
$\dfrac{a+1}{a+2} \neq \dfrac{b+3}{b+4}$

$(a+2)(b+3) = (a+1)(b+4)$

$ab + 3a + 2b + 6 = $
$ab + 4a + b + 4$

$3a + 2b + 6 = 4a + b + 4$

$a - b = 2$

$4 \cdot 2$
$5 - 3$
$3 - 1$

5

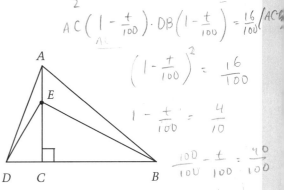

Note: Figure not drawn to scale.

In the figure above, the length of CB is t percent less than the length of DB, and the length of EC is t percent less than the length of AC. If the area of triangle EBC is 16 percent of the area of triangle ABD, then what is the value of t?

(A) 4
(B) 16
(C) 25
(D) 51
(E) 60

Handwritten (top):
$$\dfrac{\left(AC - \frac{t}{100}AC\right)\left(DB - \frac{t}{100}DB\right)}{2} = \dfrac{16}{100} \cdot \left(\dfrac{AC \cdot DB}{2}\right)$$

$AC\left(1 - \frac{t}{100}\right) \cdot DB\left(1 - \frac{t}{100}\right) = \frac{16}{100}/ACC$

$\left(1 - \frac{t}{100}\right)^2 = \frac{16}{100}$

$1 - \frac{t}{100} = \frac{4}{10}$

$\frac{100 - t}{100} = \frac{90}{100} \quad \frac{40}{100}$

$t = 60$

Handwritten (right):
$CB = DB - t\% DB$
$EC = AC - t\% AC$
$A_{EBC} = 16\% \cdot A_{ABD}$
$\dfrac{(EC \times CB)}{2} = \dfrac{16}{100}\left(\dfrac{AC \times DB}{2}\right)$

6 Questions 6–8 refer to the following sequence of steps.

1. Select a number that is greater than 40 and less than 200.

2. Divide the number arrived at in the previous step by 20.

3. Find the smallest integer that is greater than or equal to the number arrived at in the previous step.

4. Subtract 5 from the number arrived at in the previous step.

5. Print the number that results.

Which of the following numbers could be printed in step 5?

(A) 17
(B) 12
(C) 1.7
(D) –1
(E) –7

Handwritten:
$12 + 5 = 17 \qquad 17 \cdot 20 = 340$
$17 + 5 = 22$
$\frac{x}{20} = 2 \quad \frac{x}{40} \qquad \frac{x}{20} = 22$
$-7 + 5 = 2 \qquad 440$
$-1 + 5 = 4$
$\frac{x}{20} = 4$

7 If 150 is the number chosen in step 1, then what number will be printed in step 5?

(A) 2.5
(B) 3
(C) 7.5
(D) 8
(E) 70

$$\frac{150}{20} = 7.5$$

$\downarrow$

8

$\frac{-9}{3}$

8 When the number 112 is selected in step 1, the number printed in step 5 is b. When the number a is selected in step 1, the number b is printed in step 5. What is the greatest possible value of a?

(A) 112
(B) 114
(C) 120
(D) 123
(E) 134

112   9   9
$\downarrow$ $\downarrow$ $\downarrow$
b   b   1

$$\frac{112}{20} = 5.6 \qquad 1 + 5 = 6$$

$\downarrow$

6

$\frac{-5}{1}$

$\frac{x}{20} = 6$

$x = 120$

$b = 1$

GO ON TO THE NEXT PAGE

Directions: For Student-Produced Response questions 9–18, use the grids at the bottom of the answer sheet page on which you have answered questions 1–8.

Each of the remaining 10 questions requires you to solve the problem and enter your answer by marking the ovals in the special grid, as shown in the example below. You may use any available space for scratch work.

Answer: 1.25 or $\frac{5}{4}$

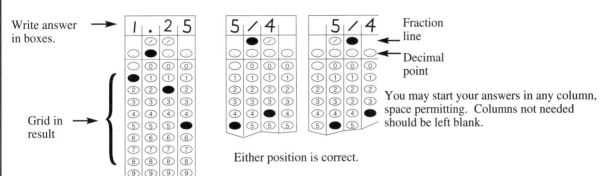

Write answer in boxes.

Grid in result

Either position is correct.

Fraction line

Decimal point

You may start your answers in any column, space permitting. Columns not needed should be left blank.

- It is recommended, though not required, that you write your answer in the boxes at the top of the columns. However, **you will receive credit only for darkening the ovals correctly**.

- Grid only one answer to a question, even though some problems have more than one correct answer.

- Darken no more than one oval in a column.

- No answers are negative.

- **Mixed numbers** cannot be gridded. For example: the number $1\frac{1}{4}$ must be gridded as 1.25 or 5/4.

(If is gridded, it will be interpreted as $\frac{11}{4}$ not $1\frac{1}{4}$.)

- Decimal Accuracy: Decimal answers must be entered as accurately as possible. For example, if you obtain an answer such as 0.1666. . ., you should record the result as .166 or .167. **Less accurate values such as .16 or .17 are not acceptable.**

Acceptable ways to grid $\frac{1}{6}$ = .1666. . .

---

9 If $a - b = 12$ and $\frac{a}{3} = 10$, then what is the value of b?

$$a = 30$$

$$30 - b = 12$$

$$b = 30 - 12 = \boxed{18}$$

10 A telephone call cost $0.35 for the first 3 minutes and $0.07 for each additional minute. How many minutes long was a telephone call that cost $1.75?

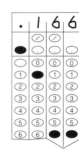

$$(0.35) + (0.07)(x - 3) = 1.75$$

$$0.35 + 0.07x - 0.21 = 1.75$$

$$0.07x = 1.61$$

$$x = \boxed{23} \text{ min}$$

GO ON TO THE NEXT PAGE

11 The points *V*, *W*, *X*, *Y*, and *Z* are located on a number line in that order. The length of *VW* is twice the length of *WX*, the length of *WX* is twice the length of *XY*, and the length of *XY* is twice the length of *YZ*. If the length of *VZ* is 30, what is the length of *WY*?

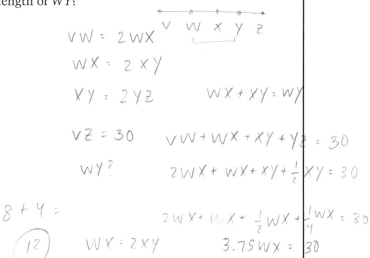

$$VW = 2WX$$
$$WX = 2XY$$
$$XY = 2YZ \qquad WX + XY = WY$$
$$VZ = 30 \qquad VW + WX + XY + YZ = 30$$
$$WY? \qquad 2WX + WX + XY + \tfrac{1}{2}XY = 30$$

$$8 + 4 =$$
$$\boxed{12} \qquad WX = 2XY \qquad 2WX + WX + \tfrac{1}{2}WX + \tfrac{1}{4}WX = 30$$
$$XY = \tfrac{8}{2} = 4 \qquad 3.75WX = 30$$
$$WX = 8$$

13 A store sells 12 different types of radios, 10 different types of television sets, and 5 different types of vacuum cleaners. How many different combinations of one radio, one television set, and one vacuum cleaner can a customer buy?

$$12 \cdot 10 \cdot 5 = \boxed{600}$$

12

```
   BB
   BB
   BB
   BB
 +BB
 �ँ▓
```

In the correctly worked addition problem above, the number covered by the shaded rectangle is a 3-digit number that is at least 250 and no greater than 400. What is one possible value of the number covered by the shaded rectangle?

$$250 \leq x \leq 400$$

$$55$$
$$66 \qquad \boxed{330}$$
$$77$$

14 If day 6 of a 30-day month lies on a Wednesday, and the last Sunday of the month occurs on day *n*, what is the value of *n*?

Sun	M	T	W	Th	F	Sat
			6			
			13			
			20			
24	25	26	27	28	29	30

$$n = \boxed{24}$$

GO ON TO THE NEXT PAGE

15 For all negative integers x other than –1, let $\lozenge x\lozenge$ be defined as the product of all the negative odd integers greater than x. For example, $\lozenge-7\lozenge = (-5) \cdot (-3) \cdot (-1) = -15$.

What is the value of $\dfrac{\lozenge-75\lozenge}{\lozenge-74\lozenge}$?

$$\frac{-73 \cdot -71 \cdot \ldots}{-73 \cdot -71 \cdot \ldots} =$$

1

17 If the median of $7x$, $5x$, $13x$, $11x$, and $8x$ is divisible by 20, what is the smallest possible value for x if x is a positive integer?

$5x, 7x, \underline{8x}, 11x, 13x$

$\dfrac{8x}{20} \rightarrow x = 5$

16

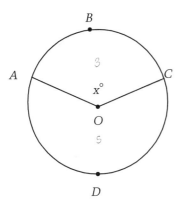

In the figure above, O is the center of the circle, and the ratio of the area of region $OABC$ to the area of region $OCDA$ is 3 to 5. What is the value of x?

$\dfrac{3}{8} \cdot \dfrac{45}{360} = 135$ $\dfrac{OABC}{OCDA} = \dfrac{3}{5}$

135

18

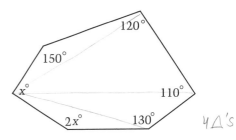

Note: Figure not drawn to scale.

What is the value of x in the figure above?

4 $\triangle$'s $\triangle = 180$

4 · 180 = 720

150
120
110
130
510

720
-510
210

$3x = 210$
$x = 70$

The following sentences test correctness and effectiveness of expression. Part of each sentence or the entire sentence is underlined; beneath each sentence are five ways of phrasing the underlined material. Choice A repeats the original phrasing; the other four choices are different. If you think the original phrasing produces a better sentence than any of the alternatives, select choice A; if not, select one of the other choices.

In making your selection, follow the requirements of standard written English; that is, pay attention to grammar, choice of words, sentence construction, and punctuation. Your selection should result in the most effective sentence—clear and precise, without awkwardness or ambiguity.

EXAMPLE:

Every apple in the baskets <u>are ripe and labeled according to the date it was picked</u>.

ANSWER:

(A) ● (C) (D) (E)

(A) are ripe and labeled according to the date it was picked.
(B) is ripe and labeled according to the date it was picked.
(C) are ripe and labeled according to the date they were picked.
(D) is ripe and labeled according to the date they were picked.
(E) are ripe and labeled as to the date it was picked.

1 Hearing that the test results exceeded state mandates, <u>a party was thrown by the math teacher</u> for the students.

(A) a party was thrown by the math teacher
(B) a party was thrown
(C) the math teacher was thrown a party
(D) the math teacher threw a party
(E) the math teacher had thrown a party

2 Many students prefer social studies over <u>science classes, another one of the preferences is that students prefer English</u> over foreign-language classes.

(A) science classes, another one of the preferences is that students prefer English
(B) science classes, which is also a preference for English
(C) science classes; another student preference is for English
(D) science classes; another preference is that students prefer English
(E) science classes; students prefer English

3 Joe Smith wrote the biography but refused <u>to be credit as the author nor in any other capacity</u> for the commercial success of the book.

(A) to be credit as the author nor in any other capacity
(B) to be credit as the author or
(C) to be credited as the author nor in any other capacity
(D) to be credited as the author or
(E) to neither be credited as the author nor

4 George Balanchine was <u>almost as skillful a dancer as he was at choreography</u>.

(A) almost as skillful a dancer as he was at choreography
(B) almost as skillful at dance as he was a choreographer
(C) almost skillful as a dancer and a choreographer
(D) almost as skillful a dancer as at choreography
(E) almost as skillful a dancer as he was a choreographer

5 Staring out over the ocean, <u>the waves gave the sailor a sense of stability</u>.

(A) the waves gave the sailor a sense of stability
(B) the sailor gave a sense of stability to the waves
(C) the sailor felt a sense of stability from the waves
(D) waving gave the sailor a sense of stability
(E) the waves gave a sense of stability to the sailor

GO ON TO THE NEXT PAGE

KAPLAN

6 Many football players vent their anger on the playing field, daily in their lives they are calm though.

(A) Many football players vent their anger on the playing field, daily in their lives they are calm though.

(B) Many football players vent their anger on the playing field, though in their daily lives they are calmer than that.

(C) Many football players are angrier on the playing field than daily.

(D) Many football players vent their anger on the playing field though in their daily lives they are calm.

(E) Many football players vent their anger on the playing field, though calm in their daily lives.

7 Certain constellations have a particular meaning for those people which have a belief in astrology.

(A) which have a belief in astrology

(B) who believe in astrology

(C) whom believe in astrology

(D) that believe in astrology

(E) who believe in horoscopes

8 Relying on its news, CNN is a television station many people watch.

(A) Relying on its news, CNN is a television station many people watch.

(B) Relying on its news, the television station CNN is the one many people watch.

(C) A television station watched by many people relying on its news is CNN.

(D) Relying on its news, many people watch the television station CNN.

(E) Many people, relying on CNN, and watching it.

9 The technique of impressionism is perhaps best seen in either Monet's or Renoir's work.

(A) in either Monet's or Renoir's

(B) either in Monet's or in Renoir's

(C) either Monet's or Renoir's

(D) within Monet's or Renoir's

(E) in Monet's or Renoir's

10 Tom hated to watch golf, of which he found the length particularly boring.

(A) golf, of which he found the length particularly boring

(B) golf; he found the length particularly boring

(C) golf, which he found particularly boring

(D) golf, to which he found the length particularly boring

(E) golf; which he found particularly boring in length

11 The government imposed sanctions on a renegade nation last month after they violated the terms of a worldwide arms-control agreement.

(A) imposed sanctions on a renegade nation last month after they violated

(B) imposed sanctions on a renegade nation last month after it was violating

(C) has imposed sanctions on a renegade nation last month after they violated

(D) imposed sanctions on a renegade nation last month after that nation violated

(E) imposed sanctions on a nation of renegades last month after they violated

Directions: The following sentences test your ability to recognize grammar and usage errors. Each sentence contains either a single error or no error at all. No sentence contains more than one error. The error, if there is one, is underlined and lettered. If the sentence contains an error, select the one underlined part that must be changed to make the sentence correct. If the sentence is correct, select choice E. In choosing answers, follow the requirements of standard written English.

EXAMPLE:

<u>Whenever</u> one is driving late at night, <u>you</u> must take extra precautions <u>against</u>
   A   B   C

falling asleep <u>at</u> the wheel. <u>No error.</u>
           D   E

ANSWER:

Ⓐ ● Ⓒ Ⓓ Ⓔ

---

12 The scientist <u>conducting</u> the experiment in the
               A
rain forest was less interested in why the

particular species was prevalent <u>than in</u> whether
                             B
<u>they have</u> <u>violently</u> taken over another species'
  C   D
habitat. <u>No error</u>
        E

13 <u>That</u> his presentation on financial strategy was
   A
criticized <u>savagely</u> by his customers <u>who</u> watched
        B   C
it <u>came</u> as a shock to the analyst. <u>No error</u>
   D   E

14 A downfall in the economy could affect the ballet

season because programs <u>performed</u> in the new
                    A
symphony hall <u>cost</u> twice <u>as much</u> in overhead as
          B   C
<u>the old performance space.</u> <u>No error</u>
       D   E

15 The <u>other</u> cyclists and <u>me</u> <u>immediately</u> started
       A   B   C
peddling when we heard the whistle <u>blown</u> by the
                           D
race organizer. <u>No error</u>
           E

16 <u>Although</u> the amount of money in the bank
    A
accounts <u>keep</u> dwindling, the account holders
        B
<u>claim that</u> their finances <u>are improving.</u> <u>No error</u>
   C   D   E

17 To compare a new investment opportunity

<u>to one's</u> previous stock losses <u>is a more</u>
   A   B
advantageous strategy <u>than</u> <u>attempting</u> to turn a
                 C   D
profit without referring back to them. <u>No error</u>
                               E

GO ON TO THE NEXT PAGE

18 Like that of many braggarts, the businessman's
A   B
success sounded impressive but in fact was not
C
because he had done no work to attain it. No error
D   E

19 The bidders for the museum-restored, newly
A
framed painting clearly wanted to purchase
B   C
artistic recognized work for their collections.
D
No error
E

20 No one dares to contradict the high school
A
principal, for she has the authority to detract from
B   C
a student's grade point average for any reason.
D
No error
E

21 The store manager telephoned the warehouse
A
manager after he failed to deliver the products on
B   C   D
the correct day. No error
E

22 During the debate, Jack attended closely to the
A
Independent Party candidate's economic plan,

which Jack thought was better structured
B   C
than the other candidates. No error
D   E

23 Edward Villella's talent enables him to stage
A
ballets that develop from and incorporate the
B   C
feeling that George Balanchine intended. No error
D   E

24 Many people claim to have seen UFOs, but
A   B
not one have proved that such objects exist.
C   D
No error
E

25 This year, the company announces Take Your
A
Daughter to Work Day in an effort to build the
B
morale of employees in the head office
C
during the recession. No error
D   E

26 Initially intended as a comment on traditional
A   B
politics, the strongly worded e-mail exerted great
C
influence on the businesses at its time. No error
D   E

27 Seniors which need help with their college
A
applications can find immediate assistance in
B   C   D
the Guidance Department. No error
E

28 Doctors have found that herbal medications,
A
when combined with a more traditional medical
B
approach, shortens the healing time for a number
C   D
of surgical procedures. No error
E

29 The complex formulas and problems of Algebra II
A
caused me more sleepless nights and test anxiety
B   C
than Algebra I. No error
D   E

GO ON TO THE NEXT PAGE

Directions: The following passage is an early draft of an essay. Some parts of the passage need to be rewritten.

Read the passage and select the best answers for the questions that follow. Some questions are about particular sentences or parts of sentences and ask you to improve sentence structure or word choice. Other questions ask you to consider organization and development. In choosing answers, follow the conventions of standard written English.

Questions 30–35 are based on the following passage.

(1) A few years ago, my high school decided to eliminate music programs. (2) My friends and I disagreed with the decision, and so we developed a pamphlet that discussed our opinions. (3) Many students approached us after reading the pamphlet and said that we changed the way they used to think about music. (4) This made us feel that we were really effecting our curriculum. (5) We hoped our actions would make the school change its policy.

(6) But we hoped in vain. (7) We weren't allowed to take chorus, band, or string classes. (8) The school said that it was because music wasn't an important skill to develop in comparison to math, English, and science. (9) The development of musical ability affects so many aspects of a person's life. (10) I disagree. (11) Music teaches you to listen for patterns and ideas that aren't in words. (12) Learning how to read music is like learning a second language—it is the same because it's another way to express yourself. (13) People should know the importance of music education and it is up to students to prove it to them.

30 In context, which is the best version of the underlined portion of sentence 3 (reproduced below)?

Many students approached us after reading the pamphlet and said that we changed the way they used to think about music.

(A) the pamphlet and said that we changed the way they used to think about music
(B) the pamphlet and said that we changed the way they thought about music
(C) the pamphlet and said that we changed the way they think about music
(D) the pamphlet and said that we change the way they think about music
(E) the pamphlet and said that we change the way they used to think about music

31 In context, which is the best version of the underlined portion of sentence 4 (reproduced below)?

This made us feel that we were really effecting our curriculum.

(A) we were really effecting our
(B) we were really influencing on our
(C) we were really having an influence on our
(D) we were really affecting our
(E) we were effecting our

32 Which of the following sentences is best inserted at the beginning of the second paragraph, before sentence 6?

(A) However, when music programs continued to be eliminated, we realized that, despite our pamphlet, students were not motivated to fight the policy.
(B) Therefore, when music programs continued to be eliminated, we realized that despite our pamphlet, students were not motivated to fight the policy.
(C) As a result, when music programs continued to be eliminated, we realized that despite our pamphlet, students were not motivated to fight the policy.
(D) However, students had too much on their minds.
(E) However, students did not fight the policy.

33 Which of the following would be the most suitable sentence to insert immediately after sentence 6?

(A) We were too optimistic.
(B) Our pamphlet was very effective.
(C) The school continued their policies.
(D) The school continued its policy.
(E) The school changed its policy.

GO ON TO THE NEXT PAGE

34 Sentence 10 would make most sense if placed
after:

(A) Sentence 7
(B) Sentence 8
(C) Sentence 11
(D) Sentence 12
(E) Sentence 13

35 In context, which is the best version of the
underlined portion of sentence 12 (reproduced
below)?

*Learning how to read music is like learning a
second language—it is the same because it's
another way to express yourself.*

(A) it is the same because it's another way to
    express yourself
(B) it is the same way to express yourself
(C) music is the same because it's another way to
    express yourself
(D) each are a way to express yourself
(E) it's another way to express yourself

**IF YOU FINISH BEFORE TIME IS CALLED, YOU MAY CHECK YOUR WORK ON
THIS SECTION ONLY. DO NOT TURN TO ANY OTHER SECTION IN THE TEST.** **STOP**

SECTION 6
Time—25 Minutes
24 Questions

Directions: For each question in this section, select the best answer from among the choices given and fill in the corresponding oval on the answer sheet.

Each sentence below has one or two blanks, each blank indicating that something has been omitted. Beneath the sentence are five words or sets of words labeled A through E. Choose the word or set of words that, when inserted in the sentence, best fits the meaning of the sentence as a whole.

EXAMPLE:

Today's small, portable computers contrast markedly with the earliest electronic computers, which were ----.

(A) effective   (B) invented   (C) useful
    (D) destructive   (E) enormous

ANSWER:

Ⓐ Ⓑ Ⓒ Ⓓ ●

1 As far as the committee was concerned, the ------- with which the braggart interjected his opinion confirmed his -------.

(A) flourish .. mediocrity
(B) reluctance .. humility
(C) ostentation .. pretentiousness
(D) severity .. exhibitionism
(E) ambivalence .. prejudice

2 Many philosophers contend that true enlightenment is found only by ------- those material objects that obstruct one's contemplation of the eternal.

(A) renouncing (B) affirming (C) considering
    (D) imbibing (E) concealing

3 The cheerfulness with which the administrator spoke to the assembly temporarily hid the ------- of her address; her jovial tenor, however, soon gave way to more sober remarks.

(A) elation (B) optimism (C) comprehension
    (D) frailty (E) gravity

4 The university chancellor finally ------- the students' concerns by showing that there was no tuition increase in the following year's budget.

(A) elicited (B) triggered (C) allayed
    (D) derogated (E) shifted

5 The biography detailed how the formerly ------- young man became a ------- who caused a great deal of harm before his eventual imprisonment.

(A) innocent .. libertarian
(B) irreproachable .. miscreant
(C) nefarious .. demagogue
(D) malicious .. reprobate
(E) hapless .. leader

6 The ------- effects of the recent record-setting blizzards were somewhat ------- by the series of sunny and pleasant days that followed.

(A) frigid .. exacerbated
(B) stimulating .. alleviated
(C) disastrous .. counterbalanced
(D) intensifying .. aggravated
(E) overwhelming .. challenged

7 Because the Senator typically appears -------, her reticent attitude last evening seemed particularly -------.

(A) sociable .. appropriate
(B) gregarious .. incongruous
(C) distraught .. sympathetic
(D) serious .. irrelevant
(E) pedestrian .. inexplicable

8 In contrast to most of the students, whose faces appeared vacant, the new student maintained a(n) ------- expression throughout the lecture.

(A) gloomy (B) rapt (C) dessiminated
    (D) imbued (E) retiring

GO ON TO THE NEXT PAGE

KAPLAN

Directions: The passages below are followed by questions based on their content; questions following a pair of related passages may also be based on the relationship between the paired passages. Answer the questions on the basis of what is <u>stated</u> or <u>implied</u> in the passages and in any introductory material that may be provided.

Questions 9–12 are based on the following passages.

Passage 1

Many national parks and monuments have seen an upgrade in their security systems over the past decade. Well-founded fears of graffiti, theft,
Line and negligent conduct by a small percentage of
(5) visitors have led the National Park Service to emphasize security, and a tremendous amount of effort has gone into the massive project of fencing and gating these precious lands. The greatest difficulties for the park system are the sites that
(10) contain artifacts and monuments, since these sites are the most difficult to secure. Nonetheless, all parks need to be well protected for future generations, whether the parks contain natural wonders or monuments to human achievement.

Passage 2

(15) One of the many duties of the National Park Service is to preserve and protect the parks themselves. However, they cannot put these concerns ahead of the needs of today's park visitors. Many parks contain artifacts and ruins
(20) that are nothing less than memorials of personal heritage. Some of these parks, like Chaco Canyon and Petroglyph National Monument, are home to great treasures of Native American culture. Park visitors have a right to access this property as
(25) their own, but barbed-wire fences send a different signal. The soundest security measure would be to give the citizens their rightly deserved sense of ownership.

9 In Passage 1 (line 6), the word "tremendous" most nearly means

(A) immense
(B) famous
(C) excellent
(D) elevated
(E) exemplary

10 On the whole, the author of Passage 1 regards the security at national parks as

(A) inevitable
(B) terrible
(C) fortunate
(D) necessary
(E) superfluous

11 The primary function of the phrase "memorials of personal heritage" (lines 20–21) is to

(A) reinforce the idea that the artifacts and ruins in parks belong to the visitors
(B) reveal the fragility of the park property most in need of protection
(C) highlight the importance of the artifacts and ruins to the park system as a whole
(D) suggest that the artifacts and ruins have already been partially destroyed by visitors
(E) raise concerns about the presence of barbed wire in national parks

12 The author of Passage 2 would most likely regard the "fencing and gating" mentioned in lines 7–8 as an example of

(A) sound security measures
(B) the duties of the National Park Service
(C) upgraded security systems
(D) signs to visitors that they are not welcome
(E) property lines

GO ON TO THE NEXT PAGE

Questions 13–24 are based on the following passages.

The following passages are excerpted from two books that discuss fairy tales. Passage 1 was written by a specialist in psychology and children's literature and was published in 1965. Passage 2 was written by a folklore methodologist and was published in 1986.

Passage 1

Most of the stories that our society tells have only enjoyed a comparatively short period of popularity in comparison with the sweep of human history, flaming into popular consciousness in books,
(5) television or film for a period reaching anywhere from a few months to a few centuries. Fads come and go as fickle as the weather, and today's hit may be tomorrow's forgotten relic. But one particular kind of story that our society tells, the fairy tale, has
(10) a kind of popularity that is uniquely persistent. Literally since time immemorial, fairy tales have been told and retold, refined and adapted across generations of human history. Folk tales that spoke to people in some deeper way, and thus proved
(15) popular, endured and were passed down through the ages. Tales that had only temporal and fleeting appeal are long since lost. Since, as we know, it is a truism that time sifts out the literary wheat and discards the chaff, fairy tales can be said to have
(20) undergone the longest process of selection and editing of any stories in human history.

Consider, for example, the story of "Snow White." Here is reflected the tale of the eternal struggle for supremacy between the generations. The evil mother
(25) queen grows jealous of the competition of the young Snow White for supremacy in the realm of youth and beauty, so she contrives to do away with her rival. The innocent Snow White survives by a twist of whim and circumstance, and then retreats into the
(30) forest—the traditional symbol of the site of psychological change—where she hides among the Seven Dwarves. Small supernatural spirits or homunculi, often depicted in folk tales as tiny elves, spirit men, trolls, or fairies, represent unconscious
(35) forces, and thus Snow White must care for and nurture the Seven Dwarves while she undergoes her psychological transformation. The dwarves' mining activities can be said to symbolize this process of mental delving into the depths in hopes of uncovering
(40) the precious materials of the developing psyche.

Yet Snow White's road to her new identity is not without incident. The breaching of the secure space by the disguised queen mother and Snow White's giving in to the temptation of the apple—
(45) representative of the same youth and beauty that the queen seeks to deprive her of—causes her to fall into the slumberous mock-death. Only the prince can deliver Snow White and metaphorically resurrect her with a kiss, itself a motif that suggests her entry into
(50) the identity of a mature person ready to leave the dwarves and forest of the unconscious behind and take on adult responsibilities.

The popularity of this tale, and others like it, across time and in widely scattered societies
(55) confirms its power in tapping into unconscious forces and common motifs that all humans share. All humans in all ages experience generational rivalry and the impact that it has on patterns of growth and maturity. The specific symbols used to
(60) represent these dynamics are less important than their universality; indeed the very adaptability of the symbolism is what allows tales to remain popular over time. By dramatizing these psychological progressions, the fairy tale helps its audience to
(65) process the ill-understood unconscious psychological forces that are a part of human life. Can it be any wonder that such powerful avenues to the cosmic unconscious can be shown to have remained popular across the eons?

Passage 2

(70) The contention that folklore represents a cosmic tale that encapsulates cross-cultural human universalities in narrative form is naïve in the extreme. The notion that folk tales somehow embody a symbolically encoded map of human
(75) consciousness suffers from a fundamental flaw: it assumes that each tale has a more-or-less consistent form. In fact, the forms of most folk tales that we have today recorded in collections and in the popular media represent nothing more than isolated
(80) snapshots of narratives that have countless forms, many of which are so different as to drastically change the interpretations that some critics want to say are universal.

Consider, for example, the story of "Little Red
(85) Riding Hood." Some psychological interpretations might conjecture, for example, that this is a tale about obedience and parental authority. Straying

GO ON TO THE NEXT PAGE

KAPLAN

from the path in the forest, in this context, might represent rebelling against that authority, and the
(90) wolf then symbolizes the dangerous unconscious forces from which parents seek to protect Little Red. The red color of the riding hood might be seen as representing the subdued emotions of anger and hostility. Being consumed by the wolf signifies a
(95) period of isolation and transformation. Finally, the rescuing huntsman at the end of the story then symbolizes the return of parental authority to deliver the innocent child from being metaphorically consumed by ill-understood emotional states.
(100) It is an apparently consistent analogy, and one that is difficult to dispute, until one investigates the circumstances of the composition and recording of the version of "Little Red Riding Hood" that we have today. Earlier editions of the story simply don't have
(105) many of the components that critics would like to present as so-called "universal symbols." For example, in the vast majority of the older and simpler versions of this tale, the story ends after the wolf eats the girl. So there can be no theme of
(110) parental rescue because, in all but a few of the examples of this tale, there is no rescue and no kind huntsman. In some versions the girl even saves herself, completely contradicting the assumption that it is a story about rescue. Story elements such as
(115) the path, the hunter, and the happy ending, which are seen as essential symbolic components of our interpretation above, were introduced to this ancient tale by the Brothers Grimm in the 19th century. Even the introduction of the "symbolic" red garment
(120) dates only from the seventeenth century, when it was put into the story by Charles Perrault.
In fact, every fairy tale known to the study of folklore has so many different versions that there are encyclopedic reference books to catalog the
(125) variations and the differences between them. A creature that is an elf in one country and era might be a troll in another. A magic object represented as a hat in one version of a tale might be a cloak in ten other tellings. If folk tales actually represent
(130) universal human truths in symbolic form, the symbols in them would have to reflect universal consistency across time. Any attempt to pinpoint a consistent symbolic meaning or underlying scheme in such a field of moving, blending, and ever-
(135) changing targets is doomed to fail before it even begins. Instead, we should embrace all such variations on a theme, searching for insights into the cultural conditions which prompt such divergence.

13 In discussing "fairy tales" in lines 17–21, the author of Passage 1 suggests that

(A) which stories endure and which are forgotten has nothing to do with the quality of the story
(B) stories written by a single author and not endlessly retold and edited may well not have the lasting appeal of fairy tales
(C) many folk tales that spoke deeply to their audiences have been lost and forgotten over the ages
(D) folk tales undergo the same degree of selection and editing as other kinds of literature
(E) the original author of "Snow White" was very careful with the selection and editing of the tale

14 According to the author of Passage 1, the experience of the "motifs" mentioned in line 56 is shared by "all humans" because

(A) they appear in the tale "Snow White"
(B) they reflect the views of critics
(C) they signify the transition from childhood to adult identity
(D) they embody unconscious forces that must be cared for and nurtured
(E) they represent experiences that all humans have undergone

15 The word "avenues" in line 67 most nearly means

(A) boulevards
(B) beginnings
(C) homecomings
(D) approaches
(E) forces

16 The statement that "there can be no theme of parental rescue...huntsman" in Passage 2 (lines 109–112) suggests that fairy tales

(A) should make a greater effort to capture universal human themes
(B) are generally not interested in historical accuracy
(C) cannot be said to have a single authoritative form
(D) are usually not concerned with themes of rescue
(E) were not solidified into final form until the 19th century

GO ON TO THE NEXT PAGE

17 The author of Passage 2 primarily takes issue with critics who extract simple symbolic interpretations from fairy tales because of what he sees as their

(A) disregard for the rigorous principles of modern psychology
(B) naïve view of the complexity of human nature
(C) failure to make proper use of reference materials pertaining to folklore methodology
(D) willingness to assume that minor details of a specific version of a folk tale are universal
(E) unsuccessful attempts to correctly interpret the symbolism of older versions of fairy tales

18 Which of the following conclusions is suggested by the final sentence of Passage 2?

(A) The variations among versions of fairy tales can tell us something about the cultures in which these versions developed.
(B) Folklore methodologists should seek out oral versions of folk tales themselves instead of getting them from books.
(C) The earliest recorded versions of folk tales are more accurate and authoritative than later versions.
(D) Only fairy tales written in modern times can be accurately interpreted.
(E) Fairy tales with many versions are more likely to survive many generations than are those that lack significant variations.

19 The authors of both passages state that fairy tales are

(A) intuitively meaningful
(B) critically misunderstood
(C) historically changeable
(D) symbolically rich
(E) essentially practical

20 With which of the following statements about fairy tales would the authors of both passages most likely agree?

(A) The popularity of fairy tales is due to their deeper meanings.
(B) Fairy tales speak to all humans in the language of universal psychological symbols.
(C) Fairy tales have resulted from a compositional process very different from that of modern literature written by a single author.
(D) The study of folklore is undergoing extensive changes because of new information about different versions of particular tales.
(E) The unique origins of fairy tales makes it possible to create symbolic schemes that link the events depicted in fairy tales with eternal human truths.

21 The author of Passage 1 would probably respond to the statement in lines 77–84 of Passage 2 with the argument that

(A) many modern folk tales originated relatively recently and haven't been subjected to centuries of editing
(B) the changes in the symbolism of more-recent revisions of folk tales are less important psychologically than the broad themes
(C) there is no evidence that the symbolism of folk tales is related to psychological forces
(D) "Snow White" is a poor example to use as evidence because it has changed so much over time
(E) better techniques and methodologies have recently allowed even less-popular tales to survive across time

GO ON TO THE NEXT PAGE

KAPLAN

22 Which of the following best describes the primary disagreement that the author of Passage 2 would most likely raise against the statement in Passage 1 (lines 32–37) that "Small supernatural spirits...transformation"?

(A) The psychologist who made this interpretation did not use the encyclopedic catalogs of different versions of this tale.

(B) The popularity of this tale is no indication of its value in expressing a psychological truth.

(C) This version of the tale is not necessarily the most accurate, because it is recent and may have deviated too much from the true version over time.

(D) Small supernatural spirits could represent many things other than unconscious forces.

(E) The specific details in different versions of this folk tale show too much variation to make any consistent interpretations based on this particular version.

23 The author of Passage 1 would most likely reply to the statement in lines 119–121 of Passage 2 by

(A) arguing that specific symbols still stem from the underlying psychological structure of the tale

(B) pointing out that the seventeenth and nineteenth centuries were still quite a while ago

(C) agreeing that the red garment probably does not represent aggressive emotions

(D) postulating that the works of Perrault and the Grimms are not valid examples of folklore

(E) stipulating that this particular tale has too many variants to be faithfully interpreted

24 Which symbolic interpretation made by the author of Passage 1 most closely mirrors the interpretation made by the author of Passage 2 in lines 94–95 ("Being consumed...transformation")?

(A) Snow White represents the queen's rival in the realm of youth and beauty.

(B) Being lost in the forest symbolizes a period of separation and change.

(C) Small supernatural homunculi signify unconscious forces.

(D) The prince delivers Snow White from her mock death with a kiss.

(E) The huntsman epitomizes parental authority.

IF YOU FINISH BEFORE TIME IS CALLED, YOU MAY CHECK YOUR WORK ON THIS SECTION ONLY. DO NOT TURN TO ANY OTHER SECTION IN THE TEST. **STOP**

SECTION 7
Time—20 Minutes
16 Questions

Directions: For this section, solve each problem and decide which is the best of the choices given. Fill in the corresponding oval on the answer sheet. You may use any available space for scratchwork.

Notes:

(1) Calculator use is permitted.

(2) All numbers used are real numbers.

(3) Figures are provided for some problems. All figures are drawn drawn to scale and lie in a plane UNLESS otherwise indicated.

(4) Unless otherwise specified, the domain of any function f is assumed to be the set of all real numbers x for which $f(x)$ is a real number.

Information

  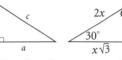

$A = \frac{1}{2}bh$ $c^2 = a^2 + b^2$ Special Right Triangles $A = \pi r^2$ $C = 2\pi r$ $V = \ell w h$ $V = \pi r^2 h$ $A = \ell w$

The sum of the degree measures of the angles in a triangle is 180.
The number of degrees of arc in a circle is 360.
A straight angle has a degree measure of 180.

---

1 If $4p^2 = 36$ and $36 > 5q$, which of the following must be true?

(A) $p^2 > 5q$
(B) $p^2 = 5q$
(C) $4p^2 > 5q$
(D) $4p^2 = 5q$
(E) $4p^2 < 5q$

2 The sum of 7 numbers is greater than 140 and less than 210. Which of the following could be the average (arithmetic mean) of the numbers?

(A) 5
(B) 12
(C) 17
(D) 20
(E) 28

$$\frac{140}{7} < \frac{sum}{7} < \frac{210}{7}$$

$$20 < \frac{sum}{7} < 30$$

GO ON TO THE NEXT PAGE

3 If $7d < 4r$ and $4r < 8p$, which of the following must be true?

(A) $7d < 8p$
(B) $8p < 7d$
(C) $p < d$
(D) $r = 2p$
(E) $2r = p$

5 If the average (arithmetic mean) of 8 numbers is greater than 10 and less than 12, which of the following could be the sum of the 8 numbers?

(A) 70
(B) 80
(C) 90
(D) 100
(E) 110

$$10 < \frac{sum}{8} < 12$$

$$80 < sum < 96$$

Location	Number of Boxes	Number of Toys in Each Box
Basement	4	10
Garage	2	6
Attic	5	7

4 The chart above shows the location of all the toys stored at Joe's house. According to the chart, what is the total number of toys at Joe's house?

(A) 23
(B) 40
(C) 57
(D) 87
(E) 123

$$(4 \cdot 10) + (2 \cdot 6) + (5 \cdot 7)$$
$$40 + 12 + 35 = 87$$

6 A certain necklace is made up of beads of the following colors: red, blue, orange, indigo, clear, and silver. The necklace contains 120 beads. According to the pie chart above, how many beads of the necklace are NOT blue?

(A) 20
(B) 24
(C) 92
(D) 96
(E) 100

$$80\%$$

$$\frac{4}{5} \frac{80}{100} \cdot 120 = 96$$

7 The hour hand of a watch rotates 30 degrees every hour. How many complete rotations does the hour hand make in 6 days?

(A) 18
(B) 12
(C) 10
(D) 8
(E) 6

1 day = 24 hrs

6 days · $\frac{24 \text{ hrs}}{1 \text{ day}}$ = 144 hrs

144 hrs. $\frac{30 \text{ deg}}{1 \text{ hr}}$ = 4320°

$\frac{4320}{360}$ = 12

8

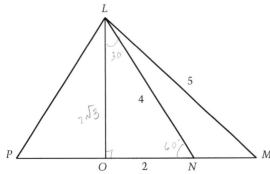

Note: Figure not drawn to scale.

Which of the following is a triangle whose angles have degree measures of 30, 60, and 90?

(A) ΔLMN
(B) ΔLMP
(C) ΔLOP
(D) ΔLMO
(E) ΔLNO

$2^2 + x^2 = 4^2$
$x^2 = 16 - 4$
$x^2 = 12$
$x = \sqrt{12} = 2\sqrt{3}$

9 Which of the following expressions can be negative?

(A) $\frac{x^2}{2}$

(B) $\frac{3}{1 + x^2}$

(C) $4x^3$

(D) $(x^3)^2$ x^6

(E) $x(x^3 + x^5)$ $x^4 + x^6$

10 The Earth makes one complete rotation about its axis every 24 hours. Assuming it rotates at a constant rate, through how many degrees would Goannaville, Australia rotate from 1:00 p.m. on January 2 to 4:00 p.m. on January 3?

(A) 202°
(B) 250°
(C) 350°
(D) 363°
(E) 405°

2   1:00 pm

3   4 p.m.

360
45
405

24 + 3 =
/27
hrs.

360°

$\frac{3}{24} = \frac{1}{8} \cdot 360 =$

45

GO ON TO THE NEXT PAGE

11 If S is the set of all numbers between –3.5 and 3.5, inclusive, T is the set of all prime numbers, and U is the set of all positive integers, then the intersection of S, T, and U contains how many elements?

(A) 0
(B) 1
(C) 2
(D) 3
(E) More than 3

(handwritten) $S: [-3.5, 3.5]$ $T: [prime]$ $U: [pos.\ int]$

13 Which of the following expressions is equal to 3^8 when $y = 3^5$?

(A) $\dfrac{y}{3}$

(B) $9y^2$

(C) $\dfrac{y^2}{3}$

(D) $\dfrac{y^2}{9}$

(E) $\dfrac{y^3}{27}$

(handwritten) $\dfrac{3^5}{3^1} = 3^4$ $y = 3^5$ $9 = 3^2$ $3^2 \cdot (3^5)^2$ $(3^5)^2 = 3^9$ $\dfrac{(3^5)^2}{3^2} = \dfrac{3^{10}}{3^2}$

12 Which of the following expressions must be positive for all values of a and b?

(A) $a + b$
(B) $a^2 - b^2 + 10$
(C) $a^2 + b^2 + 1$
(D) $a^3 + b^3 + 16$
(E) $a^4 + b^2 + a^2$

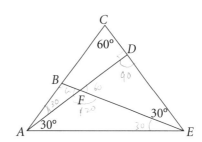

Note: Figure not drawn to scale.

14 In triangle *ACE* above, *AD* and *BE* are line segments. Which of the following is NOT a right triangle?

(A) *ABF*
(B) *ACD*
(C) *ADE*
(D) *AFE*
(E) *BCE*

GO ON TO THE NEXT PAGE

15 The initial number of elements in a certain set is p, where $p > 0$. If the number of elements in the set doubles every hour, which of the following represents the total number of elements in the set after exactly 24 hours?

(A) $24p$
(B) $48p$
(C) $2p^{24}$
(D) $(2p)^{24}$
(E) $(2^{24})p$

16 The absolute value of a certain integer is greater than 3 and less than 6. Which of the following could NOT be 2 less than the integer?

(A) −7
(B) −6
(C) 2
(D) 3
(E) 4

SECTION 8
Time—20 Minutes
19 Questions

Directions: For each question in this section, select the best answer from among the choices given and fill in the corresponding oval on the answer sheet.

Each sentence below has one or two blanks, each blank indicating that something has been omitted. Beneath the sentence are five words or sets of words labeled A through E. Choose the word or set of words that, when inserted in the sentence, best fits the meaning of the sentence as a whole.

EXAMPLE:

Today's small, portable computers contrast markedly with the earliest electronic computers, which were ----.

(A) effective   (B) invented   (C) useful
    (D) destructive   (E) enormous

ANSWER:

Ⓐ Ⓑ Ⓒ Ⓓ ●

1 The editorial highlighted both sides of the ------- ; despite its contentiousness in public discussions, the debate was fairly and objectively outlined in the newspaper.

(A) accord (B) calamity (C) disagreement
    (D) disposition (E) consensus

2 Although Jane Austen's novels are most often ------- for their eloquence and imagery, they are also highly esteemed for their subtle, yet shrewd ------- the economic and social milieu of the landed gentry of nineteenth century England.

(A) admired .. observations on
(B) denigrated .. metaphors about
(C) respected .. diversity of
(D) inclined .. interpretation of
(E) maligned .. simplicity of

3 From his early, more ------- paintings to his final, most ------- masterworks, the progression of Turner's painting style mirrored the evolution away from Romantic realism and toward increasing degrees of abstraction.

(A) obscure .. explicit
(B) misunderstood .. understated
(C) enthralling .. retrospective
(D) tame .. romantic
(E) traditional .. pioneering

4 Sylvester signed his name with a characteristic ------- that made his signature look more like art than writing.

(A) wince (B) glimpse (C) flourish
    (D) nod (E) understatement

5 To dissect vital communications, the -------, a specialist in the technology of deciphering messages, typically employs a host of complex mathematical formulas.

(A) entomologist (B) connoisseur (C) cryptologist
    (D) statistician (E) pathologist

6 Most of the guests found the hotel to be -------, listing the ------- of the amenities as one of the things they disliked the most.

(A) deficient .. paucity
(B) venerable .. expediency
(C) nascent .. petulance
(D) congenial .. convenience
(E) quaint .. antiquity

Directions: The passages below are followed by questions based on their content; questions following a pair of related passages may also be based on the relationship between the paired passages. Answer the questions on the basis of what is <u>stated</u> or <u>implied</u> in the passages and in any introductory material that may be provided.

Questions 7–19 are based on the following passage.

This passage is a work of fiction based on the real experiences of Wilma Mankiller, the first female Principal Chief of the Cherokee Nation.

During an interview for a literary magazine, I was asked why my autobiography, titled *Mankiller, A Chief and Her People*, contained so much history of
Line the Cherokee, history that occurred almost five
(5) centuries before I was born. That answer is a very simple one for me to give, but may be difficult to understand. The person that I am has been defined by my people and their experiences, whether it was a week ago or centuries ago. When I ran for Deputy
(10) Chief in 1985, I ran as a Cherokee, not as a Cherokee woman. I was shocked by how much my gender played a role in the election, because it never once entered my mind when I made the decision to run. My decision to run for office was founded on the
(15) desire to help my people recognize their own strength and realize they had the power to rebuild their lives and their communities because they had been able to accomplish these goals in the past.

I am proud to be a Cherokee and I am proud of my
(20) people, both past and present. Everything that has happened in our past has affected our present and will affect our future. But one theme remains constant—survival. Our history has been full of obstacles and hardships, yet we persevere. In the late
(25) 1830s, the Cherokee were forced to relocate from their homelands throughout the Southeast to Indian Territory in what later became Oklahoma. We were stripped of our land, our homes, and our possessions and then forced to walk to the new territory. Many
(30) others may have simply succumbed to the hardships and ceased to exist. Instead, we rebuilt our tribe and our community with a new constitution, a new tribal government including our own judicial system, businesses, schools for both girls and boys, and even
(35) newspapers printed in both Cherokee and English. This renewal occurred within seven years of our arrival in Indian Territory. These accomplishments alone show the limitless tenacity of the Cherokee people.
(40) It becomes even more clear when the story continues and the history of the early 1900s includes the destruction of everything we had rebuilt in the previous fifty years. Our schools and our courts were closed down. Our sovereignty was stripped away.
(45) From 1906 to 1971 we could not even elect our own tribal leaders. But the Cherokees did what we had always done—we survived. This second rebirth took

much longer than the first, but we found the strength to do what had been done before.
(50) You may wonder why I use "we" when I speak of Cherokee history. Again, I return to the idea that as a Cherokee, my tribe's history has defined me, just as it has defined all Cherokee. In fact, some of my personal experiences parallel the experiences of my
(55) ancestors. In 1956, my parents, siblings, and I were moved to California as part of the BIA* relocation program. We were moved away from our family, our tribe, and our community in an effort to improve our lives. Unlike the forced removal of the 1830s, the
(60) program was voluntary, but it had the same effect on the tribe as a whole. It divided us and showed us that the federal government believed we could not improve our lives without aid. But just as my ancestors survived the hardships, so did my family.
(65) We found a new community at the San Francisco Indian Center. We found a place where we belonged and where we could find strength in sharing experiences with other Native Americans.

In 1977, I began working for the Cherokee Nation
(70) as an economic stimulus coordinator. I was charged with the task of getting university training in environmental science and health for as many Cherokee students as possible so that they could return to their communities and provide service for
(75) their people. All around me, I saw a rebuilt Cherokee government working hard to restore the tribe to its earlier glory. One project in particular was a shining example of how the Cherokee are capable of finding and implementing our own
(80) solutions—the Bell Project. Bell was a small rural community where violence was a method of solving problems, where indoor plumbing was a luxury, and where many houses were on the brink of falling down. We entered the community and asked
(85) them what needed to be done and what their dreams for the future included. We asked them to define the problems, then worked with them to decide how they could rebuild their community. As a community, they decided to build a water
(90) system, rehabilitate twenty of their existing houses, and build twenty-five new ones. They would provide volunteer labor while we would provide the materials and technical resources by soliciting financial support for the project.

* Bureau of Indian Affairs

GO ON TO THE NEXT PAGE

(95) Many people doubted the project would succeed. No one believed the members of the community would work, especially as unpaid volunteers. But I had to believe that, as Cherokee we could follow the paths of our
(100) ancestors and work to rebuild ourselves. We gave the people of Bell an opportunity to take charge of their own lives and their own future and they accepted it with open arms. I still believe the Bell project was my most significant achievement for
(105) the Cherokee Nation. I proved to our tribe that we are all capable of improving our lives and our communities ourselves. It is a very powerful belief—it allows all Cherokees to dream what others would deem impossible and to know that it is very
(110) possible because we have done it in the past.

7 In lines 1–18, the author achieves each of the following goals EXCEPT

(A) identifying the author's ethnicity
(B) indicating the author's motivation for seeking election as Deputy Chief in 1985
(C) suggesting the role the author's gender played in the 1985 election
(D) describing the influences on the author's self-identity
(E) offering a detailed description of the author's autobiography

8 The author's experience of running for the office of Deputy Chief is significant to her mainly because it

(A) motivated the author to write and publish her autobiography
(B) gave her the chance to prove that a woman could be as effective as a man in the office of Deputy Chief
(C) allowed her to work toward helping Cherokees improve their own lives
(D) gave her the opportunity to work directly on improving the troubled relationship between the U.S. Government and the Cherokee Nation
(E) permitted her to serve as a symbol of the nobility of Cherokee history and culture

9 The list of accomplishments that the Cherokee people achieved after being moved to Oklahoma (lines 31–37) is significant in the passage for which of the following reasons?

I. It demonstrates that the Cherokee had a sophisticated societal structure.
II. It serves as evidence that the Cherokee were resilient.
III. It shows how the Cherokee were able to benefit from government assistance.

(A) I only
(B) II only
(C) III only
(D) I and II only
(E) I, II, and III

10 The anecdotes in lines 24–31 and lines 55–63 are closely related because

(A) the author cities them as examples of the perseverance of the Cherokee people
(B) the stories are both instances of hardships defeating the Cherokee people
(C) they express the author's horror at the actions of the federal government
(D) they are both examples of forced relocations of native people
(E) they convey the most important influences on the author's identity

11 When the author states that "my tribe's history has defined me, just as it has defined all Cherokee" (lines 52–53), she suggests which of the following about the Cherokee?

(A) They are constantly being moved around to different geographic areas.
(B) They are frequently in dispute with the U.S. government.
(C) The hardships that they have suffered in the past have profoundly affected their lives in the present.
(D) They have the persistence and determination to rebuild their own communities.
(E) Their destiny is to return to their former glory.

12 Which of the following best describes the author's attitude toward the BIA relocation program described in lines 55–63?

(A) diffident
(B) dismayed
(C) inspired
(D) agreeable
(E) mystified

13 The author mentions the San Francisco Indian Center (lines 65–66) in order to

(A) show where her family found a community after their relocation to California
(B) illustrate the size of the San Francisco Native American community
(C) describe how the government helped the author's family after their relocation
(D) argue against protecting the Native American community from majority influences
(E) emphasize the need for community centers outside of the Indian tribal lands

14 In line 70, "charged" most nearly means

(A) accused
(B) billed
(C) assigned
(D) electrified
(E) attacked

15 The author refers to the "Cherokee students" in line 73 primarily as examples of Cherokees who

(A) would eventually help coordinate work on the Bell project
(B) could help spread awareness of Cherokee culture to non-Cherokee people
(C) would contribute to the Cherokee government's economic stimulus efforts
(D) could eventually play a role in the Cherokee tradition of rebuilding the tribe from within
(E) might eventually become involved in the rebuilding of the Cherokee government

16 The Bell Project, lines 80–94, is cited as evidence that the Cherokee should be

(A) aided in solving the problems in their communities
(B) prevented from taking charge of their community projects
(C) provided with materials and resources to improve their communities themselves
(D) held up as examples of outstanding Native Americans
(E) persuaded to build a community water system wherever one is needed

17 In paragraph 6 the author draws a distinction between

(A) volunteering and being forced to do something
(B) helping others and helping yourself
(C) changing your own life and changing the lives of others
(D) following your ancestors and branching out on your own
(E) helping yourself and accepting outside help

18 Which of the following claims is most strongly supported by the author's argument?

(A) More women should run in government elections.
(B) Small-scale volunteer projects work best.
(C) Education is vital to community rebuilding efforts.
(D) Maintaining traditional cultural values is important.
(E) Cherokees should look to their history for inspiration.

19 The primary purpose of the passage is to

(A) determine the role of history in personal identity
(B) persuade readers to cherish their cultural and historical heritage
(C) describe the virtues of the Cherokee people
(D) explain the motivation for including ancestral history in an autobiography
(E) argue against federal assistance for Native Americans

IF YOU FINISH BEFORE TIME IS CALLED, YOU MAY CHECK YOUR WORK ON THIS SECTION ONLY. DO NOT TURN TO ANY OTHER SECTION IN THE TEST.

STOP

SECTION 9 Time—10 Minutes 14 Questions	**Directions:** For each question in this section, select the best answer from among the choices given and fill in the corresponding oval on the answer sheet.

The following sentences test correctness and effectiveness of expression. Part of each sentence or the entire sentence is underlined; beneath each sentence are five ways of phrasing the underlined material. Choice A repeats the original phrasing; the other four choices are different. If you think the original phrasing produces a better sentence than any of the alternatives, select choice A; if not, select one of the other choices.

In making your selection, follow the requirements of standard written English; that is, pay attention to grammar, choice of words, sentence construction, and punctuation. Your selection should result in the most effective sentence—clear and precise, without awkwardness or ambiguity.

EXAMPLE: ANSWER:

Every apple in the baskets <u>are ripe and labeled according to the date it was picked</u>.

(A) are ripe and labeled according to the date it was picked.
(B) is ripe and labeled according to the date it was picked.
(C) are ripe and labeled according to the date they were picked.
(D) is ripe and labeled according to the date they were picked.
(E) are ripe and labeled as to the date it was picked.

---

1 Walt Whitman wrote <u>poems and they express</u> the wonder of both the natural world and the human race.

(A) poems and they express
(B) poems, being the expressions of
(C) poems, they express
(D) poems that express
(E) poems, and expressing in them

2 The press secretary claimed that although the protesters in the opposing party have made valuable points, <u>the failure is in their not understanding</u> the positive effects of the new policy.

(A) the failure is in their not understanding
(B) the failure they have is in their not understanding
(C) they failed not to understand
(D) they have failed to understand
(E) failing in their understanding of

3 The air pollution levels in California could be reduced by implementing better public-transit systems, encouraging carpools, <u>and inventing new ways</u> to control exhaust fumes from automobiles.

(A) and inventing new ways
(B) and if they invent new ways
(C) also by inventing new ways
(D) and new ways being invented
(E) and if there were new ways

4 <u>Having an exceptionally big living room, the French club chose Lindsay's house</u> as the best place to hold their end-of-year party.

(A) Having an exceptionally big living room, the French club chose Lindsay's house
(B) French club members who chose Lindsay's house for its exceptionally big living room saw it
(C) Linday's house's exceptionally big living room led to its choice by the French club
(D) Because it has an exceptionally big living room, the French club chose Lindsay's house
(E) Based on its exceptionally big living room, Lindsay's house was chosen by the French club

5 Several of Cynthia Murphy's <u>photographs are inspired by the surrealism of rock concerts, taken from</u> dramatic and dizzying low angles.

(A) photographs are inspired by the surrealism of rock concerts, taken from
(B) photographs have their inspiration from the surrealism of rock concerts with
(C) photographs, inspired by the surrealism of rock concerts, are taken from
(D) photographs, which are inspired by the surrealism of rock concerts and which are taken from
(E) photographs, being inspired by the surrealism of rock concerts, taken from

GO ON TO THE NEXT PAGE

6 The neighborhood, once nearly deserted, is now a bustling, productive community.

(A) The neighborhood, once nearly deserted, is
(B) The neighborhood was once nearly deserted, it is
(C) The neighborhood that once having been nearly deserted is
(D) The neighborhood, because it was once nearly deserted, is
(E) The neighborhood was once nearly deserted, and it is

7 Ernest Hemingway absorbed the culture and events in Paris, where he lived for many years, and these are his observations that are included in his most autobiographical writing.

(A) these are his observations that are included
(B) the inclusion of these, his observations is
(C) his observations having been included
(D) his inclusion of these observations
(E) included his observations

8 The idea that a salad should be composed of iceberg lettuce and free of any more unusual greens prevailed in most of the diners along the highway.

(A) The idea that a salad should be composed of iceberg lettuce and free of any more unusual greens prevailed in most of the diners along the highway.
(B) The idea that prevailed about a salad in most of the diners along the highway was that of being composed of iceberg lettuce and free of any more unusual greens.
(C) In most of the diners along the highway, they had a prevalent idea that a salad should be composed of iceberg lettuce and free of any more unusual greens.
(D) Prevalent as an idea in most of the diners along the highway was for a salad to be composed of iceberg lettuce and free of any more unusual greens.
(E) Prevalent in most of the diners along the highway, they thought that a salad should be composed of iceberg lettuce and free of any more unusual greens.

9 New growth that was being thwarted by the poor quality of the soil, but now they are sprouting several new vines.

(A) New growth that was being thwarted by the poor quality of the soil, but now they are sprouting several new vines.
(B) The poor quality of the soil had thwarted new growth, but the plants are now sprouting several new vines.
(C) New growth was thwarted by the poor quality of the soil, and so now they are sprouting several new vines.
(D) Though the poor quality of the soil had thwarted new growth, the plant is now sprouting several new vines.
(E) Now sprouting several new vines, the plant's poor soil had thwarted new growth.

10 For many a pampered housecat, being cute is more important than being a good hunter.

(A) being cute is more important
(B) having cuteness is more important
(C) there is more importance in cuteness
(D) cuteness has more importance
(E) to be cute is more important

11 The issue we debated which was whether or not to require a minimum lot size for any house built after this year.

(A) which was whether or not to require a minimum lot size for any house built
(B) was whether or not to require a minimum lot size for any house they build
(C) was whether or not to require a minimum lot size for any house built
(D) was the requirement of whether or not a minimum lot size was needed for any house
(E) whether or not to require a minimum lot size for any house built

GO ON TO THE NEXT PAGE

12 You may choose to print your report <u>using the</u>
<u>default layout, you may choose to</u> customize your
report by clicking on the "custom" icon.

   (A) using the default layout, you may choose to
   (B) using the default layout, however, you may
        choose to
   (C) using the default layout, yet you may also
        choose to
   (D) using the default layout; you may also
   (E) using the default layout; you may have chosen
        to

13 <u>One of the symptoms of an allergy is when</u> you
develop hives on your face or torso.

   (A) One of the symptoms of an allergy is when
   (B) One of the symptoms of an allergy is that
   (C) Symptoms of an allergy include when
   (D) One of the symptoms of an allergy includes
        that
   (E) Symptoms of an allergy including that

14 <u>In addition to them we voted on at our last</u>
<u>meeting, several issues</u> remain to be decided.

   (A) In addition to them we voted on at our last
        meeting, several issues
   (B) As well as them we voted on at our last
        meeting, several issues
   (C) Additional to them we voted on at our last
        meeting, several issues
   (D) In addition to those we voted on at our last
        meeting, several issues
   (E) In addition to them which we voted on at our
        last meeting, several issues

**IF YOU FINISH BEFORE TIME IS CALLED, YOU MAY CHECK YOUR WORK ON
THIS SECTION ONLY. DO NOT TURN TO ANY OTHER SECTION IN THE TEST.** **STOP**

Diagnostic Test
Answers and Explanations

ANSWER KEY

Section 1
Essay

Section 2
1. B
2. D
3. C
4. B
5. B
6. D
7. A
8. D
9. A
10. B
11. E
12. A
13. A
14. E
15. C
16. B
17. E
18. E
19. C
20. D

Section 3
1. A
2. D
3. E
4. A
5. A
6. A
7. B
8. D
9. D
10. E
11. E
12. E
13. C
14. B
15. D
16. A
17. E
18. C
19. B
20. A
21. E
22. A

23. E
24. D

Section 4
1. C
2. D
3. E
4. C
5. E
6. D
7. B
8. C
9. 18
10. 23
11. 12
12. 275, 330
    or 385
13. 600
14. 24
15. 1
16. 135
17. 5
18. 70

Section 5
1. D
2. C
3. D
4. E
5. C
6. D
7. B
8. D
9. A
10. B
11. D
12. C
13. E
14. D
15. B
16. B
17. D
18. E
19. D
20. C
21. C
22. D
23. E

24. C
25. A
26. D
27. A
28. C
29. D
30. B
31. D
32. A
33. D
34. B
35. E

Section 6
1. A
2. A
3. E
4. C
5. B
6. C
7. B
8. B
9. A
10. D
11. A
12. D
13. B
14. E
15. D
16. C
17. D
18. A
19. C
20. C
21. B
22. E
23. A
24. B

Section 7
1. C
2. E
3. A
4. D
5. C
6. D
7. B
8. E

9. C
10. E
11. C
12. C
13. D
14. D
15. E
16. E

Section 8
1. C
2. A
3. E
4. C
5. C
6. A
7. E
8. C
9. D
10. A
11. C
12. B
13. A
14. C
15. D
16. C
17. E
18. E
19. D

Section 9
1. D
2. D
3. A
4. D
5. C
6. A
7. E
8. A
9. D
10. A
11. C
12. D
13. B
14. D

ANSWERS AND EXPLANATIONS

Section 1 (Essay)

Sample Grade 5 Essay

Every obstacle can be turned into an opportunity, if one has the right attitude or perspective. People with this attitude are buoyant, not easily discouraged, and welcome challenges and adversity.

I can think of no better example than in sixth grade, when I broke my hand. I fell off my bicycle one day and broke it, and the doctor put it into a cast.

Now the cast was a real obstacle. It was on my right hand, the one I write with. It looked like homework would be impossible, but I learned to type with one hand and did my English and Social Studies work on the typewriter, and my Mom wrote out my math homework based on answers I gave her. The experience sure helped my typing! It also made me learn the value of work, and gave me a chance to really learn to appreciate my mother.

In addition, having the cast was an excuse to improve my basketball game. I was a decent player, but most comfortable with my right hand. But with the cast on I was forced to practice dribbling with my left hand, and now I can go either way.

Finally, there was one other unexpected benefit. In Art Class, I was never very good. But one day, with my hand still in the cast, I tried drawing with my left hand. To my surprise, I was much better at it than before! The cast is long gone, but I still draw left-handed and am really quite good at it. Maybe I'd never have known about this ability if I hadn't made my obstacle into my opportunity.

Grader's Comments: The essay is scored based on four basic criteria: Topic, Support, Organization, and Language. This essay scores well on all counts, but it has too little variation in sentence structure to earn a 6.

This essay demonstrates an especially strong grasp of the writing assignment, earning high points for Topic, Support, and Organization. The author states a thesis in paragraph 1, provides several specific, relevant examples of how the obstacle was turned into a good experience in paragraph 2, and concludes with a final, highlighted example. These are discussed in a clear and convincing way.

Vocabulary is fairly strong ("buoyant," for example). There are a few minor grammatical errors (like the unparallel "I can think of no better example than in sixth grade" and the confusing pronoun in "I fell off my bicycle one day and broke it"—the kinds of error you'll avoid if you recall what you've learned for the multiple-choice questions—but these mistakes don't affect the generally high quality of the essay.

Sample Grade 3 Essay

To say that every obstacle can be turned into an opportunity is to be an optimist. Some people just always look on the bright side, and are able to overcome there obstacles.

Dorothy in the Wizard of Oz is stranded by the tornado and can't go home. So she takes the opportunity to make friends with Scarecrow etc, and to rid the world of wicked witches. Her optimism wins her the right to go back to Kansas. Ophelia in Hamlet however, is not an optimist. She and Hamlet fall in love but then he pushes her away. She doesn't understand why and kills herself.

In the real world, Marie Curie was told women couldn't be scientists but perservered and discovered radium. Now there are more women scientists than ever.

I like to think I'm an optimist too. If somebody tells me I can't do something, I just try harder until I can. Take field hockey. I went out as a freshman and barely made the team, but worked and worked and this year was a starter on the varsity. We came in second in the league. Life is like that if you look on the bright side. Don't get discouraged. Every cloud has a silver lining. So if you are an optimist, every obstacle is an opportunity.

Grader's Comments: Even though this author attempted with some success to fulfill the assignment, the examples from literature and history are underdeveloped and confused. The author doesn't really explain how the obstacles she mentions became opportunities for the individuals in question. Finally, in paragraph 3, the author's personal experience of overcoming an obstacle doesn't tell us much about how she "turned it into an opportunity."

The essay is too short to develop its ideas well. The two-sentence third paragraph gives the impression that its idea is especially neglected. In fact, there is no reason for it to be a separate paragraph—it merely adds one more example to the list already provided in paragraph 2.

The essay relies too much on clichés ("look on the bright side" and "more...than ever"). Note the effective parallelism in the first sentence, though.

Overall, it seems as if the writer had a hard time coming up with ideas and rushed to write the essay in the last few minutes. Any ideas are better than none; good ideas that never get onto the page won't help.

Sample Grade 1 Essay

I don't agree with this statement, that we can turn every obstacle into an opportunity. Some obstacles are just that. Like if I wanted to be a NBA basketball player. In the NBA you have to be tall as a tree, and I'm the shortest person in the whole school. Back in elementary school too. So I'm never going to opportunity to play the NBA.

And if you die young like from leukemia, that obstacle doesn't give you the opportunity to do anything with your life. So it depends on the obstacle. It should have said MANY obstacles or SOME obstacle. It just depends.

Grader's Comments: While the author does present a point of view clearly, this essay is deficient in both development and presentation. It's perfectly acceptable for the author to disagree with the stimulus statement, but she provides hardly any support for that position. The ideas presented are extremely thin, and there's no logical organization to them. Finally, this essay's prose leaves out words ("So I'm never going to opportunity…"), is too colloquial ("Like if I wanted to be…"), and seriously violates the rules of standard written English ("Back in elementary school too.").

Section 2 (Math)

1. B
Difficulty: Low
Strategic Advice: To solve for *a*, isolate it on one side of the equation.
Getting to the Answer:

Since $b \neq 0$, both sides of the equation $ab = \dfrac{b}{4}$ can be divided by *b*. Dividing both sides of the equation by *b*, we find that $a = \dfrac{1}{4}$. Choice (B) is correct.

2. D
Difficulty: Low
Strategic Advice: To find the least total travel time, add the least time to travel from *A* to *B* and the least time to travel from *B* to *C*. To find the greatest total travel time, add the greatest times to travel from town to town.
Getting to the Answer: To find the least total time of travel, add the two smallest times of travel. That is, add the least possible time of travel from Town *A* to Town *B* and the least possible time of travel from Town *B* to Town *C*. The least total time of travel, in minutes, is 7 + 16 = 23. To find the greatest total time of travel, add the two greatest possible times of travel. The greatest total time of travel, in minutes, is 10 + 24 = 34.

3. C
Difficulty: Low
Strategic Advice: The decimal must be moved 4 places to the right in order to go from 3.475817 to 34,758.17. Each place that the decimal point is moved to the right multiplies the decimal number by 10.
Getting to the Answer: Since the decimal point here must be moved 4 places to the right, the number 3.475817 must be multiplied by 10^4 in order to obtain 34,758.17. $10^4 = 10,000$, and choice (C) is correct.

4. B
Difficulty: Low
Strategic Advice: The median is the number in the middle when a list of numbers is arranged from least to greatest.

Getting to the Answer: Since there are 61 students, if the scores are arranged in increasing order then the middle score is the 31st score. This is because $\dfrac{61 - 1}{2} = \dfrac{60}{2} = 30$, so there will be 30 scores before the 31st score and 30 scores after the 31st score. Imagine that the first 5 scores of 46 are written down. Then the 7 scores of 54 are written to the right of the 46s. Up to now we have 5 + 7 or 12 scores. When the 18 scores of 67 are then written to the right of the 54s, we now have 12 + 18 = 30 scores written down. The next score, the 31st score, is a 78. So the median is 78.

5. B
Difficulty: Low
Strategic Advice: Carefully translate from English to math to get an equation involving the current number of lamps. Solve for the current number, but don't forget to increase it by 40% before selecting your answer.
Getting to the Answer:

Call the current number of lamps *x*. When 50 lamps are added, the new number of lamps is *x* + 50. This number of lamps, *x* + 50, is equal to $\dfrac{3}{2}$ of the original number of lamps, *x*. So we have the equation $x + 50 = \dfrac{3}{2}x$. Now solve this equation for *x*.

$$x + 50 = \frac{3}{2}x$$
$$50 = \frac{1}{2}x$$
$$x = 100$$

The current number of lamps is 100. This number is to be increased by 40%. Now 40% of 100 is 40. So if the current number of lamps is increased by 40%, the new number of lamps will be 100 + 40, which is 140.

6. D
Difficulty: Low
Strategic Advice: Think about how the sides of the two triangles in this figure are related. If they are all the same length, what kinds of triangles are in the figure? What angles does that type of triangle have?

Getting to the Answer: Since $WY = YZ = ZW$, triangle WYZ is an equilateral triangle. In an equilateral triangle, each of the 3 interior angles has a measure of 60 degrees. So angle WYZ has a degree measure of 60. Thus, $a = 60$.

Since $WX = XY = WY$, triangle WXY is an equilateral triangle. So $b = 60$. Thus $a = 60$ and $b = 60$. So $a + b = 60 + 60 = 120$.

7. A
Difficulty: Low
Strategic Advice: Although this problem doesn't involve complicated math, it's easy to get confused if you try to do it in your head. Translate carefully from English to math, and write down your work to help keep track of things.
Getting to the Answer: Subtract $3x - 7$ from $3x + 5$.

$$(3x + 5) - (3x - 7) = 3x + 5 - 3x + 7 = 12$$

8. D
Difficulty: Low
Strategic Advice: Again, remember not to stop too soon. This question asks not for the total amount the club received, but for the amount they planned to spend on the speaker.
Getting to the Answer: The percent of the budget spent on lunch is $100\% - 40\% - 25\% - 20\% = 15\%$. We're told that the club plans to spend $90 on lunch. Let x be the total amount of the budget, in dollars. Then 15% of x is 90. So $0.15x = 90$. Solve this for x.

$$0.15x = 90$$
$$x = \frac{90}{.15} = 600$$

The total budget is $600. Now 40% of this was spent for a guest speaker. So $\frac{2}{5} \times \$600 = 2 \times \$120 = \$240$.

9. A
Difficulty: Low
Strategic Advice: Translate this piece by piece.
Getting to the Answer: "When z is decreased by 3" means $z - 3$. Next, "the result is" means =. So now we have $z - 3 =$. Now let's look at "twice the square of the sum of y and 4". Now "the sum of y and 4" means $y + 4$. Then "the square of the sum

of y and 4" means $(y + 4)^2$. Then "twice the square of the sum of y and 4" means $2(y + 4)^2$. So the entire statement translated into algebra is $z - 3 = 2(y + 4)^2$. Choice (A) is correct.

10. B
Difficulty: Medium
Strategic Advice: The fastest way to get the answer here is to Backsolve. Plug the given point into each possible equation until you find one that doesn't work.
Getting to the Answer:
Choice (A): Is $2 = 1 - (-1)$ true? $1 - (-1) = 1 + 1 = 2$. Eliminate choice (A).

Choice (B): Is $2 = (-1) + 1$ true? $(-1) + 1 = -1 + 1 = 0$. So $2 = (-1) + 1$ is not true. The equation $y = x + 1$ of choice (B) cannot be the equation of line l. Choice (B) is correct.
At this point, on Test Day, you'd move on. Now, for the sake of making sure you understand the relevant math, let's check the other choices.

Choice (C): The equation $x = -1$ is the equation of the line such that every point on this line has an x-coordinate of -1. Since the point $(-1, 2)$ has an x-coordinate of -1, the point $(-1, 2)$ is a point on the line with the equation $x = -1$.

Choice (D): Is $2 = (-1) + 3$ true? $(-1) + 3 = -1 + 3 = 2$. So the equation $y = x + 1$ of choice (D) could be the equation of line l. Choice (D) is incorrect.

Choice (E): The equation $y = 2$ is the equation of the line such that every point on this line has a y-coordinate of 2. Since the point $(-1, 2)$ has a y-coordinate of 2, the point $(-1, 2)$ is a point on the line with the equation $y = 2$. So choice (E) is incorrect.

11. E
Difficulty: Medium
Strategic Advice: Don't be worried by symbols you've never seen. The test makers made them up, and they'll be defined in the question. Just plug the given values into the definition and simplify.
Getting to the Answer: Use the definition of the symbol #, which is defined by the equation $c \# d = (c + 1)(d - 1)$. Begin by finding the values of the expressions inside the parentheses first. To find the value of 5 # 2, use the defining

equation $c \# d = (c + 1)(d - 1)$. In this equation replace c with 5 and d with 2.
Then $5 \# 2 = (5 + 1)(2 - 1) = (6)(1) = 6$.

To find the value of $6 \# 4$, use the defining equation $c \# d = (c + 1)(d - 1)$. In this equation replace c with 6 and d with 4.
Then $6 \# 4 = (6 + 1)(4 - 1) = (7)(3) = 21$.

Now we know that $5 \# 2 = 6$ and $6 \# 4 = 21$.

Therefore $(5 \# 2) \# (6 \# 4) = 6 \# 21$.

It remains to find the value of $6 \# 21$.
To find the value of $6 \# 21$, use the defining equation $c \# d = (c + 1)(d - 1)$. In this equation replace c with 6 and d with 21.

Then $6 \# 21 = (6 + 1)(21 - 1) = (7)(20) = 140$.

12. **A**
Difficulty: Medium
Strategic Advice: Notice the difference between "must be" and "could be." This question wants to know which of the answer choices *could* be a prime number — so you only need to find one value of p that will give you a prime number in one of the answer choices.

Getting to the Answer: The question stem tells us that p divided by 4 yields a remainder of 0. This means that p must be a multiple of 4.
If $p = 4$, then $\frac{p}{4} = \frac{4}{4} = 1$, which is not a prime number. However, if $p = 8$, then $\frac{p}{4} = \frac{8}{4} = 2$, which is a prime number. So $\frac{p}{4}$ could be a prime number, and choice (A) is correct. Let's briefly consider the other answer choices.

Choice (B): $2\sqrt{p}$. We know that p is a multiple of 4 and that p is greater than 1. The possible values of p are 4, 8, 12, 16, 20, 24,.... It is seen that none of $2\sqrt{4} = 2(2) = 4$, $2\sqrt{8}$, $2\sqrt{12}$, $2\sqrt{16} = 2(4) = 8$, $2\sqrt{20}$, $2\sqrt{24}$,... is a prime number. Either $2\sqrt{p}$ is not an integer and therefore not a prime number, or $2\sqrt{p}$ is not a prime number when it is an integer.

Choice (C): $\frac{p}{3}$. Since p is a multiple of 4, $p = 4N$ where N is a positive integer. Then $\frac{p}{3} = \frac{4N}{3}$.

If $\frac{p}{3}$ is not an integer, then it is not a prime number.

If $\frac{p}{3}$ is an integer, then N must be a multiple of 3.

So if N is a multiple of 3, then $N = 3M$ where M is a positive integer, and $\frac{p}{3} = \frac{4N}{3} = \frac{4(3M)}{3} = 4M$. Now $4M$ is the product of 4 and the positive integer M, so $\frac{p}{3}$ cannot be a prime number.

Choice (D): p. Since p is a positive integer that is a multiple of 4, p cannot be a prime number.
Choice (E): $2p$. Since p is a multiple of 4, $2p$ must be a multiple of 8 and therefore cannot be a prime number.

13. **A**
Difficulty: Medium
Strategic Advice: This problem tests your knowledge of the Triangle Inequality Theorem, which states that the sum of *any* two sides of a triangle must be larger than the third side. Backsolve, starting with (C).
Getting to the Answer: We know that one side has to be 5, and if the total perimeter is 9, than the sum of the other two sides is 4. This is not greater than 5, so move on, applying this logic to the other answer choices. (A) is correct because, if the perimeter is 11, 6 is the sum of the other two sides. This situation is the only one that satisfies the Triangle Inequality Theorum. Note that (B) is incorrect because 5 is not greater than 5.

14. **E**
Difficulty: Medium
Strategic Advice: Remember, the ratio between the areas of circles is not the same as the ratio between their radii or their diameters.
Getting to the Answer: Problems such as this should normally be solved by Picking Numbers. To begin, note that the ratio of the areas is 1:4:8. Since we are dealing with circles, we should pick numbers for their radii. Using the simplest ratio, and assuming the areas are exactly 1π, 4π, and 8π,

respectively, begin with the first circle. If the area is 1π, the radius must be 1 since $(1^2)\pi = 1\pi = \pi$. The second circle must have a radius of $\sqrt{4} = 2$. The third circle must therefore have a radius of $\sqrt{8} = 2\sqrt{2}$. Since the question asks about diameter, we must double each radius, which yields: 2, 4, and $4\sqrt{2}$. Now, the sum of the diameters is $2 + 4 + 4\sqrt{2} = 6 + 4\sqrt{2}$. This answer isn't a choice, but remember the areas were in a ratio, so we simply have to try multiples of our answer. If each term is multiplied by 3, we get $18 + 12\sqrt{2}$, which is (E).

15. **C**
Difficulty: Medium
Strategic Advice: We know that x is a negative odd integer. We need to count how many even numbers are located between x and 0. The easiest method is to pick a number for x, then test it against the answer choices. For instance, if $x = -3$, there's only one even integer between -3 and 0: -2. Which answer choices equal 1 when $x = -3$?

Getting to the Answer:

Choice (A): $-(-3) - 2 = 3 - 2 = 1$. This is possibly correct.

Choice (B): $-\dfrac{(-3)}{2} = \dfrac{3}{2}$. Eliminate choice (B).

Choice (C): $\dfrac{-(-3) - 1}{2} = \dfrac{3 - 1}{2} = \dfrac{2}{2} = 1$. Choice (C) is possibly correct.

Choice (D): $-3 + 4 = 1$. Choice (D) is possibly correct.

Choice (E): $\dfrac{-(-3) - 2}{2} = \dfrac{3 - 2}{2} = \dfrac{1}{2}$.

Eliminate choice (E).
How do we find the right answer from among (A), (C), and (D)? We need to pick another number for x. This time we will let $x = -5$. There are two even, negative integers (-4 and -2) between -5 and 0. Which answer choice equals 2 when $x = -5$?

Choice (A): $-(-5) - 2 = 3$. Eliminate choice (A).

Choice (C): $\dfrac{-(-5) - 1}{2} = \dfrac{5 - 1}{2} = \dfrac{4}{2} = 2$. Choice

(C) is possibly correct.
Choice (D): $x + 4 = -5 + 4 = -1$. Eliminate choice (D).

Now that all four incorrect answer choices have been eliminated, we know that choice (C) must be correct.

16. **B**
Difficulty: High
Strategic Advice: To solve this question we will need to know these two things.
(i) The probability formula when the outcomes are equally likely is

$$\text{Probability} = \frac{\text{Number of favorable outcomes}}{\text{Number of outcomes}}$$

(ii) The probability that two events occur is equal to the probability that the first event occurs multiplied by the probability that the second event occurs given that the first event occurs.

Getting to the Answer: The probability of getting a rose on the wheel A is $\dfrac{1}{7}$. The probability of getting a rose on wheel B is $\dfrac{1}{7}$. The probability of getting a rose on both wheels A and B is $\dfrac{1}{7} \times \dfrac{1}{7} = \dfrac{1}{49}$. Similarly, the probability of getting a pen on both wheels is $\dfrac{1}{49}$. There are 7 different ways to get the same picture on wheels A and B. Each of these ways has the same probability of $\dfrac{1}{49}$. So the probability of getting the same picture on both wheels is $7\left(\dfrac{1}{49}\right) = \dfrac{1}{7}$. The probability of getting a candle on the third wheel is $\dfrac{1}{7}$. So the probability that a cash prize is awarded, which is the probability that wheels A and B land on the same picture and wheel C lands on a candle, is $\dfrac{1}{7} \times \dfrac{1}{7} = \dfrac{1}{49}$.

17. E
Difficulty: High
Strategic Advice: This question could trap many test takers simply because, while rushing through the late problems, they forget to test the other quadrants for positive products. If this question appears toward the end of the section, check your assumptions. Don't automatically second guess yourself, but know that "obvious" answers are seldom correct on late math problems.
Getting to the Answer: Remember the signs of the x- and y-coordinates in each quadrant. In quadrant I, they're both positive. In quadrant II, the x-coordinate is negative and the y-coordinate is positive. In quadrant III, both the x- and y-coordinates are negative. In quadrant IV, the x-coordinate is positive and the y-coordinate is negative.
Also remember:

positive $\times$ positive = positive
positive $\times$ negative = negative
negative $\times$ negative = positive

If the product of the x- and y-coordinates is +20, either they're both negative or they're both positive. So, the point could either fall in quadrant I or quadrant III. We don't have enough information to determine which one. Choice (E) is correct.

18. E
Difficulty: High
Strategic Advice: To solve for z in terms of x, you'll need to get rid of y. Solve one equation for y in terms of z, then plug that into the other equation to get an equation that includes only x and z.
Getting to the Answer:
We want to solve for z in terms of x. Looking at the equations, we can obtain an equation with just x and z by solving the second equation, $y - 1 = z^2$, for y in terms of z. Then we will substitute this expression for y in terms of z into the first equation, $x = z^2 + 3y$. This will give us an equation with just x and z. We will then try to solve this equation for z in terms of x.

Begin with the equation $y - 1 = z^2$.
Adding 1 to both sides of this equation, we now have $y = 1 + z^2$.
Now substitute $1 + z^2$ for y into the first equation, $x = z^2 + 3y$.

Then

$$x = z^2 + 3(1 + z^2)$$
$$x = z^2 + 3 + 3z^2$$
$$x = 4z^2 + 3$$

Now solve this equation for z.

$$x = 4z^2 + 3$$

$$x - 3 = 4z^2$$

$$\frac{x - 3}{4} = z^2$$

$$z^2 = \frac{x - 3}{4}$$

We know that $z > 0$, so $z = \sqrt{\dfrac{x - 3}{4}}$

Choice (E) is correct.

19. C
Difficulty: High
Strategic Advice: Add any information you have to the figure. For instance, angle ADC must be 90 degrees, since it is one corner of a square.
Getting to the Answer:

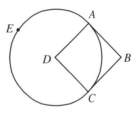

The area of the entire region is equal to the area of square $ABCD$ plus the area of region $DAEC$. (We've added point E for clarity.)

The perimeter of a square is 4 times the length of a side. Since the perimeter of this square is 24, a side of this square has length $\dfrac{24}{4} = 6$. The area of a square is its side squared. So the area of this square is 6^2, which is 36.

Sides AD and DC of the square are radii of the circle. Since the sides of the square are 6, the radius of this circle is also 6.

A sector of a circle is the region formed by two radii and the arc that they intercept. A central angle of a circle is an angle formed by two radii. Region *DAEC* is a sector of circle with a radius of 6 and a central angle having a measure of 360 − 90 = 270 degrees. The area of a sector of a circle having a radius *r* and a central angle with a measure of *n* degrees is $\pi r^2 \times \dfrac{n}{360}$. So the area of sector *DAEC* is $\pi(6^2) \times \dfrac{270}{360} = 36\pi \times \dfrac{3}{4} = 9\pi \times 3 = 27\pi$.

The area of square *ABCD* is 36, and the area of region *DAEC* is 27π. The area of the entire region is 36 + 27π.

20. D
Difficulty: High
Strategic Advice: If you have trouble keeping track of all the variables, try Picking Numbers for *x, y,* and *z*. Since you're dealing with percents, Pick Numbers that are easy to take percents of, such as 100.
Getting to the Answer: First let's find the total number of gallons in the mixture. There are *x* gallons of brand *A* drink, there are *y* gallons of brand *B* drink, and there are *z* gallons of water. So the total number of gallons in the mixture is *x + y + z.*

Next, let's find the total amount of orange juice in the mixture. There are 30% of *x* gallons of orange juice from brand *A*. The decimal equivalent of 30% is 0.3. So there are 0.3*x* gallons of orange juice from brand *A* in the mixture. There are 40% of *y* gallons of orange juice from brand *B*. The decimal equivalent of 40% is 0.4. So there are 0.4*y* gallons of orange juice from brand *B* in the mixture. The total number of gallons of orange juice in the mixture is 0.3*x* + 0.4*y.*

Now, let's find the percent of orange juice in the mixture. A percent is just a fraction. Let's find the fraction of orange juice in the mixture, and then convert that fraction to a percent. The fraction that 0.3*x* + 0.4*y* is of *x + y + z* is $\dfrac{0.3x + 0.4y}{x + y + z}$. We want to convert this fraction to a percent. To convert a fraction (or decimal) to a percent, multiply that fraction or (decimal) by 100%.

So $\dfrac{0.3x + 0.4y}{x + y + z} = \dfrac{0.3x + 0.4y}{x + y + z} \times 100\%$. Let's try multiplying 100 by (0.3*x* + 0.4*y*) and leaving the % symbol after the fraction. The percent symbol appears after the fractions of each answer choice and the denominators of the answer choices suggest that they weren't simplified.

Then $\dfrac{0.3x + 0.4y}{x + y + z} \times 100\% = \dfrac{(0.3x + 0.4y) \times 100}{x + y + z}\% = \dfrac{30x + 40y}{x + y + z}\%.$

Choice (D) is correct.

Section 3 (Critical Reading)

1.   A
Difficulty: Low
Strategic Advice: With longer sentences, you must pay even closer attention to keywords.
Getting to the Answer: *However* tells you there is a contrast between the two blanks. Look to the second blank first. It appears to refer to the absence of a skill rather than the possession of it. The phrase *to be able to use such materials effectively* suggests that these professors can't be effective because they lack such expertise.
(A) is the only one that matches your prediction for the second blank. Read both blanks into the sentence, and this confirms (A) as your answer.
(B) *Inspired* could work for the first blank, but *enjoy* doesn't provide the needed contrast.
(C) *Determined* sounds plausible for the first blank, but *require* doesn't make sense in the second.
(D) One doesn't *elect* expertise.
(E) Neither word makes sense here.

2.   D
Difficulty: Medium
Strategic Advice: Some questions will be resistant to prediction, but interpreting the keywords can help to identify the relationship between the blanks.
Getting to the Answer: Based on the keywords in the sentence *(despite, nonetheless, remained)*, you're looking for words with opposing meanings.
(A) These words are not opposites.
(B) Something *lustrous* actually could be *simple* in some ways; these are not really opposing words.
(C) To *illuminate* the symbolism would certainly make it *explicit*—no contrast here.
(D) These words have opposing meanings; if you weren't sure of their meanings, process of elimination would still lead you here.
(E) A poet could try to *cleanse* the symbolism *from* her work, but otherwise this makes no sense.
lustrous: gleaming; radiant
opaque: impenetrable by light
enigmatic: puzzling; obscure

3.   E
Difficulty: Medium
Strategic Advice: You must recognize *however* as the classic contrast keyword.
Getting to the Answer: The missing word will be opposite in meaning to "rehearsed" *(the product of a great deal of rehearsal)*—*unrehearsed* is a sufficient prediction. This leads you to (E).
(A) A speech can be *imprecise* regardless of the level of *rehearsal* involved.
(B) *Relentless* doesn't make sense in this context.
(C) This word agrees with the concept of heavy *rehearsal.*
(D) No contrast here.
premeditated: arranged in advance
impromptu: with little or no preparation

4.   A
Difficulty: Medium
Strategic Advice: Even if you can't make an exact prediction for a blank, remember the importance of word charge in two-blank sentences: do the blanks agree or contrast?
Getting to the Answer: *Acknowledging* indicates that the blanks will agree—since the *consensus was* ------, the *agreement* should also be ------. Start with the second blank; if the partners *struggled to uphold* the agreement, it can't have been very strong. Predict *weak* for the second blank, and *weakness* works for the first.
(A) provides a great match.
(B) *Persistence* doesn't make that much sense here; if anything, *persistence* would appear to strengthen agreements.
(C) Both of these words are opposite to your prediction.
(D) *Estimation* doesn't make sense here.
(E) You wouldn't speak of the *omission* of a *consensus.*
tenuous: flimsy; having little substance
paltry: trivial; lacking in worth
stalwart: firm and resolute
tractable: easily managed or controlled

5.   A
Difficulty: High
Strategic Advice: Late Sentence Completions remind you of the importance of studying and improving your vocabulary leading into Test Day.
Getting to the Answer: This is another straight definition sentence. You need an adjective that

describes someone with an *ill temper* who likes to *quarrel*; *grouchy* works fine.

(A) This works. If you weren't sure of the meaning of this word, an elimination strategy should bring you back to this choice.

(B) This word is much too positive.

(C) Urbane is also positive; if you didn't know that, you could assume that it has some relation to urban, which doesn't have the necessary negative charge.

(D) This is a tough word, but, if you had to choose between it and (A), which sounds more negative? (A).

(E) This is neutral in tone.

cantankerous: ill-tempered; disagreeable
urbane: polite; refined
perspicacious: shrewd; clear-sighted

Basking Sharks

6.   A

Difficulty: Low

Strategic Advice: Remember that the author of a passage writes every sentence for a reason. In a question like this one, put yourself in the author's shoes and ask, "If I were writing this passage, why would I write this sentence?"

Getting to the Answer: The image of a deadly shark catching rays is pretty funny, so look for something that sums this up.

(A) This fits your prediction well.

(B) Opposite; the end of the paragraph points out that these sharks are pretty dangerous, so the author wouldn't agree with this sentiment.

(C) Extreme; the passage is much too short to be considered in-depth.

(D) Out-of-Scope; boat attacks are mentioned, but the author never gives any reasons.

(E) Extreme; *menace* is a negatively charged word, and the rest of the passage doesn't have this negative tone.

7.   B

Difficulty: Medium

Strategic Advice: Even when a Detail question doesn't provide a line reference, you probably still need to go back to the passage for information.

Getting to the Answer: The author says that basking sharks can be dangerous to people, and, as an example, notes that divers and scientists

have been hurt by the denticles in the sharks' skin. Look for a choice that makes sense in that context.

(A) Distortion; the word "denticle" may make you think of teeth, but the passage says that denticles are contained in the sharks skin, not its mouth.

(B) This fits what you found in the passage.

(C) Distortion; protection, yes, but nothing in the passage indicates that the shark needs protection from the sun.

(D) Out-of-Scope; there's no support for this in the passage—there's no mention of food anywhere.

(E) Distortion; the denticles are *one* way for the shark to protect itself, but not necessarily the only way. (Those teeth have to be good for something.)

Arthur Miller

8.   D

Difficulty: Low

Strategic Advice: For Vocab-in-Context questions, be aware of multiple definitions.

Getting to the Answer: *Virtual* is a word we hear all the time today in phrases such as "virtual reality." Don't rely on that for context. The passage says that the essays are a lot like manuals—they are *almost* manuals.

(A) *Organic* manuals? That makes no sense.

(B) Here's the "virtual reality" trap. His essays may or may not be in electronic format; there's no telling.

(C) This is a play on one of the definitions of *virtue*, but it doesn't fit here.

(D) This is a reasonable match to your prediction.

(E) Another "virtual reality" trap.

9.   D

Difficulty: Medium

Strategic Advice: *Suggests* tells us that this is an Inference question. Keeping the author's overall tone in mind when you research the question.

Getting to the Answer: The relevant part of the paragraph is the very beginning. Other playwrights write about themselves or cut the other guy down. Miller doesn't do that. That must be the difference the question is asking about.

(A) Out-of-Scope; we do not learn anything about time frame.

(B) Out-of-Scope; the passage does not mention quantity.

(C) Out-of-Scope; although the author of this passage might wish that Miller is the most influential essayist, there is no indication that this is actually true.
(D) This matches the prediction nicely.
(E) Distortion; yes, this may be true, but it could also be true of other playwright-essayists.

Koalas

The passage is a survey of the issues involved in conserving the population of koalas. The first paragraph states that koalas have long been a symbol of Australia to the rest of the world. The author then conveys an important distinction: the population of koalas in the northern part of the country is still declining, but the southern part of the country has recently seen an increase. This is also causing problems since those animals are destroying their own food supply. Paragraph two mentions the degradation of the animal's food supply as a major problem for northern koalas. Paragraph three then mentions that a lack of wildfires has led to an increase in mistletoe, which has in turn hurt the koala's main food supply, eucalyptus. Paragraph four states that the gene pool of southern koalas is too small, which can lead to inbreeding and thus population decline. Paragraph five proposes making it easier for koalas to move to other areas through undeveloped corridors as well as the outright relocation of the animals by humans. Paragraph six condones investigation into the most nutrient-rich areas for eucalyptus, since trees in such areas make the best food for koalas. The passage wraps up by noting that humans are by far the largest threat to koalas.

10. **E**
Difficulty: Low
Strategic Advice: You should be predicting the author's purpose after every passage that you read.
Getting to the Answer: The passage discusses threats facing koalas and solutions to these problems. (E) best captures this.
(A) Distortion; this is too narrow in scope. The koala's *dietary habits* are mentioned to discuss the larger threats facing the population.

(B) Extreme; the author's assumption from the beginning is that koalas are important, but this is not the reason the essay was written.
(C) Opposite; the author characterizes *habitat fragmentation* as harmful.
(D) Distortion; a large chunk of the essay does focus on the importance of eucalyptus trees, but only as supporting evidence to prove that koala populations are declining.

11. **E**
Difficulty: Medium
Strategic Advice: Remember, the answer is in the passage. Be on guard against details taken from the wrong part of the passage.
Getting to the Answer: The cited lines appear in the first paragraph, where the author notes that, although the population as a whole is still endangered, the south of Australia is experiencing a boom in the koala population. This is causing a different set of problems, such as over-browsing. This fits well with (E).
(A) Misused Detail; this comes up in subsequent paragraphs.
(B) Misused Detail; this incorrectly ascribes the problem of low genetic variance to the Northern koalas, rather than to the Southern ones.
(C) Another Misused Detail; this comes from another paragraph.
(D) Yet another Misused Detail; this comes at the end of the passage.

12. **E**
Difficulty: Medium
Strategic Advice: Remember that you're looking for the one that is NOT discussed.
Getting to the Answer: This Detail question has a Global aspect. You may have to comb the entire passage to verify the appearance of the four wrong answers. Thankfully, that's not the case here.
(A) The author mentions "dog attacks" in line 33.
(B) *Habitat fragmentation* appears in line 28 among other places.
(C) This is discussed in line 22.
(D) Examples of *urban development* appear in the final paragraph.
So our answer is (E).

13. C
Difficulty: High
Strategic Advice: An Inference question with a Global aspect and an "EXCEPT"—don't be intimidated. Focus on the author's purpose and tone to predict the views he would be likely to agree with.
Getting to the Answer: The author would most likely support policies that would facilitate conservation of the koala. The four incorrect answers should be somewhere around this general concept.
(A) Opposite; this fits with the tone of the passage and specifically the last paragraph.
(B) Opposite; the author alludes to this in paragraph 6.
(C) The author never states this; this is your answer. This is, in fact, contrary to what he suggests in lines 71–75 as a possible solution to alleviate inbreeding.
(D) This ties in with the dog references in line 33.
(E) This is specifically addressed in paragraph 5.

14. B
Difficulty: High
Strategic Advice: In questions like these, the incorrect answers may not necessarily strengthen the claim; they only have to "not weaken" it.
Getting to the Answer: The best way to attack this is to first think about the argument presented: koalas are under threat of extinction. This is supported by a discussion regarding the effects of habitat fragmentation and the risk of genetic inbreeding. If either of these points is attacked, it could undermine the author's argument.
(A) Opposite; this would strengthen the argument.
(B) This works. If habitats in the south were more fragmented, but there was still a population boom as mentioned in the first paragraph, then it would seem that habitat fragmentation and degradation have little to do with whether or not koala populations would survive.
(C) Opposite; based on what the passage says about the degradation of eucalyptus, this would seem to strengthen the argument as well.
(D) Opposite; again, this would strengthen the case.
(E) Out of Scope; even if there were more genetic variance in the south, it would not necessarily prevent the risk of genetic inbreeding in the future.

15. D
Difficulty: Low
Strategic Advice: Be sure to read around the word to discern the full context within the sentence.
Getting to the Answer: Reading the sentence, you see you're looking for a word that means "preserve" or "keep the current population going," and this leads to (D).
(A) Extreme; the koalas would not necessarily need defense in the context of this part of the passage.
(B) This is another meaning of "sustain" that doesn't work here.
(C) This doesn't make sense in the sentence.
(E) Another meaning of "sustain" that doesn't work here.

16. A
Difficulty: Medium
Strategic Advice: A correct inference will not stray far from the passage; read carefully around the cited lines.
Getting to the Answer: Lines 91–93 discuss the relationship between toxin levels and nutrient availability: apparently the more nutrients available in an environment, the lower the level of toxin in the leaves. So leaves with high toxins probably lack those nutrients. You should at least look for choices that address this relationship, and (A) does so nicely.
(B) Opposite; leaves high in toxins are probably lower in nutrients.
(C) Opposite; the sentence referenced contradicts this.
(D) Distortion; the author is writing about the nutrients that trees get from their environments, not the nutrients that the trees in turn provide to the koalas.
(E) Extreme; the author does not suggest that high toxin levels are the cause for endangered species status.

17. E
Difficulty: Medium
Strategic Advice: Be sure to predict an answer with Detail questions so you won't be led astray by trap answers.
Getting to the Answer: The section cited suggests that further research should be done to *determine which habitats are richest in nutrients,*

as these tend to be preferred habitats for koalas. That makes a good prediction and leads directly to (E).

(A) Out of Scope; the author doesn't get into such *means.*

(B) Out of Scope; the author is more concerned with the koala's survival than with the reasons for its food preference.

(C) Distortion; finding ideal locations for *conservation efforts* is more important than determining the number of such locations.

(D) Out of Scope; plenty of *alternate habitats* exist. More important are selecting the ideal habitats among them.

18. **C**

Difficulty: Medium

Strategic Advice: Again, go for an inference in keeping with the tone of the author.

Getting to the Answer: Predict something "big picture" that the author believes about koalas, even something as basic as *in danger of extinction if something isn't done.* Then look for answers close to this tone.

(A) Extreme; the author never says that they're the *most vital species.*

(B) Extreme; the author writes of ways to prevent their extinction.

(D) Opposite; the author is quite concerned about this.

(E) Out of Scope; this is not the reason that the author mentioned the koalas as *symbols.*

Universal Grammar

19. **B**

Difficulty: Low

Strategic Advice: Be sure to research your answer on Detail questions, especially when, as in this case, the question stem directs you to an extended section of text or an entire paragraph. You will often find the necessary context for the specific detail immediately before or immediately after its appearance in the text.

Getting to the Answer: The first paragraph mentions the existence of Universal Grammar across all human languages, and the last sentence that discusses head parameters mentions that "all languages have it." The only answer that fits this is (B).

(A) Out of Scope; the passage never mentions the efforts of linguists to find a complete explanation.

(C) Out of Scope and Extreme; the passage never makes an outright refutation of the theory of Universal Grammar.

(D) Opposite and Distortion; these are the key features of the theory, not exceptions, and biologists do not object to the theory based on these particular features.

(E) Opposite; the features cited in the question stem are part of typical grammatical sentences.

20. **A**

Difficulty: Medium

Strategic Advice: Function questions ask about the way a particular detail works to develop the author's overall argument. Be sure you have a sense of the author's position before predicting how the cited detail fits in.

Getting to the Answer: The words "for example" beginning the second paragraph are key signifiers here. This paragraph is providing examples of something. The first paragraph is a basic introduction to Universal Grammar, and the second paragraph defines and explains a couple of pieces of theoretical evidence that support this theory, paraphrased nicely in choice (A).

(B) Opposite; the cited text provides support for the theory.

(C) Extreme; the cited text explains key evidence cited by the theory's advocates, but it never claims that most linguists accept them as definitive proof.

(D) Misused Detail; while the role of head parameters is explained, this explanation does not perform a specific argumentative function.

(E) Misused Detail; the second paragraph never disputes the theory.

21. **E**

Difficulty: Low

Strategic Advice: Remember that Vocab-in-Context questions will test secondary meanings of common words, so look to the specific context in order to make a good prediction.

Getting to the Answer: What would the theory of Universal Grammar "receive" in the "linguistic sphere"? Predict something like *attention.* (E) works, whereas all of the other choices use typical definitions of "play" and don't make sense in context.

22. A
Difficulty: High
Strategic Advice: Inference questions require you to draw your own conclusions based on your understanding of the author's argument. The answer is still in the text, though; it just isn't spelled out exactly. The cited paragraph is a good place to start.
Getting to the Answer: In the last paragraph, the author discusses the apparent lack of available biological evidence to support Universal Grammar and tells us that researchers recommend investigation of "neurobiological explanations" for the ways in which language operates, and (A) is a logical extension of this.
(B) Opposite; the last paragraph comes out on the side of investigating biological evidence, not against it.
(C) Opposite; again, the last paragraph points to the need for considering *social circumstances affecting language development.*
(D) Distortion; the last paragraph doesn't suggest that evidence is being ignored by linguists, only that more could be done to produce evidence for alternative explanations.
(E) Distortion; the paragraph suggests that advocates of the linguistics model don't consider language's evolutionary role, not that they oversimplify it.

23. E
Difficulty: Medium
Strategic Advice: Another inference. Look to the cited text, and keep clear who said what. Should this inference be based on the author's argument or on the argument of individuals cited by the author?
Getting to the Answer: This statement is basically accusing linguistics of being an incomplete method for studying human language development; it suggests that because of the complexity of language and grammar, linguistics alone might not allow for explanations that are wholly valid.
(A) Distortion, nowhere is it suggested that biological evidence is nonexistent.
(B) Out of Scope; the gathering of genetic evidence by biologists is never mentioned in the passage.

(C) Opposite; the simplest linguistic connections are what the researchers in the cited text are trying to avoid, claiming they render the network of associations around a single word *oversimplified and sterile.*
(D) Distortion; the cited text never suggests that the explanation is insufficient for specific languages

24. D
Difficulty: Medium
Strategic Advice: A single word can encompass an abstract concept; be sure to thoroughly review the context before making your prediction.
Getting to the Answer: The "marriage" follows an extended argument for the inadequacies of a purely linguistic approach to language and mentions a variety of evolutionary and social elements believed to be as significant. Look for an answer choice that reconciles the two approaches.
(A) Extreme; the suggestion that the combination could be or should be *flawless* is never made.
(B) Out of Scope; the author never discusses romantic relationships between scientists and linguists. Remember that the common definition of "marriage" is not relevant here, as the meaning has been changed by its context.
(C) Extreme; a *legal union* takes literally what is intended to be more abstract, namely a better working relationship between the two approaches.
(E) Out of Scope; the paragraph is concerned with reconciling linguistics and science, not science and social science.

Section 4 (Math)

1. C

Difficulty: Low

Strategic Advice: Be sure not to stop too soon! While you do need to find a to solve this question, it actually asks for $\dfrac{1}{a}$.

Getting to the Answer:

Substitute 3 for c into the equation $b = c^3$. Then $b = 3^3 = 3 \times 3 \times 3 = 27$. $b = 27$. Now substitute 27 for b into the equation $\sqrt{ab} = 3$: $\sqrt{a(27)} = 3$. So, $\sqrt{27a} = 3$. Now square both sides of this equation: $(\sqrt{27a})^2 = 3^2$. So $27a = 9$. Dividing both sides of this equation by 27, we get $a = \dfrac{9}{27} = \dfrac{1}{3}$. So $\dfrac{1}{a} = \dfrac{1}{\left(\frac{1}{3}\right)} = 1 \times \dfrac{3}{1} = 3$.

2. D

Difficulty: Low

Strategic Advice: Even though the figure is not drawn to scale, we know that it is a quadrilateral. The sum of the degree measures of the 4 angles of a quadrilateral is 360. So $f + g + h + j = 360$.

Getting to the Answer: We know that $h = 20$. Since $g = 4h$, $g = 4(20) = 80$. Now that we know that $g = 80$, we can find the value of f from the equation $f = 2g$. We know that $f = 2(80) = 160$. Now we know that

$$f = 160$$
$$g = 80$$
$$h = 20$$
$$j = 100$$

3. C

Difficulty: Medium

Strategic Advice: When you Pick Numbers, be sure to select numbers that obey the information in the question stem. Here, x must be negative, and y must be a fraction between 0 and 1.

Getting to the Answer: Let's begin with statement I. Since x is negative and y is positive, xy must be negative because a negative number multiplied by a positive number must be negative.

Since y is restricted to the interval $0 < y < 1$, while x can be any negative number, let's select values for y and x such that $xy = -\dfrac{1}{4}$.

Let $y = \dfrac{1}{2}$. Then, if we let $x = -\dfrac{1}{2}$, we have $xy = \left(-\dfrac{1}{2}\right)\left(\dfrac{1}{2}\right) = -\dfrac{1}{4}$. Statement I can be true.

Eliminate choices (A), (D), and (E), which contain statement I. Now look at statement II. If we use the same values in statement II that we used in statement I, $x = -\dfrac{1}{2}$ and $y = \dfrac{1}{2}$, then we get

$$\frac{x}{y} = \frac{\left(-\frac{1}{2}\right)}{\left(\frac{1}{2}\right)} = \left(-\frac{1}{2}\right) \times \frac{2}{1} = -1.$$ Statement II can be true. Eliminate choice (B), which contains statement II. Now that four incorrect answer choices have been eliminated, we know that choice (C) is correct.

We are expecting that statement III cannot be true, so that choice (C), III only, is the correct answer. Let's check statement III just to be sure. We know that $y < 1$. We also know that $x < 0$. So $x + y$ is the result of adding the negative number x to y. So $x + y < y$. Since $y < 1$ and $x + y < y$, it must be true that $x + y < 1$. So $x + y > 1$ cannot be true. Thus, statement III cannot be true. Choice (C), III only, is correct.

4. C

Difficulty: High

Strategic Advice: Again, remember the difference between "must be" and "could be." Translate the information in the question stem into math and manipulate the equation to see which of the Roman numerals must be true.

Getting to the Answer: Let's begin by writing the proportion statement of the question stem in fractional form. The ratio of $a + 1$ to $a + 2$ is the same as the ratio of $b + 3$ to $b + 4$, or $\dfrac{a+1}{a+2} = \dfrac{b+3}{b+4}$. Cross multiply. Then $(a + 1)(b + 4) = (a + 2)(b + 3)$. Multiply out both sides.

$$ab + 4a + b + 4 = ab + 3a + 2b + 6$$
$$a = b + 2$$

So, we have the requirement that $a = b + 2$. If $a = 4$ and $b = 2$, then the equation $a = b + 2$ is true, and so we see that both statements I and II can be true. However, the equation $a = b + 2$ does not require that the values of a and b be $a = 4$ and $b = 2$. We could also have the values $a = 5$ and $b = 3$, we could have the values $a = 6$ and $b = 4$, and we could have the values $a = 136$ and $b = 134$. Thus, each of statements I and II does not have to be true.

Look at statement III: $a - b = 2$.

We have the equation $a = b + 2$. Subtracting b from both sides of this equation, we have $a - b = 2$. So statement III must be true.

5.   **E**
Difficulty: High
Strategic Advice: Whenever a geometry question has information in the question stem that doesn't appear on the diagram, add it. This will often help you see how to get started. In this case, you need to translate the information from English to math before you can add it to the diagram.
Getting to the Answer:
The area of a triangle is $\dfrac{1}{2} \times$ base $\times$ height.
The area of triangle ABD is $\dfrac{1}{2} \times DB \times AC$

The area of triangle EBC is $\dfrac{1}{2} \times CB \times EC$.

We are given that $CB = DB - \dfrac{t}{100}DB = \left(1 - \dfrac{t}{100}\right)DB$

and $EC = AC - \dfrac{t}{100}AC = \left(1 - \dfrac{t}{100}\right)AC$.

Thus, $CB = \left(1 - \dfrac{t}{100}\right)DB$ and $EC = \left(1 - \dfrac{t}{100}\right)AC$.

The area of triangle EBC, in terms of DB, AC, and t is $\dfrac{1}{2} \times \left(1 - \dfrac{t}{100}\right)DB \times \left(1 - \dfrac{t}{100}\right)AC = \left(1 - \dfrac{t}{100}\right)^2\left(\dfrac{1}{2} \times DB \times AC\right)$

The area of triangle EBD is 16 percent of the area of triangle ABD, which means that

$$\dfrac{\left(1 - \dfrac{t}{100}\right)^2\left(\dfrac{1}{2} \times DB \times AC\right)}{\dfrac{1}{2} \times DB \times AC} = \dfrac{16}{100}.$$

Now $\dfrac{1}{2} \times DB \times AC$ can be canceled from the numerator and denominator on the left side of the equation. So $\left(1 - \dfrac{t}{100}\right)^2 = \dfrac{16}{100}$.

Now solve this equation for t.

$$\left(1 - \dfrac{t}{100}\right)^2 = \dfrac{16}{100}$$

$$\left(1 - \dfrac{t}{100}\right)^2 = \dfrac{4}{25}$$

$$\sqrt{\left(1 - \dfrac{t}{100}\right)^2} = \sqrt{\dfrac{4}{25}}$$

$$1 - \dfrac{t}{100} = \dfrac{2}{5}$$

$$\dfrac{t}{100} = \dfrac{3}{5}$$

$$t = \dfrac{3}{5} \times 100 = 3 \times 20 = 60$$

Thus, $t = 60$, and choice (E) is correct.

6. **D**
Difficulty: Medium
Strategic Advice: Think about what kinds of numbers you could get at each step. Try selecting the largest and smallest possible numbers in step 1, and see what they give you in step 5.
Getting to the Answer: Since the only information we have about what the number can be comes from step 1, where we start with a number between 40 and 200, we're going to try to figure out what the smallest and largest possible numbers are; the correct answer will be the only one between those two.

So we'll start with the smallest possible number, 41. (Remember, we need a number GREATER than 40.) In step 2, we divide it by 20, and get 2.05. Step 3—find the smallest integer greater than or equal to the number from step 2—is essentially just asking us to round up to the nearest integer, or do nothing if we're already at an integer. We're not, so we round up to 3. in step 4, we subtract 5, and get a final value of −2. So the smallest number that can be printed is −2.

Next we'll go for the largest possible number, 199. Divided by 20, we get 9.95, which rounds up in step 3 to 10. Subtracting 5 for step 4 leaves us with 5, so the largest number that can be printed is 5.

Looking at the answer choices, (A), (B), and (E) are all either larger than 5 or smaller than −2, so they can't possibly be the answer. Taking a closer look at the two remaining answers, choice (C) is a decimal—but step 3 specifically forces us to get to an integer; 1.7 is not allowed! We're left with (D) as the right answer.

7. **B**
Difficulty: Low
Strategic Advice: There's no complicated math here—all you need to do is follow the steps in the right order.
Getting to the Answer: Follow the instructions in the order that they are presented. The number selected in step 1 is 150, so we are finished with step 1.

Step 2 says to divide the number from the previous step by 20: $\frac{150}{20} = 7.5$.
So 7.5 is the number arrived at in step 2.

Step 3 says to find the smallest integer that is greater than or equal to 7.5. The integer 8 is the smallest integer that is greater than or equal to 7.5. So 8 is the number arrived at in step 3.

Step 4 says to subtract 5 from the number arrived at in the previous step.
Then 8 − 5 = 3. So 3 is the number arrived at in step 4.

In step 5, the number arrived at in the previous step is printed. So 3 is the number printed in step 5.

Choice (B) is correct.

8. **C**
Difficulty: High
Strategic Advice: Once you've found *b*, Backsolving works well on this question. Just plug each answer choice into the sequence of steps and see if you get *b*. Since you're looking for the greatest possible value, start with (E) instead of (C).
Getting to the Answer: Let's begin by determining what number is printed when the number 112 is selected for step 1.

The number from step 1 is 112. We are finished with step 1.

Step 2 says to divide the number from the previous step by 20. So $\frac{112}{20} = \frac{28}{5} = 5.6$. So 5.6 is the number arrived at in step 2.

Step 3 says to find the smallest integer that is greater than or equal to the number arrived at in the previous step. The smallest integer that is greater than or equal to 5.6 is 6. So 6 is the number arrived at in step 3.

Step 4 says to subtract 5 from the number arrived at in step 3. Now 6 − 5 = 1. So 1 is the number arrived at in step 4.

Step 5 says to print the number arrived at in the previous step. So 1 is the number printed in step 5.

Suppose that a is a number selected for step 1 and that b, which is 1, is the number printed in step 5. Then the number arrived at in step 2 is $\frac{a}{20}$, and the number arrived at in step 3 is $\left[\frac{a}{20}\right]$, where the notation $[x]$ means the smallest integer that is greater than or equal to x. That is, the smallest integer that is greater than or equal to $\frac{a}{20}$ is the number arrived at in step 3. In order to have the number 1 printed in step 5, the number 1 must be arrived at in step 4. In order to have the number 1 arrived at in step 4, the number $1 + 5 = 6$ must be arrived at in step 3. So we want the smallest integer that is greater than or equal to $\frac{a}{20}$ to be equal to 6. Now the number $\frac{a}{20}$ will be such that the smallest integer greater than or equal to $\frac{a}{20}$ is equal to 6 if $5 < \frac{a}{20} \le 6$. For example, if $\frac{a}{20} = 5.3$, then the smallest integer that is greater than or equal to 5.3 is 6.

If $\frac{a}{20} = 6$, then the smallest integer that is greater than or equal to 6 is 6.

Notice that if $\frac{a}{20}$ is less than or equal to 5, then the smallest integer that is greater than or equal to $\frac{a}{20}$ will have to be no greater than 5. For example, if $\frac{a}{20} = 5$, then the smallest integer that is greater than or equal to 5 is 5. If $\frac{a}{20} = 4.99$, then the smallest integer that is greater than or equal to 4.99 is 5. Also, if $\frac{a}{20}$ is anything greater than 6, the smallest integer that is greater than or equal to $\frac{a}{20}$ will have to be at least 7. For example, if $\frac{a}{20} = 6.01$, then the smallest integer that is greater than or equal to 6.01 is 7.

Thus, $5 < \frac{a}{20} \le 6$. Multiplying all members of this inequality by 20, we have that $100 < a \le 120$. The greatest possible value of a is 120. Choice (C) is correct.

9. **18**
Difficulty: Low
Strategic Advice: Solve for a using the second equation, then plug a into the first equation and solve for b.

Getting to the Answer: Multiply both sides of the equation $\frac{a}{3} = 10$ by 3.
Then $a = 3(10) = 30$.

Thus, $a = 30$. Now substitute 30 for a into the equation $a - b = 12$. Then $30 - b = 12$. Now solve this equation for b. Subtract 12 from both sides. Then $18 - b = 0$. Add b to both sides. Then $18 = b$.

10. **23**
Difficulty: Low
Strategic Advice: Set up an expression for the cost of a call that lasted x minutes, then set it equal to $1.75 and solve for x.
Getting to the Answer: Let x be the total number of minutes. Be careful here. The first 3 minutes cost $0.35. The number of <u>additional</u> minutes was $x - 3$. The cost of each of the $x - 3$ minutes that came after the first 3 minutes was $0.07. So the cost of the additional $x - 3$ minutes, in dollars, was $(x - 3)(0.07)$. The total cost, in dollars was $0.35 + (x - 3)(0.07)$. We know that the total cost was $1.75. So we can write down the equation $0.35 + (x - 3)(0.07) = 1.75$. Now solve this equation for x.

$$0.35 + (x - 3)(0.07) = 1.75$$

Multiply both sides by 100 in order to remove the decimal points:

$$35 + (x - 3)7 = 175$$
$$35 + 7x - 21 = 175$$
$$7x + 14 = 175$$
$$7x = 161$$
$$x = 23$$

11. **12**

Difficulty: Medium

Strategic Advice: When a geometry problem doesn't give you a diagram, you should probably sketch your own to better visualize the situation.

Getting to the Answer:

Among the specified segments in the question stem, YZ is the smallest. So it will be convenient to let the length of YZ be a, and then express the lengths of the other segment mentioned in the question stem in terms of a.

So we are letting the length of YZ be a.

Since $XY = 2(YZ)$, the length of XY is $2a$.

Since $WX = 2(XY)$, the length of WX is $2(2a)$, which is $4a$.

Since $VW = 2(WX)$, the length of VW is $2(4a)$, which is $8a$.

From the drawing, we see that:

$$VW + WX + XY + YZ = VZ$$

From the question stem, $VZ = 30$.

We have that:

$$YZ = a$$
$$XY = 2a$$
$$WX = 4a$$
$$VW = 8a$$

So we have the equation $8a + 4a + 2a + a = 30$.

Let's solve this equation for a.

$$8a + 4a + 2a + a = 30$$
$$15a = 30$$
$$a = 2$$

We want the length of WY

$$WY = WX + XY$$

We have that $WX = 4a = 4(2) = 8$.

We have that $XY = 2a = 2(2) = 4$.

So $WY = WX + XY = 8 + 4 = 12$.

12. **275, 330, or 385**

Difficulty: Medium

Strategic Advice: Try replacing the digit B with the integers from 1 through 9 inclusive.

Getting to the Answer:

Let's refer to the value of the number in the rectangle by N.

The sum of 5 equal numbers is equal to 5 times one of the numbers.

$5 \times 11 = 55$. 55 is less than 250, so 55 is not a possible value of N.

$5 \times 22 = 110$. 110 is less than 250, so 110 is not a possible value of N.

$5 \times 33 = 165$. 165 is less than 250, so 165 is not a possible value of N.

$5 \times 44 = 220$. 220 is less than 250, so 220 is not a possible value of N.

$5 \times 55 = 275$. $250 \le 275 \le 400$, so 275 is a possible value of N.

$5 \times 66 = 330$. $250 \le 330 \le 400$, so 330 is a possible value of N.

$5 \times 77 = 385$. $250 \le 385 \le 400$, so 385 is a possible value of N.

$5 \times 88 = 440$. 440 is greater than 400, so 440 is not a possible value of N.

There is no need to try letting $B = 9$ because 5×99 will be even greater than 5×88.

The possible values of N are 275, 330, and 385.

13. **600**

Difficulty: Medium

Strategic Advice: Think about each appliance one at a time—how many different radios could the customer buy? How many different televisions?

Getting to the Answer: For each of the 12 different types of radios that a customer can buy, the customer can buy 10 different types of television sets. So the number of different combinations of one radio and one television set that a customer can buy is 12×10. For each of the 12 × 10 different combinations of one radio and one television set that a customer can buy, the customer can buy 5 different types of vacuum cleaners. So the number of different combinations of one radio, one television set, and one vacuum cleaner that a customer can buy is 12 × 10 × 5.

Now 12 × 10 × 5 = 120 × 5 = 600.

There are 600 different combinations of one radio, one television set, and one vacuum cleaner that a customer can buy.

14. **24**
Difficulty: High
Strategic Advice: Think about calendar problems in terms of weeks—if one Sunday is day n, the next Sunday must be day $n + 7$.
Getting to the Answer: Since the first Wednesday occurs on day 6, the next Sunday of that month occurs 4 days later on day number 6 + 4 = 10.

Let's now determine on what days of the month each of the next Sundays are on until we run out of available days in this 30-day month.

Since we know that one Sunday is on day 10, the Sunday immediately after the Sunday on day 10 must occur 7 days later. So the Sunday immediately after the Sunday on day 10 occurs on day 10 + 7 = 17. The Sunday immediately after the Sunday on day 17 occurs on day 17 + 7 = 24 of this month. The Sunday that occurs on day 24 is the final Sunday of the month because the Sunday that occurs after the Sunday on day 24 occurs 7 days after day 24. Since 24 + 7 = 31, and 31 is greater than 30, there are not enough days in the 30-day month for a Sunday in this month after the Sunday on day 24.

The final Sunday occurs on day 24.

15. **1**
Difficulty: High
Strategic Advice: Don't let funny symbols scare you off—they'll be defined in the problem.
Getting to the Answer: ◊–75◊ is the product of all the negative odd integers from –1 through –73 inclusive.
◊–74◊ is also the product of all the negative odd

integers from –1 through –73 inclusive.

So ◊–75◊ = ◊–74◊.

Therefore, $\dfrac{\lozenge-75\lozenge}{\lozenge-74\lozenge} = 1$.

16. **135**
Difficulty: High
Strategic Advice: Here you have a part-to-part ratio *(OABC : OCDA)* that you need to convert into a part-to-whole ratio *(OABC : circle)*. Remember that the ratio between the interior angle of a sector and 360° is the same as the ratio between the area of a sector and the area of the whole circle.
Getting to the Answer: Since the ratio of the area of *OABC* to the area of *OCDA* is 3:5, the ratio of the area of *OABC* to the area of the entire circle is 3:(3 + 5) = 3:8. This ratio is the same as the ratio of the interior angle of sector *OABC* to 360°, or x:360. Set up a proportion using these ratios:

$$\frac{3}{8} = \frac{x}{360}$$
$$360(3) = 8x$$
$$1{,}080 = 8x$$
$$135 = x$$

17. **5**
Difficulty: High
Strategic Advice: The median of a set of numbers is the middle number when the numbers are arranged from least to greatest. Even though you don't know exactly what these numbers are, you can still put them in order and pick out the median.
Getting to the Answer: Because x is positive, the arrangement in increasing order of the five terms is $5x$, $7x$, $8x$, $11x$, and $13x$. The median of these numbers is the middle value, which is $8x$. We want the smallest possible value of x such that the median $8x$ is divisible by 20. Saying that $8x$ is divisible by 20 means that $8x$ is a multiple of 20. Now the prime factorization of the factor 8 of $8x$ is $2 \times 2 \times 2$. The prime factorization of 20 is $2 \times 2 \times 5$. So the factor 8 of $8x$ already contains the two prime factors 2 of 20 (and 8 also contains a third prime factor of 2, although this is not

needed to find the smallest possible value of x).
We now have the two prime factors 2 of 20. All we
still need is the prime factor 5 of 20 in the product
$8x$. The smallest positive multiple of 5 is 5, so if we
let $x = 5$, then $8x$ will be a multiple of 20. Just to
check, if $x = 5$, then $8x = 8(5) = 40$, which is a
multiple of 20 ($40 = 2 \times 20$). The smallest possible
value of x is 5.

18. **70**
Difficulty: Medium
Strategic Advice: If you don't remember what the
sum of the interior angles of a particular polygon
is off the top of your head, divide it into triangles.
You should always remember that the sum of the
interior angles of a triangle is 180 degrees, so just
add up the triangles to find the sum of the interior
angles of any polygon.
Getting to the Answer: We can draw in 3 line
segments that divide the 6-sided polygon into 4
triangles.

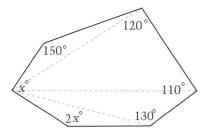

The sum of the degree measures of the 6 interior
angles of the 6-sided polygon is the sum of the
degree measures of all the interior angles of the
four triangles into which the polygon has been
divided. We know that the sum of the degree
measures of the interior angles of a triangle is
180. So the sum of the degree measures of the
interior angles of four triangles is 180(4), which is
720. Thus, the sum of the degree measures of the
interior angles of the polygon is 720.

So we can write down the equation

$$150 + 120 + 110 + 130 + 2x + x = 720.$$

Now let's solve this equation for x.

$$150 + 120 + 110 + 130 + 2x + x = 720$$
$$510 + 3x = 720$$
$$3x = 210$$
$$x = \frac{210}{3} = 70$$

Thus, $x = 70$.

Section 5 (Writing)

1. D
Difficulty: Medium
Strategic Advice: The sentence contains a modification error, eliminating choice (A). The introductory phrase cannot modify the noun that immediately follows it, *party*—a party doesn't hear things, a person does—in this case, the math teacher. The underlined portion also uses the passive voice, which is rarely part of the credited choice in the SAT.
Getting to the Answer: (B) does not correct the error and loses part of the meaning of the sentence. (C) distorts the meaning of the sentence. (D) and (E) correct the modification error, but (E) uses the past perfect (*had thrown*), which would only be correct if the sentence referred to some other past action that it preceded. So (D) is correct.

2. C
Difficulty: Medium
Strategic Advice: One of the main problems in this sentence is the comma splice: the incorrect use of a comma to connect two complete sentences. So (A) and (B) are incorrect.
Getting to the Answer: (C) correctly uses the semicolon and makes the two sentences parallel. If split into two sentences, this could read: *Many students prefer social studies over science classes. Another student preference is for English over foreign language classes.* (B) doesn't correct the run-on sentence. (D) corrects this problem but doesn't fix the wordiness or make the sentences parallel. (E) corrects the run-on sentence but eliminates any connection between the two ideas.

3. D
Difficulty: High
Strategic Advice: The question is difficult because the sentence contains two problems. First, *to be credit* is an incorrect form of the past tense. It should read *to be credited*. Second, "nor" is not correct here. Since the first part of the statement ("refused to be credit...") isn't expressed in the negative, the correct connector is "or."
Getting to the Answer: (C) and (D) correct the first problem, but only (D) eliminates the *nor*. (E) adds *neither* so that the sentence includes *neither*

and *nor*, but here the *neither* forms a double negative: *refused to neither be credited....* This is incorrect. Only (D) works.

4. E
Difficulty: Low
Strategic Advice: The sentence compares two things: Balanchine's skill as a dancer and his skill as a choreographer. The structure of the comparison must be parallel.
Getting to the Answer: (C) and (E) fix this problem—*dancer* and *choreographer* are parallel structures. (C), however, changes the meaning of the sentence. Balanchine was not *almost skillful*. He was almost as skillful a dancer as he was a choreographer. (E) is correct. (B) and (D) do not correct the parallelism problem.

5. C
Difficulty: Medium
Strategic Advice: The introductory phrase should be followed by the noun that it modifies. Remember to check modification whenever you see an introductory phrase on improving sentences questions.
Getting to the Answer: Who stares out over the ocean? The sailor. (B) and (C) both use the correct noun. However, (B) states that the sailor gave stability to the waves. This doesn't make sense. (C) is the only answer with the correct noun that makes sense... *the sailor felt a sense of stability from the waves.*

6. D
Difficulty: Medium
Strategic Advice: This sentence is a run-on, containing two independent sentences joined by a comma. Since none of the answer choices correct this by adding a semicolon, look for an answer that inserts an appropriate conjunction between the sentences or that makes one of the independent clauses a subordinate clause.
Getting to the Answer: (B), (D), and (E) all insert an appropriate conjunction *though* that shows the relationship between the two ideas. Only (D) corrects the style problems of *daily in their lives they are calm though.* (B) adds to the style problems by adding *than that.* (E) eliminates the parallelism between the two sentences. (C) omits the idea that they are calm in their daily lives, only stating that they are not as angry. Only (D) is correct.

7. **B**

Difficulty: Medium

Strategic Advice: The sentence uses the pronoun *which* to refer to people.

Getting to the Answer: (B) and (E) use the correct pronoun *who* to refer to people, but only (B) keeps the idea of the original sentence. (E) introduces horoscopes instead of astrology. (C) uses *whom* instead of *who*. (D) uses *that* to refer to people.

8. **D**

Difficulty: Medium

Strategic Advice: Check to see if the introductory phrase modifies the correct noun. It is intended to modify *many people* (many people rely on the news), but *CNN* immediately follows it.

Getting to the Answer: (C) and (D) place the correct noun directly after the introductory phrase, but (C) is inappropriately reversed, needlessly wordy, and awkward. Only (D) has the correct arrangement of words. (B) substitutes the wrong noun as modifier. CNN doesn't rely on its news; many people do. (E) is a sentence fragment; it contains no verb.

9. **A**

Difficulty: Medium

Strategic Advice: The sentence is correct as written. Don't forget answer choice (A). It is correct about as often as any other choice.

Getting to the Answer: Note the word pair *either* and *or*. (A) gives the correct usage. (B) is correct but unnecessarily complicates the sentence. (C) eliminates *in*. (D) and (E) eliminate *either* from the word pair.

10. **B**

Difficulty: Medium

Strategic Advice: The relative pronoun *which* is misused here. Tom finds the length of golf particularly boring, not golf itself.

Getting to the Answer: Instead of joining the two ideas clumsily, (B) makes each idea independent and links them with a semicolon. (C) and (E) change the meaning. Tom finds the length of golf particularly boring, not golf itself. (D) adds the preposition *to*, which does not correct the usage problem.

11. **D**

Difficulty: Medium

Strategic Advice: Take a look at the pronouns here.

Getting to the Answer: *They* has an incorrect antecedent; it should refer to the nation, but then it would have to be the singular, *it*. However, if you replace *they* with *it*, another problem arises—an unclear antecedent. Does *it* refer to the nation or the government? You have to make that distinction in your choice. Only (D) does this by replacing the pronoun with the noun *nation*. (B) is incorrect because it replaces *They* with *it* and *violated* with *was violating*. You can eliminate (C) because it changes *imposed* to *has imposed* and maintains the incorrect pronoun *they*. (E) changes the meaning of the sentence—*a renegade nation* becomes *a nation of renegades*.

12. **C**

Difficulty: Medium

Strategic Advice: This is a complicated sentence. Look to see if pronouns clearly refer to something specific.

Getting to the Answer: The pronoun *they* actually refers to a *particular species* that is singular (even though species ends in a "s"; this one is tricky). So *they* should be replaced by *it*, and the verb should be the singular *has* instead of *have*. The word *conducting* (A) is properly used. *Than* in (B) correctly parallels the idea that begins with *less interested in*. The adverb *violently* (D) correctly modifies the verb *taken over*.

13. **E**

Difficulty: High

Strategic Advice: If the relative pronoun clause confuses you, reverse the order.

Getting to the Answer: The sentence could read *The analyst was shocked that his presentation ... was criticized savagely by his customers. Criticized savagely* could be *savagely criticized*, but either is correct. Therefore, although the sentence is unusual, there is no error.

14. **D**

Difficulty: Medium

Strategic Advice: When two things are being compared (i.e., something is twice as much as something else), check to make sure that the comparison is logical.

Getting to the Answer: This sentence presents an illogical comparison: The *programs performed* *in the new symphony hall* are compared to *the old performance space.* The correct sentence reads: *A downfall in the economy could affect the ballet season because programs performed in the new symphony hall cost twice as much as programs performed in the old performance space.* The word *covered* (A) correctly describes the programs. The verb *cost* (B) agrees with programs. The phrase *as much* (C) is idiomatically correct and introduces the comparison between the programs.

15. **B**
Difficulty: Low
Strategic Advice: Pronouns are often misused in spoken English; so even if they sound correct, check to be sure.
Getting to the Answer: Try the sentence without *the other cyclists.* Would you say "me immediately started peddling"? No. The pronoun *me* is part of the subject of the sentence, so it should be "I." The word *other* (A) shows that *me* is part of the group. The adverb *immediately* (C) correctly modifies the verb *started. Blown* correctly modifies *whistle.*

16. **B**
Difficulty: Low
Strategic Advice: When you see a word like *amount,* remember that even though it refers to a number of things, it is singular.
Getting to the Answer: The subject *amount* is singular, and so the verb should be *keeps. Although* (A) connects the two parts of the sentence. *Claim* (C) is plural, agreeing with *account holders. Are improving* is the correct use of the progressive verb form.

17. **D**
Difficulty: High
Strategic Advice: Note that this sentence presents a comparison; look to see whether the comparison is logical.
Getting to the Answer: Comparisons require parallel structure; here, since the first thing being compared is *to compare,* the second should be "to attempt" (rather than *attempting*). The preposition *to* (A) is correctly placed after the verb *compare.* The verb *is* (B) agrees with the subject *to compare* (even though the word closest to the verb is the plural noun *losses*). *Than* (C) completes the idiom *is more than.*

18. **E**
Difficulty: High
Strategic Advice: Don't forget that (E) is the correct answer choice just as many times as the other answer choices are.
Getting to the Answer: Take the sentence choice by choice. The modifying phrase *like that of many braggarts* (A) correctly refers to and modifies the *businessman's success* (B). The adjective *impressive* (C) correctly refers to the success. The expression *had done no work to attain it* (D) is good, idiomatic English.

19. **D**
Difficulty: Medium
Strategic Advice: Don't get bogged down by the subject matter; look for common grammar problems.
Getting to the Answer: Here, an adjective, *artistic,* modifies a verb, *recognized.* To correct this, the adverb *artistically* should modify *recognized.* The preposition *for* (A) correctly precedes *the museum-restored... .* The adverb *clearly* (B) correctly modifies *wanted,* and the infinitive *to purchase* (C) is idiomatically correct with the verb *wanted.*

20. **C**
Difficulty: High
Strategic Advice: Don't forget that sometimes the SAT tests knowledge of vocabulary words.
Getting to the Answer: The word *detract* (which means to *disparage* or *to pull down from*) is incorrectly used here. A correct word could be *subtract.* As you build your vocabulary, pay close attention to similar words, such as "detract" and "subtract." The SAT often tests the subtle differences. The verb *dares* (A) agrees with *no one* and is in the present tense just like the rest of the sentence. The conjunction *for* (B) logically connects the two parts of the sentence. The phrase *for any reason* in (D) is good, standard English.

21. **C**
Difficulty: High
Strategic Advice: Look to see whether the pronoun clearly refers to someone.
Getting to the Answer: The pronoun *he* could refer to the store manager or the warehouse manager. Even though it would make more sense that the warehouse manager makes the deliveries,

we can't be sure. To make the sentence unambiguous, we could repeat the title in the correct position. The infrequently used verb *telephoned* (A) is correct and appropriately in the past tense. The preposition *after* (B) is correct, and *to deliver* is the correct form to follow the verb *failed*.

22. D
Difficulty: Medium
Strategic Advice: Jack, the subject of the sentence, is making a comparison. Is it logical?
Getting to the Answer: Jack improperly compares the Independent Party candidate's economic plan with the other candidate, instead of with the other candidate's plan. The verb *attended* (A) is properly in the past tense, and the adverb *closely* correctly follows. The expression *which Jack* (B) is correct standard written English, and *better structured* (C) correctly sets up the comparison between the two plans.

23. E
Difficulty: High
Strategic Advice: Don't let the fact that you may not have heard of Villella or Balanchine distract you from the grammar.
Getting to the Answer: There is no error. The expressions *to stage* (A), *that develop from* (B), and *and incorporate* (C) are standard written English. *Intended* is in the appropriate tense, as George Balanchine intended the ballets to have such feeling before Edward Villella staged them.

24. C
Difficulty: Low
Strategic Advice: This sentence includes four verbs, so check their tense agreement.
Getting to the Answer: The subject *not one* is singular, but the verb *have* is plural; it should be *has*. This is tricky because *not one* does refer to the *many people*, but only one of the many people, so it is singular. *To have seen* (A) is idiomatic in good, standard English. *But* (B) provides a logical link between the two contrasting parts of the sentence. The expression *such objects* (C) is correct.

25. A
Difficulty: Medium
Strategic Advice: Look at the sequence of events and determine whether the tenses are appropriate.

Getting to the Answer: *Announces* is incorrectly in the present tense, as the announcement took place in the past. It should read *announced*. *To build the moral* (B) is good, idiomatic English. *Of employees* (C) and *during the recession* (D) both appropriately use prepositions.

26. D
Difficulty: Medium
Strategic Advice: Read through the sentence to see if anything sounds wrong.
Getting to the Answer: *Businesses at its time* is not correct in this case. The correct idiomatic phrase is *businesses of its time*. *Comment on* (A) is correct idiomatically. The adjective *traditional* (B) properly modifies the noun *politics*. The verb *exerted* (C) is appropriately in the past tense.

27. A
Difficulty: Medium
Strategic Advice: When referring to people, *who* or *whom* are correct pronouns; context will tell you which to use.
Getting to the Answer: (A) contains the error; *which* should be *who*. (B) is the correct verb tense in context. (C) uses an adjective to modify the noun *assistance*. (D) is correct idiomatic usage.

28. C
Difficulty: Medium
Strategic Advice: The SAT will sometimes use long intervening phrases to separate a subject and verb that do not agree.
Getting to the Answer: Here, the singular verb form *shortens* does not agree with its plural subject *medications*. The error is in (C). (A) agrees with its plural subject *Doctors*. (B) properly uses the comparative form *more* to refer to two things (*herbal medications* and *a more traditional medical approach*.) (D) is correct idiomatic usage.

29. D
Difficulty: High
Strategic Advice: In a comparison, make sure the objects being compared are logical.
Getting to the Answer: This sentence compares *The complex formulas of Algebra II* with *Algebra I*. A correct comparison would either be between the two courses or their formulas and problems. (D) contains the error. (A) and (C) are correct idiomatic usage. (B) is the correct verb tense in context.

30. **B**
Difficulty: Medium
Strategic Advice: All of the verbs are in past tense but look at the sequence of events. A pamphlet in the recent past cannot change the way the students thought in the earlier past.
Getting to the Answer: (B), (C), and (D) correctly eliminate *used to*. Only (B), however, keeps the sentence in past tense (*changed the way they thought*). (C) uses *changed* and *think*, which mixes past and present. (D) uses *change* and *think*, which switches the phrase into the present. (E) keeps the incorrect phrase *used to think*.

31. **D**
Difficulty: Medium
Strategic Advice: This is a simple grammatical error substituting the noun *effect* for the verb *affect*.
Getting to the Answer: Simply substitute *affecting* for *effecting*, and (D) is your answer. The others unnecessarily complicate the situation. There is no need to substitute *influencing* for *affecting*. Also, (B) incorrectly introduces the preposition *on*, and (C) incorrectly puts the sentence in the passive voice. (E) eliminates *really*, which takes away the emphasis and thus changes the meaning of the sentence.

32. **A**
Difficulty: Medium
Strategic Advice: What can be added to make the relationship between sentences 5 and 6 clearer?
Getting to the Answer: Sentence 5 ends on a hopeful note, but sentence 6 is negative. Reading further, the policy eliminating music programs still went into effect. We need to add a sentence that explains what happened. It is possible that despite the pamphlet, students did not fight the policy, and therefore, the policy went into effect. (A), (B), and (C) all state this. Now look at the keywords. *However* in (A) correctly shows the contrasting relationship between the hope in sentence 5 and the negativity in sentence 6. *Therefore* (B) incorrectly shows a continuous relationship between sentences 5 and 6. *As a result* (C) incorrectly shows a causal relationship from the hope to the elimination of the music program. (D) introduces a new idea that is not

directly relevant to the passage. (E) contrasts the ideas but doesn't link the hope with what happened to the policy.

33. **D**
Difficulty: Medium
Strategic Advice: Sentence 6 does not adequately lead to sentence 7. We need to link the sentences.
Getting to the Answer: The link is that hope was in vain because the school continued its policy to eliminate music classes. (C) and (D) state this. (C) however, uses the plural *their* to refer to the singular *school*. Also, the passage only mentions one policy. (A) is redundant and doesn't add the missing link between sentences. (B) and (E) contradict the passage.

34. **B**
Difficulty: Low
Strategic Advice: Sentence 10 does not logically follow sentence 9. It needs to be placed elsewhere in the passage.
Getting to the Answer: The purpose of the passage is to disagree with the school's elimination of music classes. So *I disagree* should follow the last sentence about the school's view and introduce the author's view. Only (B) works. The writer disagrees with the school's idea that music wasn't an important skill, so *I disagree* should directly follow sentence 8. (C), (D), and (E) are opposite: the writer agrees with these ideas. (A) is a statement of fact, not an opinion, so the writer could not disagree with it.

35. **E**
Difficulty: Medium
Strategic Advice: The underlined portion contains a redundancy.
Getting to the Answer: The phrase before the hyphen states that learning to read music is like learning a second language, so it is redundant to state *it is the same because*. Eliminate that clause, and the sentence is correct. (B) changes the meaning. You do not express yourself in the same way by reading music and learning a second language. (C) is tricky. The SAT often includes ambiguous pronouns, so here *it* is replaced by *music*. However, that correction does not need to be made. (D) eliminates the redundancy but introduces a new error—*each* is a singular noun so it should read *each is*.

Section 6 (Critical Reading)

1.   A
Difficulty: Low
Strategic Advice: Some early Sentence Completions will simply signal a straight definition for the blank. Recognize it, accept the gift, and move on.
Getting to the Answer: *The braggart interjected his opinion* with -------, which *confirmed his* -------. You can see that both of the missing words will agree with the idea that the man is a *braggart,* so look for both to match that sentiment. (C) is the answer. If you didn't know the meanings of the two words in (C), you could still see that none of the others give you what you need.
(A) These words lack the needed similarity.
(B) These are both opposite to your prediction.
(D) *Severity* doesn't make sense in this context.
(E) *Ambivalence* is not a characteristic of a braggart.
flourish (n): an ostentatious act or gesture
ostentation: pretentious showiness
ambivalence: the coexistence of opposing attitudes or feelings

2.   A
Difficulty: Medium
Strategic Advice: Some Sentence Completions may have a relatively simple structure but contain more difficult vocabulary. Outside reading and vocab study will help with this.
Getting to the Answer: If you were looking to find something, what would you do with something that *obstructs?* You would *reject* or *get rid of* it. (A) works and is the correct answer.
(B) *Affirming* is the opposite of what you need.
(C) This is another opposite.
(D) *Imbibing,* or drinking, has nothing to do with the thrust of the sentence.
(E) *Concealing* isn't strong enough.
renounce: reject; disown

3.   E
Difficulty: Medium
Strategic Advice: While you're looking out for keywords, remember that punctuation can also help you to map the sentence.

Getting to the Answer: In this sentence, the clause following the semicolon parallels the clause before it. The administrator's *cheerfulness* concealed *something not cheerful,* just as her *jovial* tone became *sober. Seriousness* makes a good prediction.
(A) This is the opposite of your prediction.
(B) Another opposite.
(C) The word needs to have a more negative tone than the neutral *comprehension.*
(D) This word doesn't fit the context.
elation: exhilaration; a feeling of joy and pride
gravity: seriousness; solemnity

4.   C
Difficulty: High
Strategic Advice: Even "straight definition" sentences can become difficult when the choices include tough vocab.
Getting to the Answer: The key to predicting in this sentence is to understand the relationship between the *chancellor,* the *students,* and the *tuition increase.* Students wouldn't want a tuition increase, so the fact that the chancellor said there wouldn't be one should *decrease,* or *put to rest,* the students' concerns about it.
(A) This word is too neutral and has nothing to do with resolving the *students' concerns.*
(B) This is an opposite.
(C) This fits the bill. Even if you didn't know the meaning of *allayed,* you could have eliminated your way to it.
(D) This is a tough word, but it should remind you of *derogatory,* as in *make a derogatory remark;* that doesn't fit the thrust of the sentence.
(E) This is too neutral.
elicit: to draw from
allay: relieve; pacify
derogate: detract; go astray

5.   B
Difficulty: High
Strategic Advice: Remember, you don't have to start with the first blank; go to the second if it looks easier.
Getting to the Answer: *Formerly* tells you that this is a contrast sentence. The young man started out one way and wound up something different, so the two blanks will have opposite charges. The clue that he *caused a great deal of*

harm tells you that the second blank will have a negative charge, something like *menace* or *villain*.

(A) The second word lacks a negative charge.

(B) This is your answer. *Miscreant* works for the second blank; how about the first word? You would *reproach* someone for doing something bad, so *irreproachable* has the necessary positive charge.

(C) You need a positive charge for the first blank, so *nefarious* doesn't work.

(D) *Malicious* is much too negative for the first blank.

(E) You wouldn't call someone *who caused a great deal of harm a leader.*

libertarian: an advocate for the maximization of individual rights versus the rights of the state

irreproachable: blameless; faultless

miscreant: villain; evildoer

nefarious: wicked in the extreme; abominable

demagogue: a leader who gains power using impassioned appeals to the emotions and prejudices of the people

reprobate: a morally unprincipled person

hapless: unlucky; unfortunate

6. **C**

Difficulty: Medium

Strategic Advice: A sentence can set up contrast without using typical keywords like *although* and *despite;* often, as in this case, the relationship of specific words to each other will determine the relationship between the blanks.

Getting to the Answer: The first blank describes the *effects of blizzards,* while the second talks about the *sunny and pleasant days* that followed. Your prediction for the blanks should account for this contrast. A *record-setting blizzard* would probably have *catastrophic* effects, while the milder weather that followed would *reduce* them or make them seem less significant.

(A) Sunny weather wouldn't *exacerbate* the effects of a blizzard.

(B) Nothing in the sentence suggests that the effects of the record-setting storm were *stimulating.*

(D) As in (A), sunny weather wouldn't *aggravate* the effects of a blizzard.

(E) While this choice does set up a kind of contrast, it's awkward to say that sunny days *challenged* the effects of the blizzard.

frigid: extremely cold

exacerbate: increase the severity of

alleviate: make more bearable; relieve

aggravate: make worse

7. **B**

Difficulty: Medium

Strategic Advice: *Because* always indicates a cause-and-effect relationship.

Getting to the Answer: Either she was usually *reticent,* and so her reticence was normal, or she was usually not reticent, and so her reticence was unusual. If you know that reticent means quiet, then you can predict that either she's typically *talkative* or she's typically *silent.*

(A) If the senator were usually *sociable,* a reticent attitude would not be described as *appropriate.*

(C) We wouldn't typically expect a senator to appear *distraught,* and *sympathetic* in the second blank doesn't establish a strong relationship between the blanks.

(D) *Serious* has no strong connection to *reticent,* and *irrelevant* doesn't make sense in the context of the second blank.

(E) Again, *pedestrian* does not connect strongly to *reticent.*

reticent: restrained; reserved

gregarious: sociable

incongruous: incompatible

distraught: deeply agitated

pedestrian: ordinary

8. **B**

Difficulty: Medium

Strategic Advice: Cases in which the blank is in clear contrast with another element of the sentence will often draw on your knowledge of vocabulary.

Getting to the Answer: The words *in contrast to* are a pretty clear hint that this is a contrast sentence. Some of the students have *vacant* expressions, so the word in the blank will describe the opposite of that. Predict something like *attentive* or *focused.*

(A) *Gloomy* does not contrast with vacant.

(C) *Disseminated* likewise does not contrast with vacant and makes little sense in context.

(D) *Imbued* also fails to provide the contrast we are looking for and is awkwardly worded.

(E) An expression wouldn't be described as *retiring,* which also fails to contrast with *vacant.*

vacant: empty
rapt: enchanted
disseminated: scattered or distributed widely
imbued: permeated, saturated

Parks

9. A
Difficulty: Low
Strategic Advice: For Vocab-in-Context questions, always go back to the context and use your Sentence Completion skills.
Getting to the Answer: The sentence in question says a lot of work has been done, so look for a word that means *large*.
(A) This means extremely large, a good match for your prediction.
(B) *Famous* amount? That doesn't work.
(C) A common meaning for *tremendous*, but it doesn't fit here.
(D) *Elevated* generally means lofty or noble; no match here.
(E) *Exemplary* means perfect; again, no match.

10. D
Difficulty: Low
Strategic Advice: Questions about an author's attitude require you to make an inference since that information won't be directly stated in the passage.
Getting to the Answer: In the last sentence, the author says that parks need to be well protected.
(A) Extreme; the fact that something needs to be done doesn't actually mean that it will be done, so the measures are not *inevitable*.
(B) Opposite; this might apply to author 2, but not author 1.
(C) Extreme; the author obviously disapproves of the vandalism that makes the security necessary, so *fortunate* seems much too positive here.
(D) Good match.
(E) Opposite; *superfluous* means unnecessary.
inevitable: impossible to avoid
superfluous: beyond what is required or necessary

11. A
Difficulty: Medium
Strategic Advice: When looking for the function of a phrase, go back to the context and keep the author's viewpoint in mind.
Getting to the Answer: This author is arguing for access. The phrase *memorials of personal heritage* is part of the argument that the stuff in the parks really belongs to the people. Your prediction should be that the function of this phrase is to support the argument for access.
(A) This matches your prediction. The general argument is that the property on park land belongs to the visitors; therefore, they should be granted access.
(B) Misuse of Detail; this is a reference to Passage 1, which says that sites with artifacts are the hardest to protect.
(C) Out-of-Scope; Passage 2 is not concerned with the park system as a whole.
(D) Out-of-Scope; there is no implication that visitors are the reason that the sites are in ruins.
(E) Distortion; the author does not approve of the barbed wire, but this is not the function of the phrase in question.

12. D
Difficulty: High
Strategic Advice: Some of the most challenging questions for paired paragraphs ask you to infer what one author would think about something written by the other author.
Getting to the Answer: Author 2 writes that *Park visitors have a right to access this property as their own, but barbed-wire fences send a different signal.* So, to the author, fences are an example of the Park Service sending a negative signal to park visitors.
(A) Opposite; the author says that a sense of ownership would be a more effective security measure than a fence.
(B) Distortion; author 2 does say that it is the duty of the Parks Service to preserve and protect, but she also seems to regard fences as counterproductive.
(C) Misuse of Detail, it's Passage 1, not Passage 2, that mentions upgrades.
(D) Matches your prediction.
(E) Out-of-Scope; property lines are not mentioned in either paragraph.

Fairy Tales

These two passages take different viewpoints on the question of the significance of symbols in fairy tales. Passage 1 takes the position that, because of the unique circumstances under which fairy tales are composed and refined, the symbols have come to represent universal truths. Passage 2 argues that fairy tales have too many different versions to assign consistent meanings to specific symbols, so those symbols cannot be universal.

Passage 1 opens with a description of the evolution of fairy tales, retold and refined until they come to represent human universals. Paragraphs 2 and 3 present a specific example of a tale, "Snow White," and outline how its symbolism is universal. Paragraph 4 sums up and restates the argument.

Passage 2 begins by stating its position in opposition to scholars who see fairy tale symbolism as universal. Paragraph 1 outlines the basic argument—that there are too many different versions to assign specific meanings to symbols. Paragraph 2 sets up a "straw-man" argument by outlining a hypothetical interpretation of the tale of "Little Red Riding Hood." Paragraph 3 then refutes that interpretation by describing examples of different variants of the tale and how those variants invalidate the interpretations. Paragraph 4 restates and concludes the argument.

13. **B**
Difficulty: Medium
Strategic Advice: Correct answers to Inference questions will only be a step removed from what is stated in the passage.
Getting to the Answer: The lines indicated in the passage, along with those preceding them, discuss how popular fairy tales survive, while unpopular ones die out ("time…discards the chaff"). Look for an answer close to that.
(A) Out of Scope; *quality* is not discussed at this point.
(B) This answer works; it matches the passage's emphasis on "editing" and "appeal."
(C) Opposite; such tales would have "endured."
(D) Distortion; fairy tales "can be said to have" undergone an editing process, but not to *the same degree* as other forms of writing.

(E) Out of Scope; the passage doesn't address *the original author of "Snow White."*

14. **E**
Difficulty: Low
Strategic Advice: When a line reference occurs in the first line of a paragraph, you'll often need to read the following sentence to answer the question fully.
Getting to the Answer: Research the passage to find that the *motifs* mentioned are experiences from common human experience, so predict something like *all humans go through such experiences.* This prediction matches choice (E).
(A) Misused Detail; the details of the story itself appear in earlier paragraphs.
(B) Out of Scope; the author doesn't mention *critics.*
(C) Distortion; this comes up in the prior paragraph, but it doesn't fit with the author's thrust here.
(D) Out of Scope; the paragraph doesn't address this.

15. **D**
Difficulty: Medium
Strategic Advice: Read the sentence twice if you have to to nail down the meaning in context.
Getting to the Answer: The passage says that these avenues are used to get at "the cosmic unconscious," so predict something like *methods.* Choice (D) matches this prediction.
(A) This is a more standard meaning of the word that doesn't fit here.
(B), (C), and (E) don't make sense in context.

16. **C**
Difficulty: High
Strategic Advice: Beware of answer choices that pull from details in the passage but have nothing to do with the inference at hand.
Getting to the Answer: The indicated section of the passage makes the argument that an interpretation based on details about the huntsman can't be valid when most versions of the folk tale don't have a huntsman in them. Predict something along the lines of *fairy tales have too many variations to interpret.* (C) is the best match for this prediction.
(A) Distortion; this original idea comes from Passage 1.
(B) Out of Scope; the passage doesn't raise the question of historical accuracy.

(D) Distortion; *themes of rescue* are not what the author is striving for here.

(E) Opposite; the author indicates that fairy tales do not solidify *into final form.*

17. **D**

Difficulty: Medium

Strategic Advice: Remember not to confuse something said by one author with something said by the other author.

Getting to the Answer: We know that the author of Passage 2 disagrees with the kinds of symbolic interpretations made in Passage 1, and this question asks specifically why. Predict something about the way that they *fail to take multiple versions of tales into account.* Choice (D) matches this prediction.

(A) Opposite; if anything, the author of Passage 2 thinks that the author of Passage 1 pays too much attention to *psychology.*

(B) Misused Detail; it's not the *naïve view of human nature,* but rather the naïve view of folklore methodology.

(C) Out of Scope; the problem that the author of Passage 2 sees goes beyond simple *failure to use reference materials.*

(E) Distortion; the author of Passage 2 argues that there is no single *correct* interpretation of a fairy tale.

18. **A**

Difficulty: Medium

Strategic Advice: Don't range too far from the text given and the ideas in that text in drawing your conclusion.

Getting to the Answer: The final sentence of Passage 2 says that we should acknowledge the many variations among versions of fairy tales and search *for insights into the cultural conditions which prompt such divergence.* In other words, we should *question what these variations tell us about the specific cultures in which they appear.* This matches (A) nicely.

(B) Out of Scope; the passage doesn't explore the difference between written and *oral versions* of the stories.

(C) Distortion; the author of Passage 2 does not suggest that any version of a tale is more valid or authoritative than any other.

(D) Distortion; the author of Passage 2 indicates that there is no *accurate* interpretation to such tales.

(E) Out of Scope; Passage 1, not Passage 2, explores why some tales survive and others do not.

19. **C**

Difficulty: High

Strategic Advice: Some questions don't lend themselves easily to prediction; work your way through the answer choices if you need to.

Getting to the Answer: This question calls for a detail that the passages have in common, but it doesn't give you any real hints as to where to look. Eliminate wrong answers, paying special attention to those that come from one passage only. (C) is the correct choice. Both authors admit that fairy tales have changed over time.

(A) Distortion; only Passage 1 states this.

(B) Distortion; this idea appears only in Passage 2.

(D) Distortion; this appears only in Passage 1. The author of Passage 2 would not agree that *symbolic* interpretation of folk tales is valid.

(E) Out of Scope; this appears in neither passage.

20. **C**

Difficulty: Medium

Strategic Advice: On broadly stated questions, work through the choices, eliminating clearly incorrect answers, and then return to the passage to support your choice.

Getting to the Answer: Because a prediction for this question might be difficult, check and eliminate answer choices that don't match both passages. Because both authors would concur that folk tales are developed and passed down through generations (certainly a unique *compositional process*), they would agree with choice (C).

(A) Distortion; only author 1 emphasizes this.

(B) Distortion; the contention that folk tales have *universal* truth comes from Passage 1 only.

(D) Out of Scope; neither passage says anything about *new information about particular tales.*

(E) Distortion; again, the emphasis on *eternal human truths* comes out of Passage 1.

21. **B**

Difficulty: Medium

Strategic Advice: In questions asking what one author might say to the other, be careful not to confuse the respective viewpoints of the authors.

Getting to the Answer: The author of Passage 1 mentions that these motifs are common to all humans in *widely-scattered* societies across time, so he'd probably argue that the specifics of a given version are less important than these universal psychological trends. This prediction matches choice (B).

(A) Out of Scope; the author of Passage 1 makes no mention of recent versions of folk tales or advances in methodology.

(C) Opposite; the author of Passage 1 believes in the relevance of *psychological forces.*

(D) Opposite; the author of Passage 1 chooses "Snow White" as the principal example of his argument.

(E) Out of Scope; author 1 doesn't address such *techniques and methodologies.*

22. **E**

Difficulty: High

Strategic Advice: Return to the main point made by the author of Passage 2. The correct answer should be consistent with this overall idea.

Getting to the Answer: The main argument made by the author of Passage 2 is that it isn't possible to interpret the symbolism of specific tales as reflecting general psychological truth, so eliminate any answer choice that contradicts that idea. Only choice (E) captures the central argument of Passage 2 against this type of interpretation.

(A) Out of Scope; the author of Passage 2 is concerned with issues of broader significance than a particular *psychologist* or *encyclopedic catalogs.*

(B) Out of Scope; Passage 2 does not address the *popularity* of such tales.

(C) Distortion; author 2 does not believe that there is such a thing as a definitive version of a tale.

(D) Distortion; this choice doesn't reflect the overall opinion in Passage 2 that interpretations can't be made at all.

23. **A**

Difficulty: Medium

Strategic Advice: When in doubt as to what an author might say, stick with the purpose of the passage as you have first identified it.

Getting to the Answer: The author of Passage 1 says in his last paragraph that changeable symbols allow tales to adapt to different audiences while still expressing similar psychological dynamics. A prediction along these lines will match answer choice (A).

(B) Opposite; this contradicts the author's statement in the first paragraph of this passage that a period of a few centuries is, in fact, a short time.

(C) Distortion; it's not the specific interpretation that the passages disagree about, rather whether or not an interpretation can be made at all.

(D) Out of Scope; the question of which folk tales are *valid* doesn't appear in either passage.

(E) Misused Detail; this is the opinion of the author of Passage 2.

24. **B**

Difficulty: Medium

Strategic Advice: When looking for a situation similar to one given from the passage, stick to the broad themes of the first example, rather than any overly specific details.

Getting to the Answer: The interpretation indicated in the question stem connects *being consumed by the wolf* with a period of isolation and change. The correct answer choice will point to an interpretation with a similar separation and transformation, which appears in (B), the correct answer. The other answer choices are interpretations drawn from other parts of both passages, but none of them has the essential elements of disconnecting the main character from the action so that he or she can undergo some form of alteration.

Section 7 (Math)

1. C
Difficulty: Low

Strategic Advice: Since the question asks about the relationship between *p* and *q,* see if you can find a way to combine the information given about each of the variables.

Getting to the Answer: This is question 1 of 16, so look for a quick way to solve the question. Since $4p^2 = 36$, let's replace 36 with $4p^2$ in the inequality $36 > 5q$. Thus, $4p^2 > 5q$.

2. E
Difficulty: Low

Strategic Advice: The average formula says that

$$\text{Average} = \frac{\text{Sum of the terms}}{\text{Number of terms}}.$$

Getting to the Answer: We know that the sum of the 7 numbers is greater than 140. So the average of the 7 numbers must be greater than $\frac{140}{7}$, which is 20.

We know that the sum of the 7 numbers is less than 210. So the average of the 7 numbers must be less than $\frac{210}{7}$, which is 30.

So the average of the 7 numbers must be greater than 20 and less than 30. If we call the average of the 7 numbers *x*, then $20 < x < 30$. The only number greater than 20 and less than 30 among the answer choices is 28. Choice (E) is correct.

3. A
Difficulty: Low

Strategic Advice: Don't do more work than you have to. This problem does not require you to find *d*, *r*, or *p*, even in terms of each other.

Getting to the Answer:
$7d < 4r < 8p$.
Therefore, $7d < 8p$.

4. D
Difficulty: Low

Strategic Advice: Be sure to understand the information in the chart. One column gives the number of boxes in each location, whereas the other gives the number of toys in each box, not the total number of toys in that location.

Getting to the Answer:
$4(10) + 2(6) + 5(7) = 40 + 12 + 35 = 87$

5. C
Difficulty: Medium

Strategic Advice: Remember that the average of a set of numbers is equal to their sum divided by the number of numbers in the set. Therefore, the sum of a set of numbers equals their average times the number of numbers in the set.

Getting to the Answer:
$10(8) = 80$, so the sum must be greater than 80. $12(8) = 96$, so the sum must be less than 96. The only answer that fits is (C), 90.

6. D
Difficulty: Low

Strategic Advice: Be sure to answer the right question—this problem asks for the beads that are NOT blue, not the beads that ARE blue.

Getting to the Answer: According to the pie chart, 20% of the beads are blue. So 100% − 20%, which is 80%, of the beads are not blue. Thus, the number of beads that are not blue is 80% of 120. The fractional equivalent of 80% is $\frac{4}{5}$. So $\frac{4}{5}$ of 120 is $\frac{4}{5} \times 120 = 4 \times 24 = 96$. Choice (D) is correct.

7. B
Difficulty: Medium

Strategic Advice: A *complete rotation* is 360 degrees. Find the number of hours it takes for the hand to make a complete rotation, and then figure out how many complete rotations it would make in 6 days.

Getting to the Answer: Since in 1 hour, the hour hand rotates 30 degrees, the number of hours that it takes the hour hand to rotate 360 degrees is $\frac{360}{30}$, which is 12. There are 24 hours in a day. So 12 hours is $\frac{12}{24}$ of a day, which is $\frac{1}{2}$ of a day.

So, it takes the hour hand $\frac{1}{2}$ of a day to make one complete rotation. If the hour hand makes one complete rotation in $\frac{1}{2}$ of a day, then the number of complete rotations that the hour hand makes in 6 days is

$$\frac{6}{\left(\frac{1}{2}\right)} = \frac{6 \times 2}{1} = 6 \times 2 = 12.$$

8.   E

Difficulty: Medium

Strategic Advice: A triangle whose angles have degree measures of 30, 60, and 90 is a right triangle such that the leg length to leg length to hypotenuse length ratio is $1 : \sqrt{3} : 2$. So look for a triangle whose side lengths are in the ratio of $1 : \sqrt{3} : 2$.

Getting to the Answer: We can begin our search by looking for a triangle in the figure that has two sides whose lengths are in the ratio of $1 : 2$. Hopefully the length of the third side will be equal to $\sqrt{3}$ times the length of shortest side. If we can find such a triangle, we will have found the correct answer. In triangle *LNO*, the length of *LN* is 4, which is twice the length of *NO*, which is 2. The length of *LO* is $2\sqrt{3}$, which is $\sqrt{3}$ times the length of *NO*, which is 2. Thus, the sides of triangle *LNO*, which are 2, $2\sqrt{3}$, and 4 are in the ratio of $1 : \sqrt{3} : 2$. Let's note that each of these lengths of 2, $2\sqrt{3}$, and 4, is 2 multiplied by the corresponding member of the $1 : \sqrt{3} : 2$ ratio. So we have found the triangle whose angles have degree measures of 30, 60, and 90. That triangle is triangle *LNO*. Choice (E) is correct.

9.   C

Difficulty: Medium

Strategic Advice: Pick Numbers. Since the question asks about positives and negatives, you should try both a positive and a negative number.

Getting to the Answer: Any quantity raised to a positive even exponent cannot be negative.

Choice (A) is $\frac{x^2}{2}$. x^2 is the variable x raised to the even exponent 2. So x^2 cannot be negative. Therefore, $\frac{x^2}{2}$ cannot be negative because half of

a nonnegative number is nonnegative. Eliminate choice (A).

We can pick some numbers to convince ourselves that x^2 cannot be negative. If $x = -5$, then $x^2 = (-5)^2 = 25$. If $x = 0$, then $x^2 = 0^2 = 0$. If $x = 4$, then $x^2 = 4^2 = 16$. Let's note that 0 is neither positive or negative. Also, because a negative number multiplied by the same negative number is positive, 0 squared is 0, and a positive number multiplied by the same positive number is positive, x^2 cannot be negative. Thus, the square of any real number is nonnegative.

Choice (B) is $\frac{3}{1 + x^2}$. The numerator 3 is positive. Now look at the denominator. We have seen when considering choice (A) that x^2 cannot be negative. The denominator $1 + x^2$ is the sum of the positive number 1 and the nonnegative quantity x^2. So the denominator $1 + x^2$ must be positive. Since the numerator 3 and the denominator $1 + x^2$ must both be positive, the entire expression $\frac{3}{1 + x^2}$ must be positive. Eliminate choice (B).

Choice (C) is $4x^3$. The exponent 3 is odd. So x^3 can be negative. Therefore, $4x^3$ can be negative. For example, if $x = -1$, $4x^3 = 4(-1)^3 = 4(-1) = -4$. Choice (C) is correct.

Let's briefly look at choices (D) and (E).

Choice (D) is $(x^3)^2$. We said that the square of any real number is nonnegative. Therefore, the square of x^3 must be nonnegative. Also, if we use the law of exponents that says that to raise a power to an exponent, multiply the exponents and keep the same base, we have $(x^3)^2 = x^{3 \times 2} = x^6$. Now we have the quantity x raised to the even exponent 6, and we said that when a quantity is raised to a positive even exponent, the result is nonnegative. Eliminate choice (D).

Choice (E) is $x(x^3 + x^5)$. Multiply out $x(x^3 + x^5)$ in order to work without the parentheses. To multiply powers with the same base, add the exponents and keep the same base. Then, $x(x^3 + x^5) = x(x^3) + x(x^5) = x^1(x^3) + x^1(x^5) = x^{1+3} + x^{1+5} = x^4 + x^6$.

Thus, $x(x^3 + x^5) = x^4 + x^6$. Now each of x^4 and x^6 is the variable x raised to an even exponent. So each of x^4 and x^6 is nonnegative. Therefore, $x^4 + x^6$ is nonnegative. That is, $x^4 + x^6$, which is $x(x^3 + x^5)$, cannot be negative. Eliminate choice (E).

10. **E**
Difficulty: Medium
Strategic Advice: Since the Earth makes a complete rotation about its axis in 24 hours, any point on its surface must rotate through 360 degrees in that time.
Getting to the Answer:
Goannaville rotates 360 degrees in the 24 hours from 1:00 p.m. January 2 to 1:00 p.m. January 3. In the three hours between 1:00 p.m. and 4:00 p.m. on January 3, it rotates $\frac{3}{24}(360°) = 45°$ more. $360° + 45° = 405°$

11. **C**
Difficulty: Low
Strategic Advice: Sets are a topic new to the 2005 SAT. While questions about sets are more likely to be of low or medium rather than high difficulty, they will, at any difficulty level, assume that you're familiar with some of the basic terminology of sets. With that in mind, begin to absorb a few facts. The things in a set are called elements or members. The union of sets is the set of elements in one or more of the sets being united. Think of the union set as what you get when you merge sets. The symbol for union set is ∪. The intersection of sets is the set of common elements of the sets being intersected. Think of the intersection as the overlap of sets. The symbol for the intersection of sets is ∩.
Getting to the Answer:
To be in S∩T∩U—that is, the intersection of S, T, and U—a number would have to be: between −3.5 and 3.5; inclusive, prime, and positive. Given the sets in question, the only such numbers are 2 and 3. Remember that 1 is not prime; test takers who forget that fact wrongly choose (D).

12. **C**
Difficulty: Medium
Strategic Advice: Both a and b can be positive, negative, or equal to zero. The square of a negative or a positive number will be positive. Zero is neither positive nor negative.

Getting to the Answer:
(A) $a + b$ can be ruled out because a or b (or both) could be negative or zero.
(B) $a^2 - b^2 + 10$ can be ruled out because b^2 could be greater than $a^2 + 10$.
(C) $a^2 + b^2 + 1$ is correct. a^2 and b^2 are either positive or equal to zero. 1 is positive, so their sum must be positive.
(D) $a^3 + b^3 + 16$ can be ruled out because a or b could be negative, and the cube of a negative number is negative.
(E) $a^4 + b^2 + a^2$ can be ruled out because a and b could both equal zero.

13. **D**
Difficulty: Medium
Strategic Advice: To solve this question, we will have to use these 3 laws of exponents:
When you multiply powers with the same base, you add the exponents and keep the same base. Algebraically, $b^x b^y = b^{x+y}$.

When you divide powers with the same base, you subtract the exponents in the correct order and keep the same base. Algebraically, $\frac{b^x}{b^y} = b^{x-y}$. When you raise a power to an exponent, you multiply the exponents and keep the same base. Algebraically, $(b^x)^y = b^{xy}$.
Getting to the Answer: Now let's look at the answer choices. Where necessary, we will try to express numbers as a power with a base of 3.

(A) is $\frac{y}{3} = \frac{3^5}{3} = \frac{3^5}{3^1} = 3^{5-1} = 3^4$. This is not 3^8, so eliminate choice (A).

(B) is $9y^2$. Let's begin by expressing 9 as a power with a base of 3. $9 = 3 \times 3 = 3^2$. Thus, $9 = 3^2$. Then $9y^2 = (3^2)(3^5)^2 = (3^2)(3^{5 \times 2}) = (3^2)(3^{10}) = 3^{2+10} = 3^{12}$. This is not 3^8, so eliminate choice (B).

(C) is $\frac{y^2}{3} = \frac{(3^5)^2}{3} = \frac{3^{5 \times 2}}{3^1} = \frac{3^{10}}{3^1} = 3^{10-1} = 3^9$. This is not 3^8, so eliminate choice (C).

(D) is $\frac{y^2}{9}$. Let's begin by expressing 9 as a power with a base of 3. When considering choice (B), we said that $9 = 3^2$. Then $\frac{y^2}{9} = \frac{(3^5)^2}{3^2} = \frac{3^{5 \times 2}}{3^2} =$ $\frac{3^{10}}{3^2} = 3^{10-2} = 3^8$. Therefore, choice (D) is correct. Just to be sure, let's check choice (E) to confirm that it is not equal to 3^8.

(E) is $\frac{y^3}{27}$. Let's begin by expressing 27 as a power with a base of 3. $27 = 3 \times 9 = 3 \times 3 \times 3 = 3^3$.
Thus, $27 = 3^3$.
Then $\frac{y^3}{27} = \frac{(3^5)^3}{3^3} = \frac{3^{5 \times 3}}{3^3} = \frac{3^{15}}{3^3} = 3^{15-3} = 3^{12}$.
This is not 3^8, so eliminate choice (E).

14. **D**
Difficulty: Medium
Strategic Advice: Do not assume that the measurements of the angles in this figure resemble the way the figure is drawn. Any figure on the SAT that is not drawn to scale is drawn in such a way as to be deliberately misleading. To find the angles, you will need to use three pieces of information: the sum of the interior angles of a triangle is 180°, the sum of the angles along a straight line is 180°, and vertical angles—angles pointed toward each other—are equal. Using this information, you can find the measure of every angle in the diagram, as shown below. Any triangle with a 90° angle is a right triangle.
Getting to the Answer:

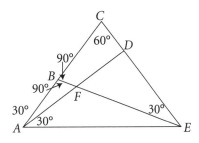

15. **E**
Difficulty: Medium
Strategic Advice: Questions about exponential growth are new to the 2005 SAT and, like this one, can be quite challenging to most test takers. You'll be the exception if you come to think about such questions in commonsense terms. To double is simply to multiply by two. The question calls for this doubling to occur 24 times. The mathematical way of expressing "doubling to occur 24 times" is 2^{24}.
Getting to the Answer: The answer is the total growth that occurs times the original population. Again, total growth is 2^{24}. The original population is p.

16. **E**
Difficulty: Medium
Strategic Advice: When you come upon absolute value questions, one great immediate reaction is to think, "Every positive number is the absolute value of two numbers: the number itself and the negative of the number."
Getting to the Answer:
Call the integer n. If the absolute value of n is between 3 and 6, n must be –5, –4, 4, or 5. Two less than each of these would be choices (A), (B), (C), and (D), respectively.

Section 8 (Critical Reading)

1. C
Difficulty: Low
Strategic Advice: What follows a semicolon expands upon the information given in the clause that precedes a semicolon.
Getting to the Answer: We have a number of clues to use in this sentence. Since we know that the second part of the sentence describes the first part in fuller detail, look at keywords such as *contentiousness, discussions,* and *debate.* The blank is going to be synonymous with *debate,* perhaps *dispute.* Choice (C) is an excellent match.
(A) *Accord* means agreement, but the second half of the sentence indicates that this was a contentious and unresolved debate.
(B) An editorial may very well describe a calamity, but the clues we do have (*contentiousness* and *debate*) describe a disagreement, not a tragedy or catastrophe.
(D) *Disposition* is a mood or temperament, which doesn't have anything to do with the clues given to us in the sentence.
(E) *Consensus* is the opposite of what we're looking for here.
accord: agreement
calamity: disaster
disposition: inclination, tendency
consensus: general agreement

2. A
Difficulty: Medium
Strategic Advice: Beginning a sentence with *although* lets you know that the second clause will contrast with the first.
Getting to the Answer: Try the first blank. If *they are also highly esteemed for -------,* then the first blank is going to be a synonym for *esteemed.* For the second blank, what features, described as *subtle* and *shrewd,* could a novel contain with regards to the *economic and social milieu* of its time? Predict an answer like insights or observations.
(B) A novel would not be *denigrated* (strong negative charge) for its *eloquence* (strong positive charge).

(C) *Respected* works in the first blank, but *diversity* in the second doesn't make sense.
(D) Conversely, *interpretation of* fits your prediction for the second blank, but *inclined* doesn't work for the first.
(E) A novel wouldn't be *maligned* (strong negative charge) for its *eloquence* (strong positive charge).
eloquence: fluency, elegance
denigrate: defame, belittle
inclined: having a preference or tendency
malign: speak evil of; malevolent

3. E
Difficulty: Medium
Strategic Advice: Sentence Completions will often test your ability to recognize parallels between two clauses.
Getting to the Answer: The *from* and *to* relationship and the keywords *progression* and *evolution* should clue you that this sentence sets up a contrast. The blanks will contrast in the same way as *Romantic realism* and *abstraction.* The first blank has to describe early paintings in the style of *Romantic realism,* and the second blank must describe *abstraction.*
(A) *Explicit* won't work in the second blank, since it is opposite to the idea of *abstraction.*
(B) While these choices might well describe the progression of an artist's work, they fail to mirror the specifics of the second clause, in which we learn that Turner moved away from *realism* and further into *abstraction.*
(C) Likewise, these choices are not in contrast and don't parallel the move from *realism* to *abstraction.*
(D) The second blank, *romantic,* is the opposite of what we predicted, since Turner's final works move increasingly toward *abstraction.*
realism: the representation of objects as they actually are
abstraction: theoretical representation; consideration apart from concrete existence
obscure: indistinct
explicit: fully and clearly expressed
enthralling: captivating
retrospective: looking back on, retroactive

4.   C

Difficulty: Medium

Strategic Advice: On one-blank sentence completions, the most straightforward questions test your ability to locate definitions for the blank within the sentence.

Getting to the Answer: The words after the blank describe the artistic manner in which Sylvester signed, so predict something associated with dramatic or artistic gestures, like *display*.
(A) Signing with a *wince* bears no relationship to the signature's artistic quality.
(B) Likewise, signing with a *glimpse* has nothing to do with the signature's character.
(D) Nor would signing with a *nod* necessarily confer any artfulness onto the signature.
(E) Again, a characteristic *understatement* would not link strongly to an artistic signature.
wince: flinch
flourish: a sweeping movement

5.   C

Difficulty: Medium

Strategic Advice: In some cases, the blank will be explicitly defined but the vocabulary may be unfamiliar. Draw on your knowledge of word roots in such cases, and remember your elimination strategies.

Getting to the Answer: In this sentence, *a specialist in the technology of deciphering messages* defines the word in the blank. The only occupation that fits that definition is (C). Think of *cryptic,* used to define something secret or mystifying.
(A) An *entomologist* is someone who studies insects.
(B) A *connoisseur* is an authority on a particular subject, such as wine or art.
(D) A *statistician* is an expert in statistics.
(E) A *pathologist* is a doctor who studies the causes of disease.

6.   A

Difficulty: High

Strategic Advice: Sometimes determining the relationships between the blanks and making good predictions hinge on one word that comes near the end of the sentence.

Getting to the Answer: This is a cause-and-effect sentence, and the keyword *disliked* in the

"effect" clues you that the guests' attitudes toward both the hotel and the amenities will be negative. This is a late Sentence Completion, and there is some formidable vocabulary in the answer choices; if you're having trouble, try eliminating any choice in which one or both words have a positive charge.
(B) Guests who disliked their stay at a hotel wouldn't describe it as *venerable.*
(C) Amenities can't be said to possess human characteristics like *petulance.*
(D) The guests' dissatisfaction with the hotel eliminates such positively-charged choices as *congenial* and *convenience.*
(E) Our biggest clue is *disliked,* and neither *quaint* nor *antiquity* relates to it.
amenities: features that increase value or attractiveness
deficient: inadequate; lacking in an essential quality
paucity: scarcity, dearth
venerable: commanding respect
expediency: appropriateness to the task at hand
nascent: emerging
petulance: quality of being ill-tempered
congenial: friendly, agreeable
quaint: charmingly odd
antiquity: ancient times

Wilma Mankiller

This narrative passage is a segment of a speech made by Wilma Mankiller discussing her autobiography. She is the only individual character, although she also talks about the Cherokee people as a group. She can be described as respectful of her heritage, proud of her tribe, and dedicated to her causes.

In the first paragraph, Mankiller explains why a large portion of her autobiography is devoted to the history of the Cherokee people—because her identity is defined by the past, present, and future of her tribe. The second and third paragraphs describe the two major disruptions of Cherokee society and the recovery from those disruptions, following the displacement from the Southeast to Oklahoma. Paragraph four compares these societal disruptions to the disturbance in Mankiller's immediate family caused by a similar relocation in the BIA program. The fifth paragraph

KAPLAN

explains Mankiller's role in Cherokee government and the Bell project. The final paragraph sums up the evidence and reaffirms the author's belief that her people are capable of improving their own lives without outside help.

The author's purpose is to demonstrate her overwhelming respect and love for her people and their history and to illustrate the persistence and strength of the Cherokee Nation and how that has affected Ms. Mankiller personally.

7. E
Difficulty: Low
Strategic Advice: With "EXCEPT" questions, don't get confused. Four of the answer choices *will be* in the passage; the correct answer choice will not be there.
Getting to the Answer: Go back to the text. Eliminate any choices that ARE supported by the first paragraph.
(A) Opposite; the author explains *I ran as a Cherokee*.
(B) Opposite; the author's motivation is stated in lines 14–18.
(C) Opposite; the author implies that gender played an important role in the election in lines 11–12.
(D) Opposite; the author explains this in the third sentence.
Only (E) is not supported by the passage.

8. C
Difficulty: Medium
Strategic Advice: If you don't get a line reference, remember that the questions will appear in order of the subject matter's appearance in the passage.
Getting to the Answer: Research the passage. The author says that her decision to run was based on *the desire to help my people recognize their own strength* and their *power to rebuild their lives* (lines 14–17). Predict something like *gave her the chance to help the Cherokees help themselves*. This prediction matches answer choice (C).
(A) and (B) are Misused Details; they include material mentioned in the same paragraph but unrelated to the correct answer.
(D) Out of Scope; Mankiller says that she wants to focus on the Cherokees themselves, not on their *relationship* with *the U.S. government*.
(E) Out of Scope; Mankiller's focus is on her people, not on herself.

9. D
Difficulty: Medium
Strategic Advice: With Roman Numeral questions, remember to start with the numeral that appears most frequently; once you have decided whether or not to include it, eliminate answer choices accordingly.
Getting to the Answer: Statements I and II appear most frequently, so choose one of them to start. Then reread the referenced lines and those directly before and after. The reference to *the limitless tenacity of the Cherokee* clearly indicates statement II as true. Eliminate (A) and (C). The many aspects of the *rebuilt...tribe* certainly sound *sophisticated,* so statement I is also true; eliminate (B). Statement III, however, contains a Misused Detail: the Cherokees recovered without *government assistance,* which eliminates (E).

10. A
Difficulty: High
Strategic Advice: When given a pair of references in the question stem, beware of answer choices that apply to only one of the references.
Getting to the Answer: Go back to the cited lines to find out how the two are closely related. Lines 24–31 describe the forced removal of the Cherokee to Indian Territory in the 1830s. Lines 55–63 describe the author's experience with the BIA relocation program in the 1950s. You could predict that *both are descriptions of relocations of the Cherokee by the federal government*.
(A) This is correct. Notice that this choice is not overly specific, but the examples do show the *perseverance of the Cherokee.*
(B) Opposite; the examples display *perseverance*, not *defeat.*
(C) Extreme; the author does not express *horror* at the government's actions.
(D) Distortion; the second reference deals with a "voluntary" relocation.
(E) Extreme; while the author might agree these historical events influenced her, we do not know that they were the *most important influences.*

11. **C**
Difficulty: Medium
Strategic Advice: The answers to Inference questions will be only slightly removed from what is said in the passage. Return to the cited lines, and work from there.
Getting to the Answer: In these lines, the author suggests that, for the Cherokee, *past and present are closely intertwined.* The experiences of them and of their ancestors have shaped their lives and outlooks. This prediction matches answer choice (C).
(A) Misused Detail; this comes from a different paragraph.
(B) Misused Detail; this has nothing to do with the statement referenced in the stem.
(D) Misused Detail; again, this point is true, but overly specific and unrelated to the quote.
(E) Extreme; the passage focuses on hardship, not their former glory.

12. **B**
Difficulty: Medium
Strategic Advice: For "author's attitude" questions, characterize the author's tone as she speaks about the detail referenced.
Getting to the Answer: Mankiller talks about the relocation as a hardship, parallel to her ancestors' removal to the Indian Territory, so predict something like *distressed* or *disturbed.* These predictions match answer choice (B), the correct choice.
(A) Out of Scope; the author is not shy about her comments here.
(C) Opposite; this is too positive.
(D) Opposite; also too positive.
(E) Out of Scope; the author seems to understand clearly the impact of the program.

13. **A**
Difficulty: Low
Strategic Advice: Return to the reference, and read closely to see how the author uses this reference and to what end.
Getting to the Answer: The author leads into this reference by describing her family's relocation experience. At the center cited, they *found a place where we belonged.* This fits with (A), the correct answer.
(B) Out of Scope; the author does not mention the *size of the community.*

(C) Out of Scope; the author makes no mention of *government* aid *after their relocation.*
(D) Extreme; while the Native American community did suffer in relation to *majority influences,* that is not the point here.
(E) Out of Scope; the author never broaches this subject.

14. **C**
Difficulty: Low
Strategic Advice: On Vocab-in-Context questions, always look to the cited text for clues. Remember that these types of questions will almost always test secondary meanings, so don't be tempted by common definitions.
Getting to the Answer: Reread the sentence beginning in line 70 to get the context for the word. To be *charged* with a task means to be *appointed* or *designated to perform* that task, both of which are great predictions. Choice (C) matches this prediction.
(A), (B), (D), and (E) all provide common definitions of charged, but none make sense in the context of line 70.

15. **D**
Difficulty: Low
Strategic Advice: On Detail questions, reacquaint yourself with the specifics surrounding the cited text. Make sure you have an understanding of the context into which the author places a particular detail.
Getting to the Answer: The students referred to here received scholarships to study environmental science and health, then went back to help their communities with what they learned. You could predict: *bettered themselves in order to help their communities.*
(A) Misused Detail; the mention of the students is near the description of the *Bell Project,* but the two aren't related.
(B) Opposite; the students are meant to focus on their own communities, not relationships to *non-Cherokee people.*
(C) Misused Detail; students will contribute to their communities, not to *the Cherokee government's* programs.
(D) is true according to the passage: *they could return to their communities and provide service for their people* (lines 73–75).

(E) Out of Scope; the sentence says nothing about the students' possible future involvement in the *Cherokee government.*

16. C
Difficulty: Medium
Strategic Advice: When a Detail question asks you to consider several lines of text or even an entire paragraph, make sure you understand the way in which the author frames the relevant section. It's often helpful to consider the text immediately before and immediately after the part(s) in question.
Getting to the Answer: Go back to the author's discussion of the Bell Project. The author describes how it is an example of a project where Cherokee citizens decided how they wanted to improve their community and then, using the resources provided by the Cherokee Nation, put in the labor to get it done. (C) expresses this idea.
(A) Distortion; while they did receive help in the form of the materials, the author is showing how they were able to solve their own problems.
(B) Opposite; the author showed how they took charge of the project.
(D) Out of Scope; the author never attempts to extend the experience or example of the Cherokee to other Native American tribes.
(E) Misused Detail; this choice too narrowly focuses on one goal of the project, not why the author described the project in the passage.

17. E
Difficulty: Medium
Strategic Advice: For open-ended questions, check the cited paragraph for context, and eliminate answer choices that don't match.
Getting to the Answer: Paragraph 6 shows how the Bell project was an example of Cherokee people helping themselves without assistance from the U.S. government or other outside agencies.
(A) Misused Detail; no one in the Bell project was *forced* to do anything.
(B) and (C) are Out of Scope; these choices describe the *helping yourself* or *changing your own life* parts of paragraph 6, but *helping* or *changing others* is never referenced in this paragraph.

(D) Misused Detail; *following your ancestors* is supported by the passage but not in reference to this question.
(E) summarizes the key relationship of the paragraph.

18. E
Difficulty: High
Strategic Advice: Inference questions will require that you draw together elements of the author's position to formulate a claim that is not specifically stated in the passage.
Getting to the Answer: Before looking at the answer choices here, predict an answer that sums up the author's central argument. Ms. Mankiller begins the passage speaking of *history of the Cherokee*, and that theme permeates the speech (lines 52–53: *my tribe's history has defined me, just as it has defined all Cherokee*). So look for an answer tying in Cherokee history, as in choice (E).
(A) Distortion; the author briefly mentions gender and politics in paragraph 1, but she never recommends a similar course of action for other women.
(B) Distortion; while the Bell project was successful largely through the work of volunteers, the author feels that this is a testament to the will of the Cherokee people, not to the effectiveness of *small-scale volunteer projects.*
(C) Out of Scope and Extreme; although the author implies that *education* played a role in rebuilding Cherokee society, this implication is insufficient to support a claim that education is *vital* to the rebuilding process.
(D) Out of Scope; the author never explicitly invokes *traditional cultural values* in the context of rebuilding the Cherokee community.

19. D
Difficulty: Medium
Strategic Advice: On Global questions, be sure to focus on the big picture. Tempting wrong answer choices will often be true according to the passage but too narrow in their focus.
Getting to the Answer: The author introduces the primary purpose of the passage in paragraph 1. She wishes to answer the question of why her book includes *so much history of the Cherokee*, an idea that choice (D) paraphrases.

(A) Out of Scope; the author only speaks about the *role of history* in *her* personal identity.

(B) Distortion; while the author clearly cherishes her heritage, she does not attempt to *persuade* the reader to do the same.

(C) Misused Detail; although the author is implicitly praising the *virtues of the Cherokee* throughout, her stated purpose in writing this passage was to explain her autobiography's focus on Cherokee history.

(E) Distortion; the author does suggest that community rebuilding is most effective in the absence of aid from outside agencies, but again, this is not her stated purpose in writing this passage.

Section 9 (Writing)

1. **D**
Difficulty: Low
Strategic Advice: If you spot two independent clauses in a sentence, make sure they are appropriately joined.
Getting to the Answer: The sentence contains two independent clauses that are not separated by either a semicolon or a comma and a conjunction, so the sentence is a run-on. The correct answer will provide either an appropriate connection or make one of the clauses a dependent clause. Choice (D) makes the second half of the sentence dependent on the first, so that's our answer. Choices (B) and (E) are excessively wordy, and choice (C) fails to correct the run-on.

2. **D**
Difficulty: Low
Strategic Advice: Always make sure the verbs in a sentence agree with each other.
Getting to the Answer: Whenever you see a sentence structured in a way that says Although this is true, that is true, make sure the verbs before and after the comma are in the same format. Since the verb before the comma is *have made*, the verb after the comma should be in the form *have (done something)*. The only answer choice that does this is (D). (B) merely adds extra words without fixing the problem; (C) introduces a double negative (*they failed not to understand* implies that they actually understood); and (E) simply changes the verb tense to another one that doesn't match the rest of the sentence.

3. **A**
Difficulty: Low
Strategic Advice: When you see a list of three or more things, double-check to see that each item is written in the same format as the others.
Getting to the Answer: The underlined item in the list is written using the same structure the other items are written in. Double check the answer choices to see if there's a more concise or more smoothly-worded one. All the answer choices but (A) distort the parallel structure of the list, so (A) is correct.

4. **D**
Difficulty: High
Strategic Advice: Make sure that each modifying phrase is as close as possible to the thing that it modifies.
Getting to the Answer: The original sentence is incorrect because it reads as though it's the *French club* that has an *exceptionally big living room*. Look for an answer choice that places the modifying phrase next to the thing it modifies. Answer choice (E) does this but incorporates unnecessary passivity (*was chosen*) that makes the sentence awkward. (B) indicates that the choice made was for more than just the end-of-year party, which isn't the case. (C) makes sense, but it changes the subject to the living room, and it's not clear whether the pronoun *its* refers to the house or the room. (D), on the other hand, is logical and concise. Instead of including a modifying phrase, (D) begins the sentence with an introductory phrase that clearly indicates the cause-and effect relationship between the attributes of the house and the French club's choice. (D) is the best answer.

5. **C**
Difficulty: Medium
Strategic Advice: Make sure each modifying phrase is as close as possible to the thing it modifies.
Getting to the Answer: As the sentence stands, *taken from dramatic and dizzying low angles* seems to be a phrase that modifies *rock concerts*, which is not the intent. Choice (B) is a run-on. Choice (D) turns the phrase into a dependant clause without a predicate, so it is a fragment. Choice (E) introduces extraneous words without fixing the initial problem. That leaves you with (C), which turns *inspired by the surrealism of rock concerts* into a phrase that modifies *photographs*, and adds a verb to make the latter part of the sentence the necessary predicate.

6. **A**
Difficulty: Medium
Strategic Advice: Remember that about one in five Improving Sentences questions will be correct already.
Getting to the Answer: The sentence seems grammatically correct, so check to see if there are any answer choices that are more concise.

(B) consists of two independent clauses that are improperly connected, so it is a run-on. (C) seems excessively wordy. (D) and (E) both seem to imply that the *neighborhood is now bustling* as a *result* of its having once been nearly deserted, which doesn't make sense. (A) is the most concise and consistent answer.

7. **E**

Difficulty: Medium

Strategic Advice: Always look for the most concise way to deliver the necessary information.

Getting to the Answer: The sentence seems grammatically correct but wordy, so look for an answer choice that is more concise. (B) says that the *inclusion* is what's in his writing, not the observations themselves, which doesn't make sense. (C) and (D) introduce new subjects (the observations or his inclusion) without giving them a verb. (E) turns the end of a sentence into a dependent clause that is correctly attached to the beginning of the sentence, and this version is more concise than (A), so (E) is the best answer.

8. **A**

Difficulty: Medium

Strategic Advice: When a sentence seems correct, check for a more concise way of writing it among the answer choices.

Getting to the Answer: The sentence seems correct but complicated. Check the answer choices for a more concise way of saying it. (B) and (D) add complication by separating the word *idea* from the description of it. (C) and (E) both add a pronoun—*they*—that seems to refer to the diners themselves having an idea, as opposed to the staff of the diners. (A) is, after all, the best way to express this concept, and so it is the best answer.

9. **D**

Difficulty: Medium

Strategic Advice: Always make sure each pronoun refers to something specific and clear.

Getting to the Answer: There are a couple of things wrong with this sentence: the first clause is merely a fragment, whereas the second clause makes a complete sentence by itself with a different subject than the first clause; it is impossible to say what the pronoun *they* is referring to. (B) fixes both these problems, but

check the rest of the answers to make sure there isn't a better one. (C) seems to indicate that the poor soil is what caused the new vines to grow, which doesn't make sense. (D) seems to fix the initial problems even better than (B); *Though* gives a clearer indication than *but* of the change in circumstance. (E) makes it sound like it's the soil that has sprouted new vines, not the plant. (D) is the clearest and most concise answer.

10. **A**

Difficulty: High

Strategic Advice: When items are being compared or listed, make sure they are written using the same structure.

Getting to the Answer: You are looking for the most effective way to draw this comparison. *Having cuteness* is awkward, so (B) is out. (C), (D), and (E) all have different verb structures for the first half of the comparison from the second half of the comparison, so (A) is the best answer.

11. **C**

Difficulty: Medium

Strategic Advice: A sentence that leaves the meaning of a clause incomplete will not be correct as written.

Getting to the Answer: The use of *which* in the second clause leaves its meaning unclear. (C) corrects the error without introducing any additional errors. (B) corrects the error but introduces an ambiguous pronoun (*they*). (D) is awkward and unnecessarily wordy. (E) eliminates *was*, creating a structure fragment.

12. **D**

Difficulty: Medium

Strategic Advice: The simplest way to correct a run-on sentence is with a semicolon splice.

Getting to the Answer: (D) corrects the run-on error without introducing any new problems. (B) and (C) do not address the run-on error. (E) uses the semicolon splice but introduces an inappropriate verb tense (*may have chosen*).

13. **B**

Difficulty: High

Strategic Advice: *When* is only appropriate when used in reference to time.

Getting to the Answer: Only (B) corrects the error without introducing any additional issues.

(C) does not address the error. In (D), *one of the symptoms* and *includes* are redundant. (E) eliminates the predicate (main) verb, creating a sentence fragment.

14. **D**
Difficulty: Low
Strategic Advice: Although *them* and *those* are frequently used interchangeably in everyday speech, they do not mean the same thing. *Them* is the objective form of the pronoun *they*; *those* is the plural form of the demonstrative pronoun *that*.
Getting to the Answer: Only (D) correctly replaces *them* with *those*. (B) simply rewords the selection. (C) and (E) do not address the error; additionally, in (C), *Additional to* is grammatically incorrect.

CHAPTER THREE

Customize
Your Study Plan

YOUR STUDY PLAN

Now that you have completed the Diagnostic Exam, it is time to assess your results. By giving yourself an idea of how well you have performed, you will be better able to identify those areas in which you need help. Study time is limited, we know, so how you spend your time is crucial.

Score Yourself

Because there are many variables affecting how well you will perform on the real test, there is no way to calculate a precise score. You can, however, get a ballpark idea. Go through the exam, and figure out how you performed.

First, look at the **Essay**. The Essay score ranges **from 0–6 (best)**. This score will be factored into the final scaled score for the Writing section. You can get a good idea if your essay is on the right track by reading your finished essay and comparing it to the sample essays in this book. Then, use the scoring criteria based on the scoring rubric at collegeboard.com to see what elements you covered and what elements you missed. Be as objective as you can; if you aren't sure, ask someone whose opinion you respect to read your essay as well. Though this method is not as precise as the official essay grading system, you will get a good idea of your performance, which will help you to focus your essay practice in the weeks ahead.

Second, turn to the multiple-choice answers. Tally the number of questions you got right and the number you got wrong.

Critical Reading Section: Calculate each question type separately (**Sentence Completion** and **Reading Comprehension**). Multiply the total number you got wrong by .25 and subtract that result from the number you got right. Round to the nearest whole number.

Math Section: Calculate each question type separately (**multiple-choice** and **Grid-ins**). Multiply the total number of multiple-choice questions you got wrong by .25 and subtract that result from the number you got right (there is no penalty for wrong answers on Grid-in questions). Round to the nearest whole number.

Writing Section: Calculate the multiple-choice questions together (**Usage**, **Sentence Correction**, and **Paragraph Correction**). Multiply the total number of questions you got wrong by .25 and subtract that result from the number you got right. Round to the nearest whole number.

For these three sections, scores range from **200–800**. Two-thirds of test takers score between 400 and 600.

Review Each Section and Identify Your Weak Areas

Now its time to review how well you did on each question type. By doing this, you will be able to build a customized study plan.

Writing
The Essay: 1 essay

There are many ways to turn a good essay into a great essay, but the best way is through focused practice with test-like prompts. To find appropriate prompts, turn to the op-ed page in your local newspaper and find an issue or an argument to write about. Or you can check out collegeboard.com for sample prompts. Before you write, keep in mind the following things:

1. Write your essay out in full. Practice writing how you will on Test Day to be sure your essay is legible.
2. When you sit down to write your essays, have an alarm clock on hand, and set it to ring after 25 minutes. This is the first task you will be required to do on Test Day.
3. Always spend a few minutes creating a plan for your essay. You'll be sorry if you jump in and just start writing.
4. When you complete your essay, put it away for a few days before you assess it. A fresh eye is key for proper evaluation. Did you answer the prompt? Is your discussion clear, and do you see the progression of ideas from start to conclusion? Compare your text to the College Board rubric.

Try another prompt the following week to see how you have progressed. You're sure to improve if you dedicate time to practicing writing a winning SAT-style essay.

Multiple Choice: 49 questions

You will see 49 Writing questions on the SAT in three different types: 25 Sentence Corrections, 18 Usage, and 6 Paragraph Corrections. You will be tested on your ability to fix or re-word part of a sentence, identify the error in a sentence, and to correct or combine sentences to fix a paragraph, respectively. Your grammar, style, and vocabulary skills will be useful in this section.

If you answered 42–49 questions correctly: This section should give you little trouble on Test Day. Skim over the questions you missed and try to understand why.

If you answered 33–41 questions correctly: You need a more focused and careful review in this area. Is there a pattern to the questions you answered incorrectly? Go back to the questions you answered correctly and review how you came up with the right answer: Did you simply know the answer? Did you make an educated guess? Review briefly the rules for the commonly tested errors.

If you answered 32 or fewer questions correctly: Your writing skills need work. Review the rules for the commonly tested errors. Then go back and work on taking a systematic approach to the questions in this section. Remember that it's best to skip a question if you can't eliminate at least one answer choice. Use Kaplan's Writing Flashcards (available exclusively at Borders) to review the basic building blocks of grammar and to sharpen your ability to recognize errors in sentences.

Critical Reading
Sentence Completion: 19 questions

You will see 19 Sentence Completion questions. Sentence Completion questions test the breadth of your vocabulary and your ability to choose from five responses the word(s) or phrase(s) that best complete the sentence, based on the rules of standard written English.

If you answered 16–19 questions correctly: You have a strong vocabulary and understand the structure of sentences. Clearly, this is an area of strength for you. Skim over the few questions you did miss and try to grasp why. Check to see that you didn't make careless errors.

If you answered 12–15 questions correctly: You're solid in this area but could use some review. Look at the questions you answered incorrectly. Check the sentence for keywords (such as *since, similarly, also, thus, because, likewise, therefore, despite, although, but, however, yet, unless, rather, while, unfortunately,* and *nonetheless*) you may have missed.

If you answered 11 or fewer questions correctly: Building your vocabulary and reviewing the fundamentals of sentence structure need to be top priorities for you if you want to score well on this section. Strengthen your vocabulary by studying word families and roots and reading books or other materials with SAT words used in context (Kaplan has a variety of SAT vocabulary-building novels).

Reading Comprehension: 48 questions

Reading Comprehension is the most time-consuming question type and, for many test-takers, the most intimidating part of the Critical Reading section. This doesn't have to be the case. There are several reading passages on the test; some are followed by as few as two questions and some by as many as 13 questions. The passages are written in difficult, often technical prose and are adapted from books and journals in the broad areas of humanities, the social sciences, the natural sciences, and fiction. These questions are designed to test whether you can quickly and accurately read for the gist of the prose (its underlying purpose and principal ideas), the role of supporting details, and the meaning of vocabulary words based on their context.

If you answered 41–48 questions correctly: You're in great shape. You are masterful at being able to understand the substance of a passage and to research a passage for specific information. Clearly, you have a talent for understanding texts. Skim over the questions you missed and try to understand why.

If you answered 32–40 questions correctly: You need some work in the area of Reading Comprehension. Review the questions you missed, going back to the original reading passage as needed. Maybe you didn't read the question carefully. Maybe you misread the text. Maybe you skipped an important detail. Being able to distinguish opinions or interpretations from factual assertions is important in Reading Comprehension.

If you answered 31 or fewer questions correctly: You'll need to learn to zero in on the *why* and the *how* of a text. Those two things make SAT reading different from everyday reading. Re-read the passages on the questions you missed. Start by focusing on the author's views. What is the main idea? Examine how each paragraph fits into the overall scope of the passage. Then practice making a Roadmap—handwritten notes at the side of each paragraph indicating the general idea. Don't sweat the details in the passage.

Math
Math: 54 questions

The Math section consists of 44 classic multiple-choice math problems (the type found on many standardized tests) and 10 student-produced response questions. The math tested on these questions mainly consists of junior and senior high school level arithmetic, algebra, algebra II, and geometry, along with median/mode/range, standard deviation, and simple probability.

If you answered 47–54 questions correctly: This section should give you little trouble on test day. Skim over the questions you missed and try to understand why.

If you answered 40–46 questions correctly: You need a more focused and careful review in this area. Go back to the questions and try to figure out how you did. Look at the questions you answered correctly, and review how you came up with the right answer. Ask yourself: Did you simply know the answer offhand? Did you make an educated guess? Review briefly the basic math concepts.

If you answered 39 or fewer questions correctly: Your problem-solving and data-interpretation skills need work. Review basic math concepts. Then go back and learn to develop a systematic approach to the questions in this section. Decide how much effort to put into each question. Learn to get comfortable using alternative methods, such as Picking Numbers or Backsolving, where you plug answer choices into the question to see which one works.

Build Your Study Plan

Now that you have reviewed all the question types and assessed your skill set, it's time to implement your study plan. To do this, you'll need to map out your objectives in a calendar. The next chapter will help you do this.

CHAPTER FOUR

Customize Your Study Schedule

YOUR STUDY SCHEDULE

Maybe you have plenty of time to devote to studying for the SAT. Maybe you're such a whiz with Sentence Completion questions that you barely need to review. Or, maybe you're like most people and need to make a study plan.

The key to effective test preparation goes beyond practice quizzes; it starts with planning. To get you from today to Test Day, we're going to work with your diagnostic test results and come up with a schedule that works for you—tailored to your skills and timetable.

Question 1: How many months until the SAT?

On the following page, you'll find a blank calendar. The page shows only one month, so if you have more time than that, photocopy it for every month you have. Ideally, you should have three full months to study. However, if you have less than two months to prepare, don't despair; just get going on your study plan today.

Study Calendar

Make a copy of this page for every month of study. Fill it out. Stick to it!

Month: _____

Sunday	Monday	Tuesday	Wednesday	Thursday	Friday	Saturday

Question 2: How much real time do I have to study?

It's easy to think that if you have three months to study, you're all set. That's all the time in the world, right? Not likely. You probably have school and a part-time job to factor in, as well as other time-consuming obligations. And don't forget your social life!

That said, let's give your calendar a good look. Block out the time you are at work or school. Next, block out any weekly meetings you have, remembering to include volunteer work, club activities, religious observances, music or athletic practice, and so on. Go ahead and write in your calendar. Carve it up, and make it your own.

If you're like most busy high school juniors or seniors, you'll see that you may not have as much time to devote to SAT prep as you thought. That might be the bad news. The good news is that you now know exactly how much study time you have to work with. Maybe it's an hour in the evening, plus four hours straight on Sunday for the next three months. Maybe it's less. Either way, you can now approach your study time more realistically.

Question 3: How should I target my study time?

Go back to your diagnostic results. Sort the question types in order of difficulty; that is, the order of difficulty that *you* experienced. Focus first on the types that gave you the most trouble. Then, focus on the subsequent types as they appear on your list.

Of course, the focus should be on the question types you found challenging, but don't totally dismiss those on which you did well. When you need to break up the intensity of the troublesome questions, put them on hold and review the questions you aced. The power of review goes a long way, even if you think you know the subject matter through and through.

In the chapters that follow, you will find practice quizzes for each SAT question type. Go right to the question type that gave you the most trouble. (For many students, it's Reading Comprehension. For many others, it's the Essay.) Complete the skill-building quiz for that topic in Week 1. Analyze your results. Compare them with how you performed on the Diagnostic. Did you improve? We hope so. If you still need more practice, Kaplan offers a comprehensive preparation guide to the SAT, available at Borders. Check out your local store.

Also in Week 1, consider all the broader topic areas you may see on the Critical Reading, Math, and Writing sections of the test. You may be shaky on grammar or obtuse angles. Make flashcards to drill yourself on math rules, word roots, and vocabulary to help you hone your skills in these areas (Kaplan makes these, too, now available exclusively at Borders). We provide a tear-out reference sheet in the front of the book for studying on the go. Tear it out and bring it with you whenever possible. Five-minute capsule reviews here and there can add up to a bonus study section.

In Week 2, start by reviewing what you studied in Week 1. Add some flashcard practice, then tackle another practice chapter—this time on your second weakest section.

For Week 3, you guessed it: Review Weeks 1 and 2, build on the skills you developed by practicing with flashcards, and then plow through another practice chapter. At this point, you're well on your way to a systemic approach to conquering the SAT.

For each of the remaining weeks until Test Day, take on another chapter from this book. If you don't make it through the whole way, that's okay—you've already tackled your weakest areas. However, don't wait until the last month to try the Essay section. It takes time to develop the skills required for this. Fine-tuning them for the needs of the SAT will take practice. Take a stab at the Essay writing prompts we include here, and then review your essay based on the grading rubric provided at collegeboard.com.

It's also a good idea to take another practice test before the real exam—ideally, just one week before. Try out the official test from the College Board—the maker of the SAT. Log onto collegeboard.com and see what study tools are available.

Use the weeks up to Test Day to continue reviewing the topics that still give you trouble: go over math topics you learned in school and word roots that are the fundamentals of most words. And keep reading—there's no better way to build your vocabulary!

Question 4: Where's the best place to study?

OK, so you know when you can study, but what about where? Some people require silence, whereas others prefer white noise. Go where you will optimize your study time. Bear in mind, though, if it takes 20 minutes to get to your favorite study location, you're cutting into valuable study time. Pick a location that's close by.

Question 5: Am I ready for the SAT?

First of all, the fact that you have set up a study schedule and stuck to it is commendable. That is more than most students do, and the discipline you applied here will prove to be invaluable on Test Day. If you suffer a lapse of focus, remember your goals. Your hard work is going to pay off one day soon when you are accepted into the college of your choice.

Many of us feel unsure of our test-taking abilities. We know the feeling of walking confidently into an exam only to blank out at the exam booklet. Maybe that's never happened, but you're thinking that it could. If you find yourself thinking thoughts like that, just put a stop to it, immediately.

If you must dwell on something in the middle of the night, dwell on an image of yourself calmly answering questions correctly on Test Day. Imagine feeling good when you walk out of the test room. Think about the progress you're making on your study schedule, or just get out of bed and run through a few flashcards. You are preparing for this exam, and that means you will score well.

As mentioned, one or two weeks before you take the SAT, wake up early on a Saturday and take a final practice test. Notice your improvement from the diagnostic test you took at the start of this book. Then review your notes, flashcards, and tear-out sheet in the days prior to Test Day. Expectations tend to be fulfilled. Be positive: think about the progress you have made. You surely will have strengthened your skills after working through this book.

Get together an "SAT Survival Kit" containing the following items:
- A calculator with fresh batteries
- A watch
- A few No. 2 pencils (pencils with slightly dull points fill the ovals better)
- Erasers
- Photo ID card
- Your admission ticket from ETS
- A snack—there are two breaks, and you'll probably get hungry

Know exactly where you're going, exactly how you're getting there, and exactly how long it takes to get there. It's probably a good idea to visit your test center sometime before the day of the test so that you know what to expect—what the rooms are like, how the desks are set up, and so on.

Question 6: Do I Study the Night Before the Test?

No! Don't cram the night before the test. Get a good night's sleep. You'll wake up prepared and ready to succeed on the SAT. Good luck, and remember to bring your "SAT Survival Kit."

Section Two:

SAT Skill-Building Quizzes

CHAPTER FIVE

Critical Reading: Sentence Completion Questions

Each sentence below has one or two blanks, each blank indicating that something has been omitted. Beneath the sentence are five words or sets of words labeled A through E. Choose the word or set of words that, when inserted in the sentence, best fits the meaning of the sentence as a whole.

EXAMPLE:

Today's small, portable computers contrast markedly with the earliest electronic computers, which were -------.

(A) effective   (B) invented   (C) useful
     (D) destructive   (E) enormous

ANSWER:

1 Because he was usually so ----, Mr. Harris shocked his students with his violent reaction to their minor misbehavior in class.

(A) knowledgeable
(B) articulate
(C) trustworthy
(D) insistent
(E) tranquil

2 Because Phillis Wheatley exposed the injustices of slavery in her poems, some of which were written as early as the 1760s, she is believed to be in the ---- of American abolitionists.

(A) vanguard
(B) service
(C) rear
(D) favor
(E) realm

3 The earth hosts a ---- of insects—a number so large that it is easy to imagine the planet's surface as a heaving mass of tiny life.

(A) dearth
(B) rehash
(C) profusion
(D) moderation
(E) jumble

4 The observation that a significant percentage of the population did not ---- the Black Plague has led scientists to study the descendants of the survivors in hopes of discovering a gene that provided ----.

(A) fear . . immortality
(B) recognize . . health
(C) struggle with . . strength
(D) contract . . immunity
(E) believe in . . responsibility

5 Although Susan B. Anthony and Elizabeth Cady Stanton came from ---- backgrounds, they overcame their differences in a ---- effort to secure for women the right to vote.

(A) conventional . . failed
(B) diverse . . joint
(C) discordant . . beleaguered
(D) dignified . . frivolous
(E) similar . . united

6 Gertrude Stein championed many ---- artists of her time because she appreciated the new and experimental nature of their art.

(A) avant-garde
(B) competitive
(C) impugned
(D) dilatory
(E) mannered

7 The ---- reputation of the publishing world was ---- in 1989 when investigators at Pompano Press discovered that one of the firm's editors was accepting books for publication not because of the merits of the books, but because he was bribed by their authors.

(A) sterling . . enhanced
(B) sacrosanct . . sullied
(C) irreproachable . . facilitated
(D) deficient . . compromised
(E) auspicious . . coveted

8 Once an independent nation, Catalonia is now a region of Spain; nevertheless, it ---- a sense of ---- because it continues to have its own language and culture.

(A) surrenders . . rebellion
(B) retains . . autonomy
(C) experiences . . privilege
(D) boasts . . arrogance
(E) suffers . . neglect

9 Finding her old dolls and toys in the attic evoked ---- in the old woman as she fondly remembered her childhood.

(A) gratitude
(B) determination
(C) regret
(D) melancholy
(E) nostalgia

10 The two giant pandas at the National Zoo in Washington, DC are closely ----: scientists record their hormone levels daily, and 24-hour video cameras constantly ---- their activities.

(A) praised . . record
(B) monitored . . document
(C) criticized . . report
(D) evaluated . . approve
(E) questioned . . verify

11 Though Benjamin Franklin's presence at salons and dinner parties in France may have appeared ---- in a time of war, he had a serious purpose; he ingratiated himself with the French court and gained its ---- for the American cause of independence from England.

(A) disrespectful . . compliments
(B) frivolous . . support
(C) irrelevant . . approval
(D) extravagant . . permission
(E) rebellious . . respect

12 In response to the students' confused expressions, the teacher attempted to ---- the subject with a clear example.

(A) extricate
(B) evade
(C) comprehend
(D) elucidate
(E) obfuscate

13 Laura's excuse appeared credible at first, but further questioning and investigation revealed that it was completely ----.

(A) valid
(B) sardonic
(C) righteous
(D) fabricated
(E) incredulous

14 The magnificent, ---- sets that depicted a futuristic city in Fritz Lang's epic film *Metropolis* are now widely regarded as an outstanding visual achievement.

(A) prolific
(B) modest
(C) reticent
(D) archaic
(E) grandiose

15 Her physician determined that her headaches were ---- by caffeine, so Liz decided to ---- coffee and other caffeinated beverages.

(A) induced . . renounce
(B) alleviated . . subtract
(C) created . . destroy
(D) exacerbated . . promote
(E) enhanced . . neglect

16 The cat demonstrated her astonishing ---- by leaping from the low porch step to the top of the five-foot fence.

(A) balance
(B) awkwardness
(C) agility
(D) height
(E) curiosity

17 Although the news he reported was ----, the anchorman remained calm, keeping his fear from his expression.

(A) confusing
(B) unexpected
(C) anxious
(D) exciting
(E) dreadful

18 While the federal government promised to ---- its tax forms, many taxpayers still find them so ---- that they have to seek professional assistance.

(A) mystify . . infuriating
(B) shorten . . expensive
(C) replace . . comprehensible
(D) simplify . . bewildering
(E) rewrite . . familiar

19 The ---- hooves of the horses, the blaring of the trumpets, and the beating of drums combined to create a ---- on medieval battlefields.

(A) thundering . . cacophony
(B) running . . danger
(C) furious . . horror
(D) thrashing . . situation
(E) plodding . . calm

20 Although the long-term effects of the council's measures could be ----, no one can deny that the city is now enjoying an increase in tourism.

(A) stated
(B) compared
(C) discussed
(D) inquired
(E) debated

21 In order to maintain the ---- for which he was well known, the manager refused a tempting offer to ignore ---- in the corporation's accounting practices.

(A) geniality . . irregularities
(B) integrity . . improprieties
(C) dishonesty . . policies
(D) cordiality . . inconsistencies
(E) frankness . . rules

22 Though the politician's inauguration was a generally ---- occasion, it was not without moments of ----, including a few jokes during her acceptance speech.

(A) grim . . cleverness
(B) exciting . . curiosity
(C) mirthful . . humor
(D) solemn . . levity
(E) sober . . gravity

23 The novelist shocked his editor by ---- the book on which he had been working for seven years and starting over.

(A) abridging
(B) supplemented
(C) abandoning
(D) truncating
(E) praising

24 Advocates of free speech argue that, in order to ---- the right of Americans to express their opinions, no citizen who expresses unpopular sentiments should be ----.

(A) maximize . . divulged
(B) ensure . . ostracized
(C) diminish . . inhibited
(D) elucidate . . restricted
(E) embellish . . praised

Answers and Explanations

1. E
Difficulty: Low
Strategic Advice: Since the first few questions in a section are usually the easiest, be sure to avoid careless mistakes, and get those points.
Getting to the Answer: The students were shocked at Mr. Harris's outburst, so he must usually be pretty *calm*.
(A) The students probably wouldn't be surprised that their teacher was *knowledgeable*.
(B) Like (A), this wouldn't necessarily be a surprise to the class.
(C) Again, not a surprise.
(D) This doesn't contrast with having a violent reaction.
(E) Good match.
articulate: well-spoken
tranquil: calm

2. A
Difficulty: Low
Strategic Advice: Remember that only one choice can be correct. If several choices have the same meaning, none of them can be correct.
Getting to the Answer: The poems were written a long time ago, so Wheatley must have been something of a *pioneer* in the movement.
(A) This fits.
(B) Her actions were indeed in the *service* of the cause of abolitionists, but this choice ignores the part of the sentence that says she wrote these poems a long time ago.
(C) This is the opposite of what you're looking for. She was in the front, not the *rear*.
(D) Like (B), this makes sense with the first half of the sentence, but it ignores the fact that her poems were written so long ago.
(E) "The *realm* of the abolitionist" might mean she is part of the movement, but then this would have the same meaning as (B), and perhaps (D). They can't all be right!
vanguard: frontline

3. C
Difficulty: Medium
Strategic Advice: Your prediction doesn't have to be fancy. It should just give you an idea of what you're looking for.
Getting to the Answer: Apparently there are a whole lot of insects. In fact, *a lot* is a pretty good prediction.
(A) This is the opposite of what your looking for.
(B) This makes no sense in the sentence: "A *rehash* of insects"?
(C) Perfect.
(D) Not as much an opposite as (A), but it is still very different from your prediction.
(E) This doesn't create the impression that insects cover the entire earth's surface, as the question suggests.
dearth: shortage
profusion: abundance

4. D
Difficulty: Medium
Strategic Advice: As you go through the choices, you might keep a choice like (C), even though it feels a little funny, until you find a better choice, like (D).
Getting to the Answer: The Black Plague was an epidemic disease, so the percentage of the population being discussed must have either contracted the disease or not. Unless the scientists are truly evil, they are probably looking for people who didn't get the disease. So *contracted* is a good prediction for the first blank (remember, it is preceded by the word "not"), while *protection* fits well in the second one.
(A) Fear almost makes sense, but respectable scientists aren't going to be looking for *immortality*.
(B) If some people didn't *recognize* the plague, then their descendents wouldn't be of any help in the search for *health*.
(C) This one is tempting, but *struggle with* the plague doesn't quite match your prediction. When you get to (D), below, you should recognize it as a much better match.
(D) Good match for your predictions for both blanks.
(E) Why wouldn't people *believe* in the Plague? Also, why would a gene lead to *irresponsibility*?

5. B
Difficulty: Medium
Strategic Advice: The correct answer isn't necessarily the one with the most challenging vocabulary.
Getting to the Answer: The women had differences, so they probably came from *different* backgrounds. Since they overcame these differences, they must have made a *combined*, or perhaps a *successful*, effort.
(A) *Failed* definitely doesn't match your prediction for the second blank.
(B) This matches your predictions for both blanks.
(C) The words are tough, but neither one fits your predictions.
(D) A campaign to earn women the right to vote certainly wouldn't be considered *frivolous*.
(E) The second blank fits well, but the first is the opposite of what you're looking for.
diverse: varied, different
discordant: harsh, dissonant
beleaguered: stressed

6. A
Difficulty: High
Strategic Advice: Straight definition-style questions can still be challenging if the word being defined is tough.
Getting to the Answer: What kind of artists create *new and experimental* art? A good prediction is *experimental* or *creative*.
(A) This fits perfectly.
(B) Artists might be *competitive*, but this doesn't match the rest of the sentence.
(C) This word is challenging but doesn't have anything to do with the rest of the sentence.
(D) Like (C), this word is tough but doesn't belong.
(E) Artists might be *mannered*, but this doesn't match the second half of the sentence.
avant-garde: experimental, forward-thinking; from the French for *front line* or *front guard*
impugned: attacked verbally, called into question
dilatory: slow, lazy
mannered: artificial, pretentious

7. B
Difficulty: High
Strategic Advice: With the most challenging two-blank questions, you may need to guess when you only know one of the words in an answer choice.
Getting to the Answer: The publishers were up to no good, so this news must have hurt their reputation—in fact, *hurt* is a great prediction for the second blank. Since their reputation was hurt, it must have been pretty *good* to begin with, another solid prediction.
(A) Great match for the first prediction, but the second one is the opposite of your prediction.
(B) Great match for both blanks.
(C) The first word fits, but the second one falls flat.
(D) If the reputation was *deficient*, then it wouldn't have been changed by the news of shady business practices.
(E) You might not be sure if the first word fits, but the second one makes no sense. If a reputation is *coveted*, it has to be coveted by someone, and no such person is mentioned in the sentence.
sterling: pure
sacrosanct: pure, above reproach
sullied: compromised, dishonored
irreproachable: blameless, perfect
facilitated: made possible
auspicious: favorable, lucky
coveted: desired

8. B
Difficulty: Low
Strategic Advice: Don't settle for a choice that kind of works, like (C). Make sure it captures the entire meaning of your prediction.
Getting to the Answer: Catalonia is not an independent nation anymore, but it continues to have its own language and culture. So a good prediction might be *keeps a sense of independence*.
(A) If Catalonia were *surrendering*, the word *nevertheless* wouldn't make sense.
(B) This matches your prediction and makes sense.
(C) This is not out of the question, since the people of Catalonia might feel *privileged*, but it doesn't have much to do with the issue of independence.

(D) This is too extreme—there's nothing to indicate that the people of Catalonia are *arrogant*.
(E) This is the opposite of what you're looking for. If the people have their own language and culture, they probably don't feel *neglected*.
autonomy: self-government, independence

9. **E**
Difficulty: Low
Strategic Advice: In order to get the most points, move quickly and carefully through the easier questions, and save time for the tough ones later on.
Getting to the Answer: Another definition sentence. The woman "fondly remembered her childhood," so look for a choice that fits this definition.
(A) She might feel *gratitude*, but that doesn't mean fondly remembering something.
(B) There's not much support for this choice in the sentence. What would she be *determined* about?
(C) *Regret* is too negative; she's "fondly" remembering.
(D) *Melancholy* is also too negative.
(E) This is a perfect fit.
nostalgia: wistful remembering, bittersweet memories

10. **B**
Difficulty: Low
Strategic Advice: Keep an eye out for straight definition questions like this one—they can lead to quick points on Test Day.
Getting to the Answer: In order to predict what goes in the first blank, look at the explanation following the colon. The scientific records and video cameras suggest that *watched* or *observed* would work for both the first and second blanks.
(A) *Record* is great, but *praised* doesn't work here—cameras can't praise the pandas.
(B) Both *monitored* and *document* fit your prediction.
(C) *Criticized* is too negative; you're looking for neutral words.
(D) *Evaluated* isn't bad, but how could a camera *approve* activities?
(E) Anyone who *questioned* the pandas would be in for a very one-sided conversation.

11. **B**
Difficulty: Medium
Strategic Advice: Sometimes the correct answer to a two-blank Sentence Completion hinges on just one of the blanks.
Getting to the Answer: Four of the five answer choices here have OK choices for the second blank, so the question hinges on finding a word that contrasts with *serious*. The keyword *though* signals that the first blank will contrast with *serious*. *Trivial* and *playful* are good predictions. In the second half of the sentence, you might predict that Franklin gained the *support* of the French.
(A) *Disrespectful* looks possible for the first blank, but the second word doesn't quite work—why would a government give its *compliments* to a cause?
(B) *Frivolous* is a fine match for the first blank, and *support* is what you predicted for the second blank.
(C) *Irrelevant* doesn't contrast very clearly with *serious*; its tone is not sufficiently negative.
(D) *Extravagant* kind of works for the first blank, but it doesn't make sense that one government would need to get the *permission* of another government.
(E) *Rebellious* is not a very good match for your prediction—it doesn't contrast with *serious*.
frivolous: thoughtless, inconsequential
extravagant: excessive, over-generous

12. **D**
Difficulty: Medium
Strategic Advice: Don't give up when you see a few tough vocab words. Even if you don't know the answer right away, you can get closer by eliminating clearly wrong choices.
Getting to the Answer: The students are *confused*, so the teacher is trying to use an example. *Clarify* is a good prediction. Note, too, that you could eliminate two choices, even if you didn't know the meaning of *extricate*, *elucidate*, or *obfuscate*.
(A) A tough vocabulary word, but to *extricate* the subject makes no sense.
(B) The teacher is definitely not trying to *evade* the subject.

(C) Tempting if you're in a hurry, but notice that it's the students, not the teacher, who need to *comprehend* the subject.

(D) Great fit for your prediction.

(E) This is the opposite of what you're looking for.

extricate: free, extract

elucidate: explain, make clear

obfuscate: confuse, conceal

13. D

Difficulty: Medium

Strategic Advice: As you get to the more difficult questions, watch out for tempting choices like (E). Make sure the word works when you read it in the sentence.

Getting to the Answer: This is a contrast sentence, and the blank contrasts with the word *credible*. In this context, that means believable or valid, so a good prediction might be *unbelievable*.

(A) *Valid* is the opposite of what you want.

(B) A *sardonic* excuse doesn't contrast with credible.

(C) Like (A), *righteous* is the opposite of your prediction.

(D) *Fabricated* fits well. Her excuse wasn't *credible*—it was actually completely made up.

(E) Interesting, but watch out! *Incredulous* would describe people who don't believe the excuse, not the excuse itself.

credible: believable, trustworthy

valid: legitimate, compelling

sardonic: sarcastic

righteous: upright, moral

fabricated: fictitious

incredulous: disbelieving, skeptical

14. E

Difficulty: High

Strategic Advice: For most Sentence Completions, either the vocab or the prediction is challenging, but not both. Here, it's not too difficult to make a prediction.

Getting to the Answer: The sets are *magnificent* and *an outstanding visual achievement*, so the correct answer will be very positive.

(A) The artists who made the sets might be *prolific*, but the sets themselves can't be.

(B) If the sets were *modest*, they probably wouldn't be considered such a visual achievement.

(C) Like (A), this is something that could only apply to people. The sets couldn't be *reticent*.

(D) The sets should evoke the future, but *archaic* sets would do just the opposite.

(E) *Grandiose* fits perfectly. (You might recognize the word grand, even if you're not familiar with *grandiose*.)

prolific: abundantly creative

reticent: unwilling to talk

archaic: ancient, very old-fashioned

grandiose: extravagant, impressive, grand

15. A

Difficulty: High

Strategic Advice: Challenging Sentence Completions may define the relationship between the words in the blanks but not give you much of a hint about the words themselves.

Getting to the Answer: The sentence is somewhat ambiguous. Perhaps the headaches were *relieved* by caffeine, in which case Liz would decide to *drink* or *have more* coffee. Or, maybe the headaches are *caused* by caffeine, in which case Liz would decide to *quit drinking* coffee.

(A) This makes sense; if caffeine were giving her headaches, she would want to give up coffee.

(B) It doesn't make sense to *subtract* coffee.

(C) It also doesn't make sense to *destroy* coffee.

(D) If caffeine were making her headaches worse, Liz wouldn't want to *promote* coffee.

(E) *Enhanced* wouldn't be used with something negative like headaches. Also, Liz could neglect to drink coffee, but simply neglecting coffee doesn't make much sense.

induce: cause, provoke

renounce: give up, surrender

alleviate: ease, improve

exacerbate: make worse

16. C

Difficulty: Low

Strategic Advice: Don't fall for commonly paired words, like *cat* and *curiosity*.

Getting to the Answer: Look for something that describes the impressive leap of this cat.

(A) *Balance* might help the cat stay on top of the fence, but it wouldn't help her jump up there.

(B) Opposite; an astonishing leap does not reveal *awkwardness*.

(C) Good match.

(D) The fence, not the cat, is tall.

(E) Well, a cat might show *curiosity*, but the leap doesn't reveal this.

17. **E**

Difficulty: Low

Strategic Advice: Use word charge to quickly determine whether you are looking for a positive or a negative word.

Getting to the Answer: The anchorman felt fear, so the news must have been pretty *frightening*.

(A) This doesn't address the anchor's *fear*.

(B) Something could be *unexpected* without being frightening.

(C) The newscaster might be *anxious*, but the news itself cannot be.

(D) Like (B), this word lacks the negative charge of your prediction.

(E) This fits well.

18. **D**

Difficulty: Medium

Strategic Advice: The word *while* indicates that the two missing words must be opposite, or nearly opposite, in meaning.

Getting to the Answer: The government probably promised to make the forms easier to use, or to *simplify* them. The second blank should contrast with that, so *complicated* is a good prediction.

(A) These words don't show a contrast between the blanks.

(B) *Shorten* works pretty well for the first blank, but *expensive* doesn't contrast with that. Be careful here; it's the taxes themselves, not the tax forms, that people might find *expensive*.

(C) If the forms were *comprehensible*, people wouldn't need professional help.

(D) Good match.

(E) If the forms were *familiar*, taxpayers would not seek help.

infuriating: angering, frustrating

bewildering: extremely confusing

19. **A**

Difficulty: Medium

Strategic Advice: Be sure that your choice captures the full meaning of the sentence—here, several of the choices make some sense but don't involve sounds.

Getting to the Answer: The sentence begins with a list of sounds. For the first blank, *loud* is a

good prediction. The second blank needs to sum up this noise, so look for something that means *big noise*.

(A) *Thundering* is a great match for the sound of the horses, and *cacophony* perfectly captures the noise of the battlefield.

(B) *Running* doesn't describe a sound, and *danger* doesn't fit either. (Why would trumpets and drums be dangerous?)

(C) A battlefield might be a *horror*, but this term doesn't capture the sounds described.

(D) *Situation* doesn't describe the sounds and is too neutral to fit here.

(E) It seems unlikely that you would find many *plodding* horses in a battle, and *calm* is the opposite of your prediction for the second blank.

cacophony: dissonance, unpleasant noise

plodding: moving slowly and methodically

20. **E**

Difficulty: Medium

Strategic Advice: Trust your ear. If a choice doesn't sound right, eliminate it.

Getting to the Answer: The sentence sets up a contrast between the short- and long-term effects of some measures. The short-term effects are positive, but the long-term effects are uncertain. Look for a choice that captures this idea.

(A) Simply *stating* the long-term effects wouldn't contrast the short-term benefits. (You don't know if the long-term effects will be good or bad.)

(B) *Compared* with what? This choice doesn't make sense here.

(C) Like (A), *discussed* bears no relation to the increase in tourism.

(D) You could say that the council *inquired into the effects*, but *inquired* by itself doesn't fit here.

(E) Correct; *debated* fits well. It conveys that people don't know what the long-term effects will be and that those effects might differ from the positive, short-term effects.

21. **B**

Difficulty: Medium

Strategic Advice: If you didn't know the word *improprieties*, you could probably still eliminate the four wrong answer choices.

Getting to the Answer: It looks like the corporation wanted the manager to ignore some shady accounting policies, so *illegal actions* is a good prediction for the second blank. The manager refused to ignore this, so he must have been maintaining his honesty.

(A) *Irregularities* fits well in the second blank, but *geniality* would not make him ignore those irregularities.

(B) This fits your prediction well.

(C) *Dishonesty* is the opposite of the word you're looking for.

(D) *Cordiality* would not make someone ignore inconsistencies in accounting.

(E) If the manager ignored accounting *rules*, that wouldn't indicate *frankness*. In fact, it would indicate the opposite.

geniality: friendliness

improprieties: improper actions, infractions

cordiality: polite friendliness

frankness: directness, forthrightness

22. **D**
Difficulty: High
Strategic Advice: Remember to attack the blanks in the order you find easiest—it's often helpful to start with the second blank.
Getting to the Answer: The second blank must have something to do with the *few jokes*, so *humor* is a good prediction. The word *though* indicates contrast, so the first blank might be *serious*.

(A) *Cleverness* and *grim* both work okay by themselves, but they don't contrast one another, so they don't work in the sentence.

(B) It seems unlikely that the inauguration would be particularly *exciting*, but, even if it were, the word *curiosity* doesn't provide the contrast that the sentence demands.

(C) *Humor* is great for the second blank, but *mirthful* doesn't give the contrast you need.

(D) Good match.

(E) *Sober* works fine, but jokes wouldn't provide *gravity*.

mirthful: full of humor and cheer

solemn: serious

levity: humor, lightness

sober: serious

gravity: importance, seriousness

23. **C**
Difficulty: Low
Strategic Advice: Make sure you use *all* of the clues in a sentence.
Getting to the Answer: The key here is the phrase *starting over*, so *abandoning* and *throwing away* are good predictions.

(A) He wouldn't need to start over after *abridging* the book.

(B) He wouldn't need to start over after *supplementing* the book.

(C) This works.

(D) He wouldn't need to start over after *truncating* the book.

(E) He wouldn't need to start over after *praising* the book.

abridge: shorten, abbreviate

truncate: shorten, often abruptly

24. **B**
Difficulty: High
Strategic Advice: Take the time to analyze a complex sentence and piece its meaning together.
Getting to the Answer: Since the sentence deals with *advocates of free speech* you can predict that they want to protect the right to express opinions. So a good prediction for the first blank would be *guarantee*. What would they feel about citizens who express unpopular sentiments? They would want these citizens to have the right to speak freely: they wouldn't want them to be *censored*.

(A) It doesn't make sense to say that a person is *divulged*. You could say that their *name* is divulged, but that's not what appears in the sentence.

(B) This works well for both blanks, although it's not what you predicted for the second blank.

(C) The advocates would not want to *diminish* freedom.

(D) *Restricted* works pretty well for the second blank, but it doesn't make sense to say that not restricting people will *elucidate* freedom.

(E) It doesn't make sense to say that freedom is *embellished*.

divulge: reveal (information)

ostracize: cast out, banish, exclude

elucidate: clarify, explain

embellish: decorate, adorn

CHAPTER SIX

Critical Reading: Reading Comprehension Questions

The passages below are followed by questions based on their content; questions following a pair of related passages may also be based on the relationship between the paired passages. Answer the questions on the basis of what is <u>stated</u> or <u>implied</u> in the passages and in any introductory material that may be provided.

Questions 1–2 refer to the following passage.

Carousels have long been a favorite fairground attraction in both Europe and America. Although the carousels of France and Hungary are better known, the most elaborate carousels were found in America, not Europe. During the first decade of the 1900s, there were more than 7,000 working carousels in the United States. They were larger, better crafted, and had more realistic wooden horses and more ornate exteriors than the carousels in Europe, and attracted adults and children alike to the fairgrounds. Although only 300 carousels remain in existence today, they remain popular at county fairs and allow people to recall wonderful childhood memories.

1 The sentence in lines 7–11 ("They were larger... fairgrounds") implies that Americans

(A) went to the fairgrounds predominantly because of the well-crafted carousels
(B) were proud that their carousels were superior to the ones in Europe
(C) traveled to the fairgrounds in order to ride the large, well-crafted carousels
(D) enjoyed riding on large carousels only at fairgrounds
(E) found the realism of the wooden horses particularly compelling

2 Which of the following questions is answered by the passage?

(A) Why has the number of carousels in America declined?
(B) What are the most common locations for the remaining carousels?
(C) Why are the carousels of France and Hungary better known than those of America?
(D) Where were the first carousels built?
(E) In what ways are the American and European carousels different?

Question 3–4 are based on the following passage.

In the early days of computer speech technology, programmers attempted to synthesize speech. They programmed computers to create an electronic "carrier" tone and then to alter the harmonic content of that tone to match the component sounds of human speech known as phonemes. Although this synthesized speech was often understandable, it was quite stiff and unmusical, and few listeners would mistake it for the real thing. Recently, some researchers have abandoned this technique in favor of sample-based speech production. In this promising approach, actual recordings of human speech are broken down into individual phonemes to create samples. A sophisticated analysis program then selects the appropriate samples and strings them together to create entire words and sentences.

3 As used in the passage, the "real thing" (line 10) most likely refers to

(A) human speech
(B) a promising technique
(C) sample-based speech production
(D) synthesized speech
(E) a sequence of appropriate phonemes

4 According to the passage, the two forms of speech production differ in that synthesized speech

(A) was often understandable
(B) made use of phonemes
(C) relied on recordings of actual human speech
(D) began with an artificial tone
(E) was the result of a sophisticated analysis

Questions 5–6 are based on the following passage.

In the history of Western music, no composer has written so few routine and insignificant works as Johann Sebastian Bach. Equally adept at both instrumental and choral composition, he wrote countless works in many different forms and orchestrations while keeping the quality of these compositions extremely high. In most of his pieces, one can hear a pervading sense of vitality and energy in all voices. Today, the true mark of his success is the frequency with which his works have been successfully transcribed* for different instruments and ensembles, indicating that musicians and audiences of all kinds enjoy his beautifully crafted music.

Line (5)

(10)

transcribed: rewritten to be played by a different instrument or voice

5 The author most likely includes the phrase "routine and insignificant" to emphasize

(A) how successful Bach was during his lifetime
(B) the high quality of Bach's compositions
(C) that Bach wrote for many different instruments
(D) that all of Bach's pieces were completely different
(E) the regular rhythms of Bach's choral works

6 According to the passage, which of the following is NOT a reason that Bach should be considered a significant composer?

(A) He wrote both choral and instrumental works.
(B) His pieces have been adapted for different instruments.
(C) His pieces have a sense of liveliness.
(D) He created a large number of excellent pieces.
(E) He was very innovative in his approach.

Questions 7–8 refer to the following passage.

San Francisco's cable cars get their name from the long, heavy cable that runs beneath the streets along which the cars travel. This cable system resembles a giant laundry clothesline with a pulley at each end. Electricity turns the wheels of the pulleys, which in turn make the cable move. Under its floor, each car has a powerful claw that grips the cable when the car is ready to move, and releases the cable when the car needs to stop. The cars themselves are not powered and don't generate any locomotion. Instead, they simply cling to the cable, which pulls them up and down San Francisco's steep hills.

Line (5)

(10)

7 The author includes the image of a laundry clothesline in order to

(A) amuse the reader
(B) provide helpful visual imagery
(C) compare the everyday importance of cable cars and laundry
(D) show the extreme simplicity of the cable's mechanism
(E) stress that clotheslines also work on a pulley system

8 Which of the following questions is answered by the passage?

(A) What provides the energy to turn the wheels of a common laundry clothesline?
(B) How is the pulley system used to steer the cars from one street to another?
(C) How long has the cable car system been in use?
(D) Which component of the cable car system provides the force for movement?
(E) What special challenges for the cable cars are presented by San Francisco's steep hills?

Question 9–10 refer to the following passage.

Though the detective story began with the work of Edgar Allan Poe and Emile Gaboriau, Arthur Conan Doyle must be credited with
Line creating the most popular detective in the history
(5) of the genre. Sherlock Holmes first appeared in the novel *A Study in Scarlet* (1887). His sharp wits, keen eyes, and compelling personality made him an overnight sensation. In fact, when Doyle pushed Holmes over a cliff to his death in an 1893
(10) story, readers were so outraged that the writer was forced to resurrect his hero. Doyle's blueprint of an all-knowing protagonist, tantalizing clues, and a tidy, moralistic conclusion has since become the foundation of an entire literary tradition.

9 According to the passage, Doyle is unlike Poe and Gaboriau in that Doyle

(A) invented the detective story genre
(B) created the most popular fictional detective
(C) used tantalizing clues in his stories
(D) created a compelling protagonist
(E) wrote popular novels

10 The description of the "blueprint" (line 11) serves to convey

(A) the care with which Doyle's stories were crafted
(B) that Doyle's stories are quite enjoyable
(C) that Doyle's work was too formulaic
(D) the extent to which Doyle was influenced by Poe and Gaboriau
(E) that the Holmes stories served as a precedent for the detective genre

Questions 11–14 refer to the following passages.

Passage 1

Sarcophagi are elaborate coffins in which the kings and queens of Egypt were buried. These coffins served several important functions for the
Line ancient Egyptians, including recording
(5) biographical and historical information, conveying social status, and, of course, housing the remains of the deceased. Today, however, it is as art objects that they are most valued. The sarcophagi are decorated with superbly carved reliefs,
(10) paintings, and statuaries and often serve as a focal point of a museum's collection of art and artifacts from ancient Egypt. Visitors rarely fail to marvel at the exquisite and somber beauty of these elegant examples of sculptural artistry.

Passage 2

(15)   Artifacts in museums are often displayed in stark rooms, surrounded by white or pale walls. This lack of context leads the viewer to look at the artifact solely as art: a thing of beauty, form, and line. Unfortunately, such a setting divorces
(20) the object from its original context, robbing the viewer of a deeper understanding of the work. One leading museum recently attempted to address this problem by recreating an entire Egyptian temple as a setting in which to display many of
(25) the objects in its collection. One can only hope that other museums will begin to adopt similar approaches so that visitors can appreciate not only just beautiful artifacts, but also the meanings that these artifacts held for the cultures that created
(30) them.

11 The author of Passage 1 regards sarcophagi primarily as

(A) a practical solution to a number of problems
(B) intimately related to their context
(C) important sources of historical information
(D) a wise investment for museums
(E) beautiful objects of sculpture

12 According to the author of Passage 2, museum displays should convey

(A) a sense of the beauty of the objects on display
(B) biographical and historical information
(C) a sense of cultural context for artifacts
(D) the sense of being in an Egyptian temple
(E) information about social status

13 As used in line 22, "address" most nearly means

(A) reposition
(B) locate
(C) improve
(D) solve
(E) worsen

14 The author of Passage 2 would most likely regard the description of sarcophagi as "elegant examples of sculptural artistry" (line 14) as

(A) incomplete
(B) fortunate
(C) inaccurate
(D) apt
(E) misleading

Questions 15–18 refer to the following passages.

Passage 1

Marvin Freeman's groundbreaking new study of the plays of Henrik Ibsen will alter the course of Ibsen scholarship forever. Previously, scholars
Line limited the areas of their studies to a particular
(5) phase of Ibsen's career, since a different scholarly approach seemed to fit each of the phases. Freeman has instead taken on the entirety of Ibsen's work. Happily, this breadth of scholarship does not diminish the depth with which Freeman
(10) explores each work. The career of Ibsen is now liberated from arbitrary divisions and stands before us as a complete picture. It will be years before we can appreciate fully the service that Freeman has rendered.

Passage 2

(15) In his new tome on the plays of Henrik Ibsen, Marvin Freeman presumes to consider all of the 26 plays, a period of writing that spanned some 50 years. This experiment, while yielding some interesting observations, does not serve as a useful
(20) scholarly model. Over the course of Ibsen's career, the playwright's approach evolved so drastically that it is impossible to fully consider all of his works in the confines of a single study. Freeman is forced to simplify where complexity would be
(25) more apt. While Freeman exhibits tremendous dedication to his subject, this devotion ultimately cannot save the project from its own ambition.

15 In Passage 1, the "arbitrary divisions" in line 11 refer to

(A) the unsuccessful scholarly approaches that have been applied to Ibsen's work
(B) the breaks that Ibsen took between writing his plays
(C) a rift that Freeman has created among Ibsen scholars
(D) distinctions between various phases of Ibsen's career
(E) Freeman's dissatisfaction with previous Ibsen scholarship

16 The last sentence of Passage 1 functions primarily to

(A) imply that the book is very difficult to read
(B) highlight the lasting importance of the book
(C) celebrate Freeman's triumph over obstacles
(D) argue that additional scholarship will clarify Freeman's intent
(E) paraphrase the closing argument of Freeman's book

17 The author of Passage 2 implies that Freeman's attempt to write about Ibsen's entire career in a single book is

(A) overwhelming but not idealistic
(B) feasible but not sufficient
(C) admirable but not successful
(D) viable but not important
(E) desirable but not achievable

18 The author of Passage 2 would most likely regard the approach of the scholars mentioned in lines 3–6 as

(A) being of appropriate scope
(B) inferior to that of Freeman
(C) being of lasting importance to future generations
(D) unsuitable for Ibsen's career
(E) difficult to assess

The passages below are followed by questions based on their content and on the relationship between the passages. Answer the questions on the basis of what is <u>stated</u> or <u>implied</u> in the passages and in any introductory material that may be provided.

Questions 19–30 are based on the following passages.

The following adaptations from recent scholarly articles offer different perspectives on the harsh conditions faced by nineteenth century female factory workers in the urban centers of the United States. Both passages reflect the oppressive working environment created by the Waltham-Lowell system of organization in textile factories.

Passage 1

The Waltham-Lowell system, a business philosophy and manufacturing strategy, was named for its creator and the Massachusetts town
Line in which it was first implemented in 1815. As a
(5) manufacturing system, it combined the various stages of the textile manufacturing process under one roof, while as a business system, it detailed a set of comprehensive rules and regulations for workers. To implement the Waltham-Lowell
(10) system, factory owners preferred to employ female workers—often called factory girls—because women would work for lower wages and were then considered easier to control than men.

Many of the system's regulations, including a
(15) requirement that the women live in company-owned boarding houses, had been created primarily to assure families that their daughters would not be corrupted by factory life. Ironically, however, many of the women employed were actually forced
(20) to leave their families' homes, even when those families lived within easy commuting distance of the factories, and even when the women were married. Needless to say, living away from home and among strangers was a stressful and
(25) disorienting experience for many.

The extremely poor living conditions of the boarding houses created further problems. Most factory houses were overcrowded, dirty, and infested with vermin. These conditions, combined
(30) with shared beds and poor ventilation, allowed diseases to spread and caused health problems for many of the workers. However, it's important for modern researchers to note that American factories were not alone in maintaining boarding
(35) houses for workers. In fact, conditions in company-run American boarding houses were actually

uniformly superior to those in Europe, where conditions were even more cramped and the ethics
(40) of the owners more base.

While these living conditions were regrettable, some economists have advanced that the managers of the textile factories had little choice. The American textile market of the last century
(45) was extremely competitive, since the supply of textiles created by the nation's numerous domestic factories far exceeded consumer demand. Furthermore, foreign competitors, including English and Indian factories, began selling excess
(50) textile products in America at the beginning of the 1800s. Compounding the problem, foreign textile factories could often afford to sell their products in the American market for less than domestic manufacturers, because foreign factories set their
(55) wages far below what Americans found tolerable. American factories were thus constantly facing the risk of bankruptcy, and many managers felt that taking measures to preserve the health, comfort, and safety of their factory workers would have
(60) been financial suicide.

Passage 2

Widely utilized in the mid-nineteenth century, the Waltham-Lowell system encompassed a set of atrocious working rules that created a dismal environment for workers in textile factories.
(65) Many factory practices had ill effects on the health of workers, the majority of whom were young women. Loud machines running all day long in a small space affected the hearing of the workers, while poor ventilation filled the air with cotton
(70) lint and toxins from the whale-oil lamps used to light the factories.

Problems were not limited to purely environmental factors. Workers also lived in constant fear of the factories' agents—supervisors
(75) who would punish them severely for any time spent not working. In fact, agents could fire workers almost at whim because of the seemingly endless supply of labor willing to replace the young women on the factory floor. The workers were
(80) usually not permitted to speak while operating the machines because the agents feared that talking would distract the women from their work and slow production. Not surprisingly, breaks were

also infrequent, or absent altogether—even
(85) bathroom breaks were strongly discouraged.
Ironically given these conditions, workers were
expected to be neatly dressed in clean clothes at all
times in case someone of note came to visit the
mill. As a result, much of what little free time the
(90) young women had was spent washing or mending
clothes.

Some aspects of the Waltham-Lowell system
were not only degrading but downright dangerous.
The factory management's obsession with keeping
(95) workers at their tasks extended to keeping all
factory doors locked during working hours. As a
result, emergency evacuations were difficult or
impossible. In 1911, a fire broke out in New York
City's Triangle Shirtwaist Factory, and many
(100) workers died. Though one might hope that such a
tragedy would have finally brought about changes,
the factory owners were actually acquitted of
criminal charges, and required to pay damages of
only seventy-five dollars to each of twenty-three
(105) victims' families that sued. Sadly, the practice of
locking factory doors remained common for
several years.

Though some charge that the Waltham-Lowell
system was a result of economic necessity, we
(110) must realize that the factory managers who
implemented this system made deliberate
decisions to increase profits at the expense of their
workers, and that these workers—even those who
fell ill or died—were treated by factory managers
(115) as objects to be replaced. Owners should instead
have replaced the reprehensible Waltham-Lowell
system with another: that of common decency, to
be respected above the baser "ideals" of
nineteenth-century capitalism.

19 The attitude of the author of Passage 1 toward the
factory workers who endured harsh conditions is
best described as

(A) reserved sympathy
(B) complete disinterest
(C) ironic contempt
(D) spirited befuddlement
(E) unreserved appreciation

20 The word "base" as used in line 40 most nearly
means

(A) elevated
(B) immoral
(C) absent
(D) harmful
(E) foundational

21 According to Passage 1, the primary reason that
factories required factory workers to live in
boarding houses was to

(A) placate the fears of the workers' families
(B) ensure that the girls were not corrupted by city
   life
(C) prevent disease among factory girls
(D) restrict the social activities of female factory
   workers
(E) separate girls from their families

22 "Advanced" as used in line 42 most closely means

(A) proceeded
(B) argued
(C) denied
(D) progressed
(E) concealed

23 Which of the following, if true, would most
weaken the assertion in Passage 1 about the
necessity of subjecting factory girls to unsafe
conditions?

(A) Textile factories in France were financially
   successful even though they refused to make
   factory girls endure harsh conditions.
(B) The Waltham-Lowell system actually produced
   a smaller increase in profit than did the
   competing Bennington system.
(C) The estimated costs of increasing worker
   safety and health in the nineteenth century
   to acceptable levels would have been more
   than the total profits of factories in that era.
(D) Many twentieth-century factories treated
   factory workers with care and dignity and
   still had higher profits than nineteenth-
   century factories.
(E) An early nineteenth-century workers' rights
   activist approached all American and foreign
   factories with a plan to improve working
   conditions while maintaining profits, but
   this plan was rejected by all factories.

24 In the second paragraph of Passage 2, the description of the conditions imposed by factory agents serves to

(A) argue that American factory conditions were superior to those in Europe
(B) illustrate the role of factory agents in creating the poor working conditions discussed
(C) argue that such conditions were immoral by modern standards
(D) explain why factory agents were responsible for the 1911 fire
(E) illustrate the economic necessity of the harsh conditions

25 In the context of Passage 2, the reference to the Triangle Shirtwaist Factory fire in lines 98–99 serves to

(A) illustrate the prevalence of fires in factories that used the Waltham-Lowell system
(B) elicit unwarranted sympathy for the victims of a tragic factory accident
(C) demonstrate the dangerous conditions created by the uncaring attitude of factory owners toward their workers
(D) exemplify the extent to which factories tried to protect the safety of female workers
(E) illustrate the negligent behavior common among factory workers in New York City

26 According to Passage 2, the "tragedy" mentioned in line 101

(A) claimed twenty-three victims
(B) led to imprisonment for those responsible
(C) remained common for several years
(D) resulted from the whale-oil lamps used to light the factories
(E) failed to bring about immediate reform in working conditions

27 Which of the following most accurately describes the organization of the final paragraph of Passage 2?

(A) Evidence is questioned but ultimately accepted, leading to the main conclusion.
(B) An assertion is made and then supported with statistical evidence.
(C) A view is mentioned, then argued against.
(D) A widely held view is dismissed, and a new view is defended with historical evidence.
(E) Past circumstances are described in both moral and economic terms, resulting in a contradiction.

28 The passages differ in their evaluations of factory owners in that Passage 1 claims that

(A) market conditions partially excuse the poor work environment created by factory owners
(B) factory owners compensated society for their reprehensible actions in the factory through philanthropic work
(C) the use of the Waltham-Lowell system enabled American factories to compete with European and Indian factories
(D) factory regulations caused many health problems for workers
(E) the Waltham-Lowell system was superior to previous factory organization schemes

29 Which of the following is an aspect of the Waltham-Lowell System emphasized in Passage 2, but not in Passage 1?

(A) the difficult conditions in factory boarding houses
(B) the role of agents in factory life
(C) health hazards faced by factory girls
(D) the demands of the families of factory girls
(E) the role of safety supervisors on the factory floor

30 Both passages mention which of the following aspects of nineteenth-century factory life?

(A) the extensive demands of factory agents
(B) the health problems caused by factory life under the Waltham-Lowell system
(C) the demand that workers dress neatly
(D) the superiority of working conditions in factories outside of New York State
(E) the generosity of factory owners toward workers

Questions 31–43 refer to the following passages.

The following passages concern the novel Moby Dick by American author Herman Melville (1819-1891), which tells the story of the hunt by Captain Ahab for the whale named Moby Dick. Passage 1 is adapted from a 1852 review from a literary magazine, and Passage 2 is by a modern literary critic.

Passage 1

In *Moby Dick*, Mr. Melville is evidently trying to ascertain how far the public will consent to be imposed upon. He is gauging, at once, our
Line gullibility and our patience. Having written one or
(5) two passable extravagances, he has considered himself privileged to produce as many more as he pleases, increasingly exaggerated and increasingly dull. In vanity, in caricature, in efforts at literary innovation—generally as clumsy as they are
(10) ineffectual—and in low attempts at humor, each one of his volumes has been an advance among its predecessors. Mr. Melville never writes naturally. His sentiment is forced, his wit is forced, and his enthusiasm is forced. And in his attempts to
(15) display to the utmost extent his powers of "fine writing," he has succeeded, we think, beyond his most optimistic expectations.

The work is an ill-compounded mixture of romance and matter-of-fact. The idea of a
(20) connected and collected story has obviously visited and abandoned its writer again and again in the course of composition. The style of his tale is in places disfigured by mad (rather than bad) English; and its conclusion is hastily, weakly, and obscurely
(25) written. The result is, at all events, a strange book—neither so compelling as to be entertaining, nor so instructively complete as to take place among documents on the subject of the Great Whale, his capabilities, his home, and his capture.
(30) Our author must be henceforth numbered in the company of those writers who occasionally tantalize us with indications of talent, while they constantly summon us to endure monstrosities, carelessness, and bad taste.
(35) The truth is, Mr. Melville has survived his reputation. If he had been contented with writing one or two books, he might have been famous, but his vanity has destroyed all his chances for

immortality, or even of a good name with his own
(40) generation. For, in sober truth, Mr. Melville's vanity is immeasurable. He will either be first among the book-making tribe, or he will be nowhere. He will center all attention upon himself, or he will abandon the field of literature at
(45) once. From this morbid self-esteem, coupled with a most unbounded love of fame, spring all Mr. Melville's efforts, all his rhetorical contortions, all his declamatory abuse of society, all his inflated sentiment, and all his insinuating licentiousness.

Passage 2

(50) Many readers have dismissed Herman Melville's epic novel *Moby Dick* as "a treatise on whaling" because it contains so many chapters that explore the intricacies of the whaling trade in the mid-nineteenth century. Such passages make no direct
(55) mention of the events that make up the novel's plot, and instead provide a wealth of factual information on topics such as undersea plant life and the anatomy of great whales. Such critics feel that alternating such discursive material with the
(60) narrative detracts from the compelling account of the hunt for Moby Dick, the eponymous white whale. However, these critics fail to realize that Melville is slyly, if paradoxically, advancing the plot through these admittedly dry passages of
(65) purely factual data.

The whale Moby Dick is—unsurprisingly, given the book's title—pivotal to the plot. The story concentrates on the pursuit of the whale by Captain Ahab, a master whaler who has long been
(70) obsessed with his prey. In order to portray the hunt as a titanic struggle, Melville needed to paint a detailed portrait of the whale—a worthy rival for the ruthless and skilled Ahab. How could Melville create such a sense of personality and agency for a
(75) mute animal? How could he make the character of Moby Dick as compelling and fully-realized as Ahab?

Melville met these challenges by educating the reader. Melville had served on a whaling ship
(80) himself, and had also read much of the most current scientific information available about the creatures. Drawing on this deep understanding, Melville interspersed a number of instructional chapters throughout the book which conveyed a
(85) sense of the intelligence and majesty of these animals. As with any literary portrait, Melville

also saw the need to create a palpable sense of the place the character inhabited. Several chapters describe the climate and environment of the

(90) whale's underwater world, including an entire chapter on the plants to be found on the ocean floor. Just as Melville's contemporary Charles Dickens created vivid portrayals of London to cast a sense of light and shade on his characters, so did

(95) Melville describe the sea in order to more fully reveal the character of Moby Dick. Melville set before himself not only the task of describing whales and their environments, but also the task of whaling and the culture of its practitioners.

(100)   At its core, *Moby Dick* is the chronicle of a man's obsession. In order to paint a convincing picture of Ahab's fixation, Melville needed the reader to appreciate the tremendous financial and psychic prize such an enormous and unusual whale

(105) would represent to a master whaler such as Ahab. Melville also takes considerable pains to clearly portray the techniques and culture of whaling; several chapters are devoted entirely to describing the process of hunting and killing a whale.

(110) Although these chapters don't advance the plot directly, they help the reader appreciate the foolishness and bravery of a crew aboard a small ship, armed with only a few harpoons, attempting to bring down a creature as gigantic and powerful

(115) as Moby Dick.

31 The phrase "an advance among its predecessors" (lines 11–12) indicates that the author of Passage 1 believes that

(A) Melville's works have steadily decreased in quality
(B) Melville's literary innovations were based on the work of others
(C) *Moby Dick* is the finest novel that Melville wrote
(D) Melville was a talented, innovative writer
(E) the descriptive passages about whaling detract from the novel's plot

32 The author of Passage 1 most likely uses quotation marks around the phrase "fine writing" (lines 15–16) in order to convey

(A) the high esteem that he has for *Moby Dick*
(B) his contempt for Melville's writing style
(C) that the words were first written by another critic
(D) the success of Melville's literary ambitions
(E) that Melville used the term to refer to his own writing

33 The discussion of "a connected and collected story" (lines 19–20) in Passage 1 implies that

(A) Melville mixed a narrative plotline with instructional material to help readers appreciate the characters
(B) *Moby Dick* has more literary merit than Melville's previous work.
(C) more of the novel is devoted to instructive rather than entertaining material
(D) the author believes that the novel lacks a continuous plotline
(E) Melville had moments of inspiration separated by periods of doubt

34 The author of Passage 1 notes that *Moby Dick* is "a strange book" (lines 25–26) because

(A) whaling is an unusual subject
(B) Melville's writing style is forced rather than natural
(C) it fails to be effective as either a novel or an informational work
(D) one of the main characters is an animal
(E) the ending of the book is not well constructed

35 The author of Passage 1 would most likely agree that

(A) the discussion of the whale's environment contributes positively to the novel
(B) Melville's greatness stems from his ambition to be considered among the finest novelists
(C) it's unwise to write novels with instructional elements
(D) readers who criticize the nonfiction elements of *Moby Dick* fail to appreciate the importance of the factual information
(E) Melville's earlier works were of higher quality than *Moby Dick*

36 As used in line 64, "dry" most nearly means

(A) dehydrated
(B) ironic
(C) tedious
(D) fascinating
(E) accurate

37 The questions at the end of the second paragraph of Passage 2 ("How could he ...as Ahab?" lines 75–77) serve to

(A) cast doubt on the success of Melville's narrative techniques
(B) echo the questions asked by the novel's characters
(C) imply that Melville's characters are not believable
(D) define a problem addressed by Melville
(E) illustrate an unusual approach to the form of the novel

38 According to the author of Passage 2, Melville's description of the underwater environment and Dickens's portrayal of London are similar in that both

(A) create a dark, mysterious aura
(B) serve to educate the reader
(C) are unusual narrative techniques
(D) detract from the plot of each author's novels
(E) help to illuminate each author's characters

39 As used in line 106, the phrase "takes considerable pains" most nearly means

(A) makes a deliberate effort
(B) undergoes unpleasant experiences
(C) unsuccessfully attempts
(D) makes it possible
(E) wisely endeavors

40 The author of Passage 2 would most likely react to the description of *Moby Dick* as "an ill-compounded mixture" in Passage 1 by asserting that

(A) Melville failed to fully integrate the fictional and instructional elements in the novel
(B) the description of ocean plant life creates a sense of place for the character of the whale
(C) the nonfiction passages in the novel help the reader fully appreciate the story
(D) Melville's vanity prompted him to attempt such an ambitious novel
(E) many readers find the information about whales and whaling fascinating

41 The authors of both passages agree that the techniques used by Melville in *Moby Dick*

(A) are highly effective
(B) are similar to those of Charles Dickens
(C) create a vivid sense of place
(D) combine fictional and informational elements
(E) are bolder than those of his previous works

42 The author of Passage 1 would most likely regard the "critics" mentioned in line 58 as

(A) correct
(B) impatient
(C) unsophisticated
(D) misguided
(E) ambitious

43 Which statement best describes how the authors of the two passages differ in their views on Melville's writing?

(A) The author of Passage 1 views it as excellent, while the author of Passage 2 has a more moderate view.
(B) The author of Passage 1 criticizes it as vain and tedious, while the author of Passage 2 describes it as innovative and admirable.
(C) The author of Passage 1 feels that it is flawed but noteworthy, while the author of Passage 2 offers unqualified praise.
(D) The author of Passage 1 describes it as declining in quality, while the author of Passage 2 feels that it improved steadily over the course of Melville's career.
(E) The author of Passage 1 feels that it contains narrative and informational elements, while the author of Passage 2 describes it as purely narrative.

Questions 44–54 are based on the following passage.

In this passage, the author describes a man's contemplation of his childhood on a farm that his family has recently sold.

Yesterday there was a forest of corn here. Thomas remembered racing through it blindly, his forearms raised to protect his face from the rough
Line leaves. Playing in the corn was one of his pastimes,
(5) a pastime of any boy who lived on a farm that planted it. He would run until he was out of breath, gasping and disoriented by the spears of green towering over his head. It's easy to become lost in a corn field, to walk in endless circles. It's
(10) easier still, by picking a row of corn and following it out, to leave. Leaving the corn was easy.

For eighty years the family had grown corn on its hundred-acre plot. In his grandfather's day, even in his father's, wheat and timothy were also sown
(15) to help feed cattle and pigs. While there had been no animals on the land in Thomas's time, Thomas's father spoke at length about those days, when he himself had been a child. Back then, Thomas's father had dedicated every one of his free
(20) hours to taking care of the farm: grinding chop, cleaning up after the animals, mending fences, and performing innumerable other taxing chores. Later, it was just corn, sold to some big company out East that his father said paid them a little less every
(25) year. It wasn't about the money though; his father would have made do with just enough to keep things going. His concern was family and tradition, the agricultural way of life.

During harvest, Thomas would ride on the
(30) enormous thresher with his father. In the cabin, above the green sea parting before them, he would listen as his father explained the significance of a life dedicated to agriculture. As Thomas nibbled on a lunch packed by his mother, his father
(35) expounded upon his philosophy that a man must not be separated from the land that provides for him, that the land was sacrosanct. He would say, time and again, "A man isn't a man without land to call his own."
(40) He was not an uneducated man, Thomas's father. He had completed high school and probably could have gone to college if he wanted, but he was a man of the earth, and his spirit was tied to the soil. Agriculture was not his profession; it was his
(45) passion, one that he tried to seed in the hearts of his three boys. Thomas's two older brothers had little time for farm work, however. What chores they were not forced to do went undone or were done by Thomas; their energies were focused on
(50) cars, dating, and dance halls.

Even at a young age, Thomas was able to see in his father's eyes the older man's secret despair. The land that had been in his family for three generations was not valued by the fourth. Not even
(55) little Tommy, who always rode in the cabin with him and helped out as much as he was able, would stay and tend the fields. The world had grown too large, and there were too many distractions to lure young men from their homes. Boys these days did
(60) not realize they had a home until it was too late.

Sitting on the hood of his jeep, Thomas gazed out over dozens of acres of orange survey stakes that covered what was once his family's farm. The house, barn, and silos were all gone, replaced by
(65) construction trailers and heavy equipment. The town that lay just five miles up the road had grown into a city, consuming land like a hungry beast. Thomas's father had been the last farmer left in the county, holding out long after the farm became
(70) unprofitable. He farmed after his sons left and his wife died; he farmed until his last breath, on principle.

Now a highway and several shopping malls were going to take his place, Thomas thought. His
(75) brothers both said it was inevitable, that progress cannot be halted. They argued that if the family did not sell the land, the city would claim Eminent Domain and take it from them for a fraction of what they could get by selling it. Thomas did not
(80) feel he had any right to disagree. After all, he had chosen to leave the farm as well, to pursue his education. Though he didn't stand in their way, and though his profit from the lucrative sale was equal to his brothers', Thomas was sure he felt
(85) something that they could not. The money didn't matter much to him; he had enough to get by. It was something about the land. Now that he had finally found his way back to it, he was losing it. He was losing his home.

44 The opening sentence primarily serves to introduce a sense of

(A) urgency
(B) immediacy
(C) accurate recollection
(D) purposeful contemplation
(E) passing time

45 In line 7, the word "spears" most nearly means

(A) spires
(B) structures
(C) weapons
(D) shoots
(E) thorns

46 The final sentence of the first paragraph most clearly conveys

(A) a foreshadowing of developments that are described later in the passage
(B) the ease with which one can avoid getting lost in a cornfield
(C) the simplicity of Thomas's childhood
(D) the importance of corn to Thomas's father
(E) the joy Thomas took as a boy in wandering the cornfields

47 In line 22, the word "taxing" most nearly means

(A) monetary
(B) expensive
(C) rejuvenating
(D) tiring
(E) unskilled

48 Which of the following terms would Thomas most likely use to describe his father?

(A) Aristocratic
(B) Naive
(C) Autonomous
(D) Cosmopolitan
(E) Dogmatic

49 Based on the passage, a thresher (line 30) is most likely used to

(A) mend fences
(B) harvest crops
(C) construct shopping malls
(D) plant seeds
(E) survey land

50 Thomas's father's statement in lines 38–39 ("a man . . . own") primarily shows the father to be

(A) discouraged because he is getting less money for his corn each year
(B) overwhelmed by the number of tedious chores he must complete each day
(C) convinced that his life as a farmer is worthwhile
(D) pleased that his youngest son is with him as he threshes the corn
(E) grateful that he is making enough money to support his family

51 The description in lines 46–50 of Thomas's brother's interests ("Thomas's . . . dance halls") highlights

(A) the difference between the brothers as young men and as adults
(B) reasons that Thomas performed the brothers' neglected chores
(C) the considerable conflict between the brothers and their father
(D) the brothers' desire to profit from the sale of the farm
(E) the dichotomy between the brothers' values and those of their father

52 The most likely cause of the "secret despair" (line 52) that Thomas sees in his father's eyes is the father's

(A) disappointment that Thomas didn't help as much as he could have with the farm chores
(B) worry about his sons' preoccupation with cars, dating, and dancing
(C) regret that he didn't attend college even though he could have done so
(D) unhappiness with his marriage
(E) sadness that his sons would not care for the family farm in the same way that he had

53 An important function of the sixth paragraph is to

(A) establish that the narrative to this point has been a flashback
(B) contrast Thomas's current life with his past life
(C) show that the timeline of the story has been in reverse chronological order
(D) summarize the plot
(E) foreshadow Thomas's future

54 The last sentence of the passage ("He . . . home") suggests that Thomas feels

(A) regretful nostalgia
(B) excited anticipation
(C) righteous anger
(D) overwhelming despair
(E) unaccustomed relief

Questions 55–61 refer to the passage below.

This passage, adapted from the arts column of a prominent national newspaper, discusses the art movement known as Impressionism, which developed primarily in France in the second half of the 1800s.

Though he would one day be considered a innovator and founding father of the artistic movement known as Impressionism, Claude
Line Monet (1840–1926) began his career as a fairly
(5) traditional representational artist. His painting gradually changed, however, as he became interested in light and how it affects perception— an interest that led him to attempt to paint light itself rather than the objects off of which light
(10) reflected. Monet also rejected the tradition of painting in a dedicated studio, and left the confines of his dusty room to paint outside. Many of his friends and fellow artists, including Pisarro, Renoir, and Cezanne, were also interested in working
(15) alfresco and joined him in painting outdoors. This group, the core of the movement that would later be classified as Impressionism, made it a common practice to paint the same scene many times in a day to explore the changes in the light, using small
(20) patches of color rather than the large brush strokes and blended color that had characterized artistic technique until that time. The Impressionists were thus attempting to evoke a mood rather than document a specific scene or event, as had been the
(25) aim of earlier painters.
      This move away from representation was also effected by a technological development, as photography became more affordable and popular. Before the development of photography, painting
(30) was the primary means of documenting the marriages, births, and business successes of the wealthy. Photographers soon took over much of this role because photographs were faster, more accurate, and less expensive than paintings. This
(35) freed the Impressionists to find new roles for their medium and encouraged the public to think about painting in a new way. It was no longer just a means of recording significant events; it now reflected an artist's unique vision of a scene or
(40) moment.
      Today, Impressionism enjoys a privileged position with many art historians and critics, although this was certainly not always the case. As the movement was developing, most critics were at
(45) best uninterested and often appalled by the work. Even the name of the movement was originally a derisive critique. A critic who, like most of his

colleagues, prized realism in paintings, declared the movement "Impressionism" after the name of the
(50) painting *Impression: A Sunrise*, by Monet. The critic considered the Impressionists' works unfinished—only an impression, rather than a complete painting. It is safe to say that such a critic would be in the minority today, however.
(55) Impressionist paintings are now some of the most prized works in the art world. Museums and individuals pay huge sums to add these works to their collections, and the reproductions of the artworks are among the most popular fine art
(60) posters sold.

55 The primary purpose of the passage is to

(A) condemn the critics who prevented the Impressionists from exhibiting their work
(B) contrast Monet's work with that of Pisarro, Renoir, and Cezanne
(C) describe the primary characteristics of Monet's paintings
(D) explain the origins of Impressionism and Monet's role in the movement
(E) argue that photography is a better medium than painting for representing events

56 According to the passage, the Impressionists did all of the following EXCEPT

(A) paint the same scene at different times of the day
(B) painting the light reflected by objects
(C) use small areas of color rather than large, blended areas
(D) receive acclaim from their contemporaries
(E) reconsider the role of painting in society

57 In line 20, the author most likely mentions "patches of color" to describe

(A) the light that the Impressionists encountered when they worked outdoors
(B) a shortcoming of traditional paintings
(C) a distinguishing characteristic of modern painters
(D) an innovative technique used by Impressionist painters
(E) an artistic feature present in paintings but lacking in photography

58 The discussion of photography (lines 28–34) serves as

(A) a contrast to the discussion of traditional painting

(B) the most important context in which to understand Impressionism

(C) a description of an innovation that affected the development of Impressionism

(D) a clarification of the public's dislike of Impressionism

(E) a demonstration of its similarities to painting

59 The author of the passage would most likely describe the medium of photography as

(A) expensive
(B) precise
(C) false
(D) inconsistent
(E) prestigious

60 The "critic" mentioned in line 47 would most likely agree that

(A) Impressionist paintings are inferior because they fail to clearly represent their subjects

(B) Impressionism now enjoys a much more prestigious place in the art world than it once did

(C) Monet's Impression: A Sunrise was a highly influential work

(D) the use of photography to document important events freed painters to explore other roles

(E) Impressionist paintings are now rightly recognized by the public as important works

61 In line 48 "prized" most nearly means

(A) awarded
(B) discovered
(C) valued
(D) decorated
(E) sought

Answers and Explanations

Carousels
1. **B**
Difficulty: Medium
Strategic Advice: Inference questions don't require you to bend over backwards to make the correct answer choice work. Instead, look for the choice that follows directly from the information in the sequence or part of the paragraph to which the question refers.
Getting to the Answer: The paragraph's last sentence states that people can go on a carousel at a country fair to recall wonderful childhood memories. Look for an answer choice that matches this.
(A) Out of Scope; although it is stated that adults enjoy going on carousel rides, the author does not say that adults enjoy carousels more than children.
(B) Matches the prediction nicely.
(C) Extreme; although people enjoy the rides, the passage doesn't imply that this is people's primary reason for going to fairgrounds.
(D) Misused Detail; the author does not state exactly when carousels gained popularity. (Maybe they were even more popular in 1890, for example.)
(E) Out of Scope; we know that they were popular, but we don't know that they were the most popular attraction.

2. **E**
Difficulty: Low
Strategic Advice: Don't waste time predicting with such open-ended questions. Quickly summarize the author's viewpoint, then move on to the answer choices.
Getting to the Answer: Go through each choice, and compare it to the passage.
(A) Out-of-Scope; the passage states that the number has declined, but doesn't say why.
(B) Out-of-Scope; the author does state that *they remain popular at county fairs*, but that doesn't mean that county fairs are the most common location for the carousels.
(C) Out-of-Scope; the author says that the European carousels are better known but doesn't explain why.

(D) Out-of-Scope; the author never mentions the origins of the carousels.
(E) The American carousels *were larger, better crafted, and had more realistic wooden horses and more ornate exteriors*. That sums up the differences.

Speech Synthesis
3. **A**
Difficulty: Low
Strategic Advice: Use keywords (like *although* here) to help you prephrase.
Getting to the Answer: The whole idea of these speech technologies is to make computers sound like people, so the *real thing* must be just that—real human speech.
(A) Good Match
(B) Misused Detail; the author describes sample-based speech production as *promising*.
(C) Misused Detail; this comes later in the paragraph, but the author isn't referring to it here.
(D) Opposite; this is what the author says *won't* be mistaken for the real thing.
(E) Misused Detail; like (C), this comes later in the paragraph.

4. **D**
Difficulty: Medium
Strategic Advice: In a question like this one, be careful not to pick choices that are true of *both* processes.
Getting to the Answer: Summarize the features of each process. Synthesized speech starts with an electronic tone, which is then modified. Sample-based speech is made by stringing together recordings of phonemes from actual people.
(A) Distortion; well, it was often understandable, but this is probably true of sample-based speech also. (At least the author doesn't say it *isn't* true.)
(B) Opposite; careful—phonemes are mentioned in the description of both processes (in the second and next-to-last sentences).
(C) Misused Detail; this is true of sample-based speech, not synthesized speech.
(D) This matches the passage, since synthesized speech begins with a tone generated by the computer.
(E) Misused Detail; like (C), this is true of sample-based speech, not synthesized speech.

Bach

5. B

Difficulty: Medium

Strategic Advice: Questions often concentrate on tricky or unusual statements of simple ideas, like the first sentence of this passage.

Getting to the Answer: The author uses the phrase *routine and insignificant* to illustrate the type of compositions that Bach did *not* create— that is, the author wanted to show what a great composer Bach was.

(A) Out-of-Scope; there is no mention of Bach's success during his lifetime.

(B) Good match.

(C) Misused Detail; this is true, but it doesn't follow from the phrase *routine and insignificant*.

(D) Extreme; although the author certainly believes that Bach was a great composer, he never indicates that every work was completely different.

(E) Out-of-Scope; the author never mentions the rhythms of Bach's music.

6. E

Difficulty: Medium

Strategic Advice: On a Detail question, the details will appear directly in the passage. Here, (E) is the kind of thing the author seems likely to agree with, but it's never actually mentioned anywhere.

Getting to the Answer: Since the passage asks which choice is *not* a reason from the passage, go through each of the answer choices to eliminate all the reasons that *are* listed.

(A) This is mentioned in the second sentence: *He wrote countless works for both instrument and voice.*

(B) This is mentioned in the last sentence: *transcribed for different instruments and ensembles.*

(C) This is mentioned in the third sentence: *vitality and energy.*

(D) This is mentioned in the second sentence: *keeping the quality of these compositions very high.*

(E) Good Match; although the author would likely agree with this statement, it is never mentioned in the passage, and so is the correct answer.

Cable Cars

7. B

Difficulty: Low

Strategic Advice: Beware of choices like (D); don't make assumptions about the author's point of view that aren't warranted by the passage.

Getting to the Answer: The author is describing how the cable cars work and uses the image of a laundry line because it's likely to be familiar to most readers.

(A) Out-of-Scope; although you may find the image amusing, the author's purpose is to inform, not amuse.

(B) Good match.

(C) Out-of-Scope; the paragraph doesn't discuss laundry.

(D) Distortion; the author never indicates that the mechanism is simple, although you might think it so from the description.

(E) Out-of-Scope; the passage is not about clotheslines.

8. D

Difficulty: Medium

Strategic Advice: Read Detail questions carefully. Choices like (A) begin just fine, then *veer off course*.

Getting to the Answer: Don't waste your time trying to make a prediction for a question like this, jump right into the answers.

(A) Out-of-Scope; the laundry line is mentioned only briefly, and the author doesn't say much about how it works.

(B) Out-of-Scope; the author describes what makes the cars start and stop but never mentions steering.

(C) Out-of-Scope; the paragraph provides no historical context.

(D) Yes, this is discussed. The moving cable provides the force, and the cars simply hang on.

(E) Out-of-Scope; the hills are mentioned in passing in the last sentence, but no special challenges are mentioned.

Sir Arthur Conan Doyle

9. **B**
Difficulty: Low
Strategic Advice: Remember that Reading Comprehension questions are not ordered by difficulty, so easy questions can appear at the end of a section.
Getting to the Answer: The author writes that the detective story began with Poe and Gaboriau, but Doyle *must be credited with creating the most popular detective*.
(A) Opposite; Poe and Gaboriau invented the genre, not Doyle.
(B) Good match.
(C) Misused Detail; you don't know that Poe and Gaboriau did not also use tantalizing clues.
(D) Misused Detail; Poe and Gaboriau might also have created compelling protagonists.
(E) Misused Detail; the novels of Poe and Gaboriau may have also been popular.

10. **E**
Difficulty: Medium
Strategic Advice: Remember that the correct answer must directly answer the question. A choice can fit with an author's point of view and still be wrong.
Getting to the Answer: The author writes that this *blueprint ... has since become the foundation of an entire literary tradition*. Search for an answer choice that refers to Doyle's influence on later writers of detective fiction.
(A) Out-of-Scope; the author never states that Doyle's stories were unusually well-crafted.
(B) Distortion; the author would likely agree with this statement, but this answer choice leaves out the sense that Doyle influenced other writers.
(C) Out-of-Scope; although Doyle's work might have been somewhat formulaic, the word *too* doesn't fit with the author's positive point of view.
(D) Out-of-Scope; the author never discusses the extent to which Doyle was influenced by the inventors of the detective story.
(E) Good match.

Sarcophagi

11. **E**
Difficulty: Low
Strategic Advice: Some questions that ask about an author's attitude require you to summarize the main idea of the passage.
Getting to the Answer: The author describes the sarcophagi as *elegant examples of sculptural artistry*. Look for a choice that sums this up.
(A) Distortion; although the sarcophagi served many functions for the ancient Egyptians, *it is as art objects that they are most valued today*.
(B) Distortion; this is the opinion of author 2, not author 1.
(C) Distortion; the sarcophagi conveyed *biographical and historical information* to the *Egyptians*, but today they are primarily sculptural objects.
(D) Out-of-Scope; although the pieces *often serve as a focal point of a museum's collection*, the author never indicates that this is a wise investment.
(E) This sums up the author's attitude.

12. **C**
Difficulty: Low
Strategic Advice: On Paired Passage questions, watch out for questions that include details from the wrong passage.
Getting to the Answer: Author 2 says that displaying an artifact in a stark room *divorces the object from its original context, robbing the viewer of a deeper understanding of the work*. So, the author thinks that museums should help viewers understand the original context of an object.
(A) Opposite; the author thinks that museums should highlight the meaning of objects, rather than just displaying them as works of art.
(B) Misused Detail; this phrase comes from Passage 1, not Passage 2. Although author 2 argues for more context and thus might condone the *historical information*, there's nothing in Passage 2 to suggest the need for *biographical information*.
(C) Perfect.
(D) Distortion; the author cites the example of the temple, but this doesn't mean that all displays should include Egyptian temples. It wouldn't be

appropriate for an exhibition of, say, Native American artifacts.
(E) Misused Detail; this phrase comes from Passage 1, not Passage 2, which contains no mention of *social status*.

13. **D**

Difficulty: Medium
Strategic Advice: Beware of a choice like (C) that fits the general sense of the passage but doesn't match the exact word in question.
Getting to the Answer: The museum *attempted to address* the problem by constructing a temple. This was a solution to the problem, so here *address* means solve.
(A) It doesn't make sense to *reposition* a problem.
(B) This answer choice might trap people who are thinking of an *address* as an indicator of a location, but the meaning doesn't fit here.
(C) This choice is tempting, but be careful. You can say that the museum is *improving* a situation but not that they are *improving* the problem itself.
(D) Sounds good.
(E) This is the opposite of what you're looking for.

14. **A**

Difficulty: High
Strategic Advice: Tough questions hinge on subtle shades of meaning, so examine the exact meaning of the choices carefully.
Getting to the Answer: Author 2 feels that artifacts should not be treated simply as beautiful objects; rather, they also should be displayed in order to show the meaning of the objects. The description in Passage 1 concentrates on the beauty of the objects and therefore doesn't tell the whole story.
(A) This fits well.
(B) Opposite; author 2 would probably say that it's unfortunate that author 1 is missing out on the sarcophagi's *deeper meaning*.
(C) Opposite; the author feels that the objects are *beautiful artifacts* and would agree with the description but would feel it's incomplete.
(D) Distortion; this answer choice leaves out the idea that the description doesn't tell the whole story.
(E) Distortion; although the description is incomplete, it's not actually *misleading*, since the objects are in fact beautiful.

Henrik Ibsen

15. **D**

Difficulty: Medium
Strategic Advice: Several questions test your ability to understand references from a word or phrase to another part of the passage.
Getting to the Answer: What are the divisions that Freeman has left behind? *Previously, scholars limited themselves to a particular phase of Ibsen's career.* Freeman doesn't do this, so the divisions are between the phases of Ibsen's writing.
(A) Extreme; the author wouldn't describe previous scholarship as *unsuccessful*.
(B) Out-of-Scope; there is no discussion of Ibsen himself taking breaks.
(C) Out-of-Scope; the author doesn't mention any result that has followed from Freeman's book.
(D) This matches your prediction.
(E) Out-of-Scope; the *arbitrary divisions* refer to the previous scholarship, not Freeman's reaction to that scholarship.
rift: divide

16. **B**

Difficulty: Medium
Strategic Advice: Let the author's tone help you quickly eliminate wrong choices.
Getting to the Answer: Considering this author's positive attitude towards Freeman's book, the sentence must be high praise. The author is pointing out that this book will be important for a long time.
(A) Opposite; this negative tone doesn't fit at all.
(B) Good match.
(C) Out-of-Scope; the author doesn't discuss obstacles that Freeman faced.
(D) Opposite; the author never states that Freeman's work is unclear.
(E) Out-of-Scope; the author makes no attempt to paraphrase Freeman.

17 **C**

Difficulty: High
Strategic Advice: For an Inference question that covers the entire passage, keep the author's main point in mind. At the same time, make sure that you can defend your answer with a specific point in the passage.
Getting to the Answer: Author 2 does find some nice things to say about Freeman's book: *This experiment, while yielding some interesting*

observations, does not serve as a useful scholarly model. But, his overall opinion is that the book lacks depth—too much simplification.

(A) Opposite; *overwhelming* is ok, but *not idealistic* is the opposite of the author's viewpoint. The author does think Freeman's project is too idealistic.

(B) Opposite; *feasible* means possible or attainable, just the opposite of author 2's view.

(C) Correct; author 2 says that Freeman *exhibits tremendous dedication*, so *admirable* fits well. The author also thinks Freeman's project is too ambitious or, in other words, *not successful*.

(D) Opposite; author 2 thinks that the attempt is *not viable*.

(E) The author never indicates that a work covering Ibsen's entire career is *desirable*. *viable*: feasible, possible

18. **A**

Difficulty: Medium

Strategic Advice: When a question involves several different viewpoints, take a moment to get everything straight before you attack the answer choices.

Getting to the Answer: Before Freeman, scholars concentrated on a particular phase of Ibsen's career. These are the scholars mentioned in Passage 1. Since author 2 feels that Freeman tried to cover too much, he probably feels that scholars before Freeman took the right approach.

(A) Good match.

(B) Opposite; this is the opinion of author 1, not author 2.

(C) Misused Detail; author 1 describes the scholarship of Freeman in this way, but author 2 never speculates about the future.

(D) Opposite; author 2 feels that the scholars' approach is more appropriate than Freeman's.

(E) Out-of-Scope; there's no reason to believe that author 2 finds the scholars' work *difficult to assess*.

Waltham-Lowell System

Passage 1

The first paragraph of Passage 1 introduces the Waltham-Lowell system. It is described as a system of factory organization and rules implemented in the nineteenth century to increase profits. Then, you learn that, for economic reasons, women were preferred as factory workers. The second paragraph discusses the requirement that factory girls live in company boarding houses. The adverse consequences of this rule are described, but it is also pointed out that one of the reasons for this rule was to placate the girls' families. The third paragraph describes another problem with the boarding house regulation: health issues related to overcrowding and unsanitary conditions. The final paragraph concludes the passage with a partial justification of the Waltham-Lowell system and the factory leadership. The author argues that economic demands, including the threat of bankruptcy, made the poor conditions in American factories necessary.

Passage 2

The first paragraph of Passage 2 describes the Waltham-Lowell system as mandating atrocious factory conditions. The health risks of the system are detailed. The second paragraph then describes factory agents as supervisors who enforced regulations and often fired workers with little provocation. The third paragraph describes the practice of locking factory doors to keep workers inside the building. This led to a tragic accident at a factory in New York City, but the owners of the factory were not punished significantly. The final paragraph makes clear the author's opinion that the working conditions of the factories were inexcusable, regardless of economic conditions.

19. **A**

Difficulty: Low

Strategic Advice: In questions about the author's attitude, beware of extreme answer choices. The answer is often quite moderate.

Getting to the Answer: From the description of boarding-house life in the third paragraph, you know that the author feels sorry for the women. But the last paragraph suggests that the author also feels the conditions were perhaps necessary in order for the factories to be economically successful. Look for something that sums up these mixed feelings.

(A) *Sympathy* fits well, and *reserved* conveys the sense that the author feels the conditions were necessary.

(B) Opposite; the author is sympathetic, not *disinterested*.

(C) Opposite; again, the author is sympathetic, not *contemptuous*.

(D) Out of Scope; the author doesn't seem at all confused, so *befuddlement* doesn't fit.

(E) Extreme; the author might be appreciative of the workers, but *unreserved* is too extreme and doesn't fit the mixed feelings of your prediction.

contempt: attitude of regarding something as inferior

befuddlement: confusion

20. **B**

Difficulty: Medium

Strategic Advice: Treat a challenging Vocab-in-Context like a Sentence Completion problem.

Getting to the Answer: In the sentence in question, the author says that European boarding houses were even worse than their American counterparts. So even if you've never seen the word *base* used in this way, you know that it must be negative since it applies to the European boarding-house owners. Look for a negative word that could describe ethics, and keep in mind other meanings for the word *base*, like the base of a mountain.

(A) In this context, this word indicates that something is highly moral, the opposite of what you're looking for.

(B) *Immoral* ethics, that sounds good.

(C) Tempting meaning, but *absent* doesn't seem to match any of the other, more familiar meanings of *base*.

(D) Again tempting, but it's the actions that were *harmful*, not the ethics that motivated the actions.

(E) This matches *base*, but doesn't fit in the sentence. *Foundational* ethics? That makes no sense.

21. **A**

Difficulty: Medium

Strategic Advice: *According to Passage 1* tells you that this will ask about a specific detail. Use your Roadmap to find where the detail appears—don't try to answer from memory.

Getting to the Answer: Your Roadmap tells you that this detail appears in the second paragraph. Check out lines 16–18: "Primarily to assure families that their daughters would not be corrupted by factory life."

(A) Good match.

(B) Distortion; the passage discusses *factory* life, not *city* life.

(C) Misused Detail; the boarding houses spread— rather than prevented—disease.

(D) Out of Scope; the social activities of the workers are never discussed.

(E) Distortion; this was indeed an effect, as shown in the second sentence of the second paragraph, but it's not the reason that factory owners instituted the policy.

placate: soothe or calm.

22. **B**

Difficulty: Low

Strategic Advice: The correct answer in a Vocab-in-Context question won't just work in a particular sentence—it will also make the sentence work in the entire passage.

Getting to the Answer: Since *the economists advanced* an idea, *advanced* must be something that you can do with an idea. The final paragraph presents this idea, and the author seems to regard the idea as reasonable, so look for something that says the economists stated the idea.

(A) Typical meaning of *advanced*—but it doesn't fit here.

(B) When you read this back, it makes perfect sense.

(C) The word makes sense in the sentence, but then the sentence doesn't work with the rest of the paragraph. The author wouldn't talk about a group denying an idea that hasn't even been stated yet.

(D) Can you *progress* an idea? That doesn't make much sense.

(E) Like (C), this one sounds OK in the sentence, but that sentence then doesn't make sense in the paragraph as a whole.

23. **E**
Difficulty: High
Strategic Advice: For Reasoning questions, summarize the author's argument in your own words before looking at the answer choices.
Getting to the Answer: The author thinks that factory owners had no choice because they would have lost money and gone out of business if they had instituted better working conditions. Look for an answer choice that would weaken this argument.
(A) Out of Scope; tempting, but no. Conditions in France don't necessarily have anything to do with conditions in America. Maybe it's easier to run a factory in France for some reason that just doesn't apply in America.
(B) Out of Scope; maybe this Bennington system is even crueler to workers. We don't know anything about this Bennington system, so this fact doesn't weaken the argument.
(C) Opposite; this doesn't weaken the argument— it strengthens it. It just proves that it would have been a poor business strategy to improve working conditions.
(D) Out of Scope; maybe twentieth-century factories had technologies or other advantages not available to nineteenth-century factories. Since the situations are not the same, the improved twentieth-century conditions don't weaken the argument that poor conditions were necessary in the nineteenth century.
(E) This one fits. If factory owners had a way to improve conditions without lowering profits, then this weakens the author's argument that poor conditions were necessary.

24. **B**
Difficulty: Medium
Strategic Advice: In paired passages, it's extremely important to keep the authors straight. Don't fall for choices that mix up the authors' points of view.
Getting to the Answer: What part does this paragraph play in the passage as a whole? The author feels that the system created poor working conditions, and the second paragraph explains the part of agents in this process.
(A) Misused Detail; this comes from the author of Passage 1, not Passage 2.
(B) Matches your prediction.

(C) Misused Detail; the author speaks of the immorality of the system in the final, but not in the second, paragraph.
(D) Misused Detail; the fire isn't mentioned until the third paragraph.
(E) Misused Detail; again, this comes from Passage 1, not Passage 2.

25. **C**
Difficulty: Low
Strategic Advice: Read each answer choice carefully, and don't get caught in a trap: for example, (E) is wrong because of a single word.
Getting to the Answer: The third paragraph, which describes the fire, says that "the Waltham-Lowell system ...[was] downright dangerous." So, look for something that says the factory owners created dangerous conditions.
(A) Out-of-Scope; the author only mentions a single fire and doesn't suggest that such events happened often.
(B) Distortion; the author feels the accident was a tragedy, so sympathy wouldn't be *unwarranted*.
(C) Matches your prediction.
(D) Opposite; the author feels that factory owners didn't do enough to protect workers.
(E) Distortion; it's the factory owners, not the workers, who were negligent.
prevalence: frequency
negligent: careless
unwarranted: uncalled for

26. **E**
Difficulty: Medium
Strategic Advice: On Detail questions, watch out for answer choices that bring in irrelevant information from other parts of the passage.
Getting to the Answer: Reread the sentence in which the word appears. The author notes that one would hope that the tragedy would bring about change but that nothing much happened to the factory owners, and factories continued to lock their doors for several years.
(A) Distortion; the passage mentions twenty-three families, not twenty-three victims. There might have been victims whose families did not sue.
(B) Opposite; the next-to-last sentence in the third paragraph states that the owners were acquitted of criminal charges, so they *didn't* go to jail.

(C) Distortion; the practice of locking doors remained common, but we don't know that tragedies of this sort remained common since we don't know if fires continued to happen frequently.

(D) Misused Detail; the whale-oil lamps in the first paragraph created pollution, not fires.

(E) Matches the last two sentences of the paragraph.

27. C

Difficulty: Medium

Strategic Advice: If you're asked about the structure of a paragraph, go back and quickly reread each sentence to figure out what's going on.

Getting to the Answer: Author 2 mentions the view also held by author 1—that factory owners had to create poor working conditions in order to make money and stay in business. Author 2 then goes on to disagree and proposes that a system *of common decency* should have been used instead.

(A) No evidence is introduced in the final paragraph.

(B) No statistical evidence is introduced in the final paragraph.

(C) This matches your prediction.

(D) We don't know how widely held any of the views discussed are, and no historical evidence is presented in the final paragraph.

(E) The author doesn't say that there is a contradiction. To the author, the choice is clear: the factory owners were in the wrong.

28. A

Difficulty: Low

Strategic Advice: With paired passages, you will almost always see a question that asks you to pinpoint an issue or issues on which the two authors disagree.

Getting to the Answer: Both authors agree that the working conditions were bad, but they disagree in their final paragraphs. Author 1 states that the conditions were necessary in order for factories to stay in business, whereas author 2 states that the conditions were unacceptable and that another system should have been implemented.

(A) Here, the phrase *market conditions* means the economic situation, so this matches your prediction.

(B) Out-of-Scope; neither author mentions philanthropy.

(C) Opposite; both authors seem to agree that the system made American textile mills more competitive.

(D) Opposite; the authors agree that health problems arose from the system.

(E) Out-of-Scope; neither author mentions previous systems.

philanthropy: literally, love of humankind; charitable actions

29. B

Difficulty: Low

Strategic Advice: When asked about the differences between two authors, watch out for opposite answer choices.

Getting to the Answer: Both passages talk about poor conditions, but Passage 1 deals more with boarding houses, while Passage 2 deals with working conditions in the factories.

(A) Opposite; boarding houses are discussed in Passage 1, not Passage 2.

(B) Correct; this appears in the second paragraph of Passage 2 but never appears in Passage 1.

(C) Opposite; this is discussed by both authors.

(D) Opposite; this appears in Passage 1 but not Passage 2.

(E) Out-of-Scope; safety supervisors are not mentioned in either paragraph.

30. B

Difficulty: Low

Strategic Advice: Remember to consult your Roadmap if you need to find a detail quickly.

Getting to the Answer: There are too many possibilities here to make a prediction, so get your Roadmaps of the passages ready and eliminate anything that doesn't appear in both passages.

(A) Opposite; this is mentioned in Passage 2 but not Passage 1.

(B) The final paragraph of Passage 2 and the third paragraph of Passage 1 both mention that health problems were caused by factory conditions.

(C) Opposite; this is mentioned in Passage 1 but not Passage 2.

(D) Out-of-Scope; this is not mentioned in either passage.

(E) Opposite; both authors stress that factory owners were anything but generous.

Moby Dick

Passage 1

This is a very challenging passage. Because it was written a long time ago, the style is old fashioned and a lot of the vocabulary is difficult. Remember, though, that you don't need to understand every word to do well on the questions for a passage. In fact, you can often skip an entire sentence and still do just fine.

In paragraph 1, the author indicates that he's not at all fond of *Moby Dick*. He says that it seems like Melville is testing the reader's patience and that this book is more *exaggerated* and *dull* than Melville's previous works. Paragraph 2 notes that the book is a strange blend of story and fact, and the writer feels that the book doesn't work as either. In paragraph 3, the author writes that the first couple of Melville's books were okay, but, in his subsequent works, he has gone downhill. Melville should have stopped while he was ahead, but he ruined his reputation with *Moby Dick*.

Passage 2

This passage is modern and a little easier to handle. Paragraph 1 cites the opinions of critics (like author 1) who feel that *Moby Dick* has too much information unrelated to the plot. Author 2 disagrees, and the rest of the passage describes why. Paragraph 2 notes that Melville needed the reader to consider the whale to be a worthy rival for Ahab. This was a challenge, since the whale can't speak. In Paragraph 3, the author notes that Melville chose to educate the reader in order to illuminate the character of the whale. Consequently, the book has lots of information about whales and the sea. Paragraph 4 notes that there is also plenty of information about the process of whaling—hunting and killing whales. The author feels that this information gives the reader a better picture of Ahab's obsession.

31. **A**

Difficulty: High

Strategic Advice: Be careful with questions that ask about a term or phrase that the author uses sarcastically.

Getting to the Answer: This appears in the first paragraph, where author 1 states that each of Melville's works has gotten worse. They have *advanced* only in negative qualities such as *vanity*

and being *clumsy* and *ineffective* So, the author is using the term sarcastically.

(A) This matches your prediction.

(B) Out-of-scope; there is no mention of other authors anywhere in the passage.

(C) Opposite; this is tempting if you didn't read paragraph 1 carefully.

(D) Distortion; author 1 says that the novel was an advance in efforts at innovation, but he means it in a negative way. The innovation was clumsy and ineffective.

(E) Misused Detail; the author would agree with this, but it doesn't come up until paragraph 2.

32. **B**

Difficulty: Medium

Strategic Advice: Especially on tough passages, you can often get several questions right just based on the author's tone.

Getting to the Answer: Since the author hates *Moby Dick* so much, the quotes around *fine writing* are used to show that he doesn't really believe it to be fine at all.

(A) Opposite; even if you don't understand much of the passage, it should be clear that the author doesn't hold the novel in high esteem.

(B) Good match.

(C) Out-of-Scope; the author doesn't mention any other critics.

(D) Distortion; tempting, but the author is using the word *success* sarcastically. Melville was successful only in showing that his writing was poor. Even if you didn't fully understand this sentence, you could eliminate it because it is far too positive.

(E) Out-of-Scope; there is no indication that Melville actually used the term *fine writing* himself.

33. **D**

Difficulty: Medium

Strategic Advice: Like Detail questions, Inference questions often require you to go back and read several sentences to understand the context of a phrase.

Getting to the Answer: The author believes that the book is *an ill-compounded mixture* of a novel and an instructional work. So, when he says that *the idea of a connected and collected story has obviously visited and abandoned its writer again and again*, he is implying that the plot appears

and disappears as you read the book since it's interrupted by the factual sections.
(A) Distortion; this is the opinion of author 2, but it's much too positive for author 1.
(B) Opposite; in paragraph 1, the author makes exactly the opposite claim.
(C) Out-of-Scope; the author says that the novel is a strange blend of both kinds of material but doesn't describe one as more prevalent.
(D) Good match.
(E) Distortion; this interpretation is too literal. Also, since the author describes Melville as vain and over-confident, it seems unlikely author 1 would attribute *periods of doubt* to Melville.

34. **C**
Difficulty: Medium
Strategic Advice: Some sentences from Reading Comp passages are constructed much like Sentence Completions. A word is immediately followed by a phrase that provides a definition.
Getting to the Answer: Right after the quoted phrase, you read *neither so compelling as to be entertaining, nor so instructively complete as to take place among documents on the subject of the Great Whale*, In other words, the book doesn't work as a novel or an instructional document.
(A) Out-of-scope; the author never says that whaling is an unusual subject for a book.
(B) Misused Detail; the author does say this in paragraph 1, but not in paragraph 2, where the *strange book* reference occurs.
(C) Good match.
(D) Out-of-Scope; this is mentioned in Passage 2, but not in Passage 1.
(E) Misused Detail; the author does say this, but it's not mentioned in the sentence that explains why he considers *Moby Dick* a strange book.

35. **E**
Difficulty: High
Strategic Advice: Treat Inference questions about tone like global questions—consider the entire passage.
Getting to the Answer: Look for a choice that captures the writer's highly critical tone.
(A) Opposite; this is the opinion of author 2, not author 1.
(B) Distortion; the author does note that Melville was ambitious but would not agree with the word *greatness*.

(C) Extreme; the author doesn't like *Moby Dick*, but that doesn't mean it's *always* a bad idea to include instructional elements.
(D) Distortion; this is the thesis of Passage 2, not Passage 1.
(E) This is supported in two places. In paragraph 1, the author notes that Melville's novels are getting worse, and in paragraph 3, he writes that Melville should have stopped while he was ahead.

36. **C**
Difficulty: Low
Strategic Advice: Remember that you can usually answer Vocab-in-Context questions, even when you don't understand the passage as a whole.
Getting to the Answer: the word *admittedly* indicates that the author feels that, though the passages are important, the author knows that they are a little *dry* or *boring*.
(A) This is a common meaning of dry, but it makes no sense here.
(B) The context doesn't suggest that the passages are *ironic*.
(C) Good match.
(D) This is the opposite of what you're looking for.
(E) This doesn't make sense after the word *admittedly*.

37. **D**
Difficulty: Low
Strategic Advice: Function questions often focus on features of a passage that stand out, such as the rhetorical questions at the end of paragraph 2.
Getting to the Answer: In paragraph 2, the author illustrates the importance of making the whale a well-developed character, and the questions at the end of paragraph help to describe the problems involved in this task.
(A) Opposite; the author feels that Melville's techniques are highly effective.
(B) Distortion; these are questions asked by author 2, not by Melville's characters.
(C) Opposite; this choice is too negative in tone to fit with the passage.
(D) Good match.
(E) Distortion; this is tempting, but be careful. The questions at the end of paragraph 2 show a problem. It's Melville's solution to that problem that forms *an unusual approach to the form of the novel*.

38 **E**
Difficulty: Medium
Strategic Advice: In questions that ask you to find a similarity between two things, watch out for Out-of-Scope choices that refer to only one of the entities.
Getting to the Answer: The passage notes that Dickens described London in order to *create a sense of light and shade on his characters*, and Melville described the sea *in order to more fully reveal the character of Moby Dick*. So, both authors described places in order to add to the descriptions of their characters.
(A) Out-of-Scope; the author doesn't describe London or the underwater environment as *dark or mysterious*.
(B) Misused Detail; this is true of Melville, but the author never indicates that this is true of Dickens.
(C) Distortion; although some of Melville's techniques may be unusual, the author never says this about Dickens's work.
(D) Opposite; the author feels that it adds to each author's novel in a positive way.
(E) Good match.

39. **A**
Difficulty: Low
Strategic Advice: It's rare, but not unheard of, for a Vocab-in-Context question to ask about a very short phase rather than a single word.
Getting to the Answer: Melville devoted several chapters to describing the process of hunting and killing a whale, so a good prediction would be that he worked hard to clearly portray the techniques and culture of whaling.
(A) Good match.
(B) The word *pains* might make this a tempting choice, but it doesn't fit in the sentence.
(C) The author feels that the attempts to describe whaling were successful.
(D) He doesn't just make it possible, he actually does the describing.
(E) The author would agree that Melville was wise to describe whaling, but this doesn't follow from the phrase *takes considerable pains*.

40. **C**
Difficulty: Medium
Strategic Advice: As the questions shift to focus on both passages, be especially careful to keep straight the viewpoints of the two authors.

Getting to the Answer: Author 1 feels that *Moby Dick* was unsuccessful both as a novel and as an information work. In paragraph 2 of Passage 2, author 2 argues against exactly this point. He says that critics who dismiss *Moby Dick* as a treatise on whaling *fail to realize that Melville is ... advancing the plot*. In other words, critics like author 1 just don't get it.
(A) Opposite; this is the opinion of author 1, not author 2.
(B) Misused Detail; this addresses only the issue of the descriptions of ocean plant life and not the bigger issue of the many parts of *Moby Dick* that convey information about whales and whaling.
(C) Good match.
(D) Opposite; again, this is the view of author 1, not author 2.
(E) Opposite; author 2 says that the information is important, but *dry*.

41. **D**
Difficulty: Low
Strategic Advice: Open-ended questions like this one often yield best to elimination rather than a prediction.
Getting to the Answer: The authors don't agree about much, so go through the answer choices and eliminate anything that applies only to one of the authors.
(A) Opposite; this applies only to author 2.
(B) Misused Detail; this is only mentioned in passage 2.
(C) Opposite; only author 2 discusses sense of place.
(D) Correct; this is discussed in paragraph 2 of Passage 1 and is the main focus of Passage 2.
(E) Misused Detail; only Passage 1 discussed Melville's previous works.

42. **A**
Difficulty: Low
Strategic Advice: Note that this question asks about the reaction of author 1 to the critics cited in Passage 2. It's *not* asking about his reaction to author 2.
Getting to the Answer: The *critics* feel that *Moby Dick* is a *treatise on whaling* and *that alternating such discursive material with the narrative detracts* from the work. Author 1 would agree with this, since he also feels that the book doesn't have a continuous narrative.

Critical Reading: Reading Comprehension Questions

(A) Correct; author 1 would agree with the critics.
(B) Opposite; author 1 doesn't feel that readers should be more patient with Melville.
(C) Opposite; author 2 might agree with this assessment, but author 1 would not.
(D) Opposite; author 1 thinks that the critics are right on track.
(E) Distortion; author 1 says that it's Melville who is too *ambitious*, not his readers.

43. **B**

Difficulty: Low
Strategic Advice: Global questions on tough passages often require only that you understand the general gist of the passage or passages.
Getting to the Answer: Sum up the positions of each author in your mind. Author 1 feels that Melville is lousy, while author 2 thinks Melville is great.
(A) Opposite; author 1 would definitely deny that Melville is *excellent*.
(B) Perfect.
(C) Distortion; author 1 doesn't seem to find the work particularly *noteworthy*.
(D) Out-of-scope; *Moby Dick* is the only Melville work that author 2 discusses, so there's no evidence that this is an improvement over other works.
(E) Opposite; author 1 states that *Moby Dick* is a blend of a plotline and other, nonfictional elements.

Thomas and the Farm

Paragraph 1 establishes the location and characterizes Thomas's feelings about growing up on a farm. Paragraph 2 gives a bit of the history of the farm and Thomas's family's experience with it, while in the paragraph 3, Thomas's relationship with his father is explored. In paragraph 4, you learn more about Thomas's family, especially his father. Paragraph 5 provides you with the root of the conflict in the story: despite his father's efforts, the farm would not survive another generation in the family. In paragraph 6, you learn that Thomas is an adult, looking over the farm (now a construction site) one last time, while a flood of associated thoughts and feelings wash over him. Paragraph 7 conveys the conclusion that Thomas reaches: like his father, Thomas has discovered a personal investment in, and a connection to, the land, and he will miss it.

As is true in many narrative passages, it is important here to monitor the feelings of the main character (in this case, Thomas) and what those feelings tell you. Without being aware of the emotional undercurrent of Thomas's thoughts, you could overlook the realization he reaches at the end of the story and its relationship to the various moments he contemplates in the narrative.

44. **B**

Difficulty: High
Strategic Advice: Function questions sometimes require you to go beyond what appears on the page and speculate about the author's motivation in writing something.
Getting to the Answer: Once you understand that the first part of the passage takes place at various times in the main character's past, you can infer that *yesterday* does not literally mean the day before today, but is used metaphorically to indicate a compression of time, as in the phrase *it felt like it was just yesterday*.
(A) Distortion; *urgency* implies a sense of pressure and, perhaps, danger. There is no particular urgency in observing an empty field.
(B) This matches the sense of *just yesterday* you predicted.
(C) Distortion; Thomas may be recollecting accurately, but the author isn't writing the sentence in order to convey this—after all, Thomas's powers of recollection are never referred to in the passage.

(D) Distortion; although Thomas is *contemplating* in a very general way, it doesn't seem very *purposeful*. That is, he's not contemplating in order to accomplish something.

(E) Distortion; there is a strong sense of the passage of time in the story as a whole, but the first sentence alone does not convey this.

45. **D**
Difficulty: Medium
Strategic Advice: Always be suspicious of the everyday, primary meanings of words in Vocab-in-Context questions.
Getting to the Answer: The paragraph describes Thomas as a young boy running through a forest of corn. The sentence in which *spears* is found describes the corn as towering and green. So, you are looking for a word that fits in with this general description of the corn.

(A) This fits with the word *towers*, with no relation to corn.

(B) This is a little too vague, since *structures* doesn't convey that the corn stalks were tall and thin.

(C) This is the primary meaning of *spears*, but not the correct one in this context.

(D) This is a good fit with the word spears and with the general description of the corn.

(E) Like (B), this sounds too dangerous to fit.
spire: a tall tower, often in a castle or church

46. **A**
Difficulty: High
Strategic Advice: Some Function questions can't be answered without considering the passage as a whole.
Getting to the Answer: Why would the author repeat the idea *leaving the corn was easy*? It may not make much sense when you first read it, but by the time you finish the passage, you see that the entire story is about Thomas leaving life on the farm. So the author is giving you a hint ahead of time.

(A) Good match.

(B) It may convey this, but the author probably also has some other, more important, meaning in mind. Otherwise, it probably wouldn't be the subject of a question.

(C) The author never indicates that Thomas's life was particularly simple. Also, it's hard to see how a sentence about cornfields could convey this.

(D) This is a theme of the passage, but it's not discussed in the first paragraph.

(E) Thomas did seem to enjoy himself, but the idea that it's easy to leave a cornfield doesn't have a very direct relationship to this.

47. **D**
Difficulty: Medium
Strategic Advice: Vocabulary-in-context questions send you back to the passage; read the sentences before and after the sentence in which the word appears.
Getting to the Answer: All of the chores listed look pretty tough, so look for a word that means something like tiring.

(A) Related to a common meaning of *taxing*, but not appropriate here.

(B) Again, related to a more common meaning of taxing.

(C) Opposite; these chores sound anything but *rejuvenating*.

(D) Exactly.

(E) No, all of these chores sound like skills one would need to learn.
rejuvenating: making young and energized

48. **C**
Difficulty: High
Strategic Advice: The answer to this question will come from the passage as a whole, not from one particular sentence or word.
Getting to the Answer: Throughout the passage you are given clues, from both Thomas's father's words and actions, about what the father believes: a person should work hard and own land. In other words, the father is *self-reliant*.

(A) Opposite; in the fourth paragraph, we read that Thomas's father is *a man of the earth*. This is the opposite of *aristocratic*.

(B) Opposite; Thomas's father seems quite wise.

(C) Good match.

(D) Opposite; again, *man of the earth* doesn't seem very compatible with this choice.

(E) Distortion; while Thomas's father seems to have had strong opinions, the passage doesn't suggest that he was inflexible.
aristocratic: belonging to the nobility
autonomous: self-ruling
cosmopolitan: highly sophisticated and at home all over the world
dogmatic: inflexible and overbearing

49. B
Difficulty: Medium
Strategic Advice: Wrong answer choices on questions like this one will almost certainly contain details from the wrong part of the passage.
Getting to the Answer: In the sentence in question, you learn that Thomas and his father would ride the enormous thresher during harvest time.
(A) Misuse of Detail; mending fences is mentioned in the second, not the third, paragraph.
(B) It's used during harvest time, so this makes sense.
(C) Misuse of Detail; shopping malls are mentioned in the final paragraph, not paragraph 3.
(D) Distortion; planting seeds would happen at the beginning, not the end, of a growing cycle.
(E) Misuse of Detail; surveying land is mentioned in the paragraph 6, not paragraph 3.

50. C
Difficulty: Medium
Strategic Advice: Inference questions require you to put information together and draw a conclusion.
Getting to the Answer: The quote indicates that Thomas's father feels strongly about the need to own land—so strongly, in fact, that he defines manhood by whether or not a man has land of his own.
(A) Misuse of Detail; while it's true that the corn is fetching lower prices each year, there's no indication that the father is discouraged by this fact.
(B) Opposite; the father seems like he enjoys the farm work—in any case, we certainly can't infer that he is discouraged by the amount of work he needs to do.
(C) This fits nicely with the summary above.
(D) Out-of-Scope; Thomas's father may indeed be pleased that Thomas is with him, but the passage doesn't say so, and the quote doesn't refer to this.
(E) Out-of-Scope; again, this may or may not be true—the passage does not discuss the topic.

51. E
Difficulty: Medium
Strategic Advice: Questions like this one are particularly susceptible to elimination strategies.
Getting to the Answer: The paragraph in which this sentence appears emphasizes that the father knew his sons did not share his own interest in

farm work. Instead, the brothers were into having a good time.
(A) Misuse of Detail; we don't hear about the brothers as adults until the end of the passage, and then, their interests don't necessarily contrast with those of their youth.
(B) Misuse of Detail; actually, you are never given reasons for why Thomas performed his brothers' chores—you are only told that he sometimes did so.
(C) Distortion; although the brothers and father didn't share the same values, there's no mention of actual conflict between them. Maybe they just agreed to disagree.
(D) Distortion; this doesn't appear until the final paragraph.
(E) There is indeed a dichotomy between the values of the brothers and the father. If you didn't know the word, you could instead eliminate the other four choices.
dichotomy: a division between two, usually conflicting, parts

52. E
Difficulty: Medium
Strategic Advice: Remember that inferences on the SAT follow very directly from the evidence. You shouldn't do too much work to make a choice fit.
Getting to the Answer: Immediately following the line about Thomas's father's *secret despair*, you read, *The land that had been in his family for three generations was not valued by the fourth*. From that, you can infer that the father is sad that the farm will not be cared for by Thomas and his brothers.
(A) Opposite; in the fifth paragraph, the author states that *little Tommy helped out as much as he was able*.
(B) Distortion; although Thomas's brothers did have these interests, we don't know that the father was worried about them.
(C) Distortion; while the author says that Thomas's father could probably have gone to college, you don't know that he regrets not having done so.
(D) Out-of-Scope; we don't hear anything about the marriage.
(E) This is a good paraphrase of your prediction.

53. **A**

Difficulty: High

Strategic Advice: As always with function questions, answer the question "Why?"

Getting to the Answer: The author goes to some trouble in paragraph 6 to show that the farm is now gone and that many things have changed. Everything in the first five paragraphs happened in the past.

(A) This reflects the shift in time described above.

(B) Distortion; you don't learn much about Thomas's present life in the sixth paragraph, so it doesn't make sense to say the author is contrasting the past and present of Thomas's life.

(C) Opposite; reverse chronology would be from the present to the past, but this story goes from the past to the present.

(D) Out-of-Scope; if paragraph six were a summary of the plot, then it would contain references to the action that took place in the previous paragraphs.

(E) Out-of-Scope; there's no indication in this paragraph of what lies ahead for Thomas. *foreshadow*: to indicate what will happen in the future

54. **A**

Difficulty: Medium

Strategic Advice: Inference questions require you to put information together and draw a conclusion.

Getting to the Answer: By the end of the passage it's clear that Thomas is more in sympathy with his father's feelings about the farm than he had perhaps realized and certainly more than his brothers are. He feels he's losing his home, and he's sad about that; he wishes that it were still his home.

(A) Both *nostalgia* and *regretful* fit well.

(B) Opposite; Thomas seems a bit melancholy, the opposite of this choice.

(C) Out-of-Scope; there's nothing in Thomas's thoughts or behavior that indicates anger.

(D) Extreme; while Thomas may be a bit sad, this is way too extreme.

(E) Out-of-scope; nothing in the passage suggests relief.

Monet and Impressionism

The passage traces the development of Impressionism, noting especially the contributions of Claude Monet. Paragraph 1 describes the gradual development of Impressionism under Monet and his colleagues. The author concentrates on the artistic goals and techniques of the artists. Paragraph 2 explores how the development of photography helped create a new role for painting—a role embraced by the Impressionists. Paragraph 3 explores the critical reception of the Impressionists. Their contemporaries disparaged their works, but these paintings today *are some of the most prized works in the art world*.

55. **D**

Difficulty: Medium

Strategic Advice: A quick scan at the first word of each answer choice can often help you rule out several choices.

Getting to the Answer: With answer choices like these, look at the beginning verbs. Think first of the tone of the passage, which in this case is pretty neutral—the author gives a brief history of Impressionism with a focus on Claude Monet. Eliminate all verbs that are not in keeping with that tone.

(A) Extreme; the word *condemn* is too negative.

(B) Out-of-Scope; the author doesn't talk about the other painters enough for the word *contrast* to work here.

(C) Distortion; the word *describe* sounds good, but this choice is too specific. The author doesn't talk too much about the paintings themselves, and this choice leaves out the bigger picture of Impressionism in general.

(D) This explains the overall purpose pretty well.

(E) Distortion; the author never really *argues* for anything here. The purpose is simply to describe or explain.

56. **D**

Difficulty: Medium

Strategic Advice: In EXCEPT questions, you're looking for four *true* statements and one *false* one; the *false* one is the correct answer to the question.

Getting to the Answer: Hunt for each of these details in the passage.

(A) *This group ... made it a common practice among them to paint the same scene many times in a day....*
(B) *...an interest that led him to attempt to paint light itself rather than the objects off of which light reflected.*
(C) *...using small patches of colors rather than the large brush strokes and blended color...*
(D) This is the opposite of what happened, as described in paragraph 3. People didn't like the paintings at first.
(E) *This freed the Impressionists to find new roles for their medium and encouraged the public to think about painting in a new way.*

57. D
Difficulty: Medium
Strategic Advice: In Function questions, be sure to consider the role of a detail in both the paragraph and the passage as a whole.
Getting to the Answer: At the end of paragraph 1, where this phrase occurs, the author mentions that the Impressionists used a technique— patches of colors—to capture the light. This is different, she states, from the large brush strokes and blended color that characterized painting techniques to this time.
(A) Distortion; while it's true that the Impressionists painted outdoors, the author never offers a description of the light they encountered there.
(B) Extreme; the author says that the Impressionists were innovators but never implies that the old paintings were inferior.
(C) Extreme; you don't know from the passage that *all* modern painters used this technique—you only know that the Impressionists did.
(D) This is a good fit.
(E) Out-of-scope; this comes from the wrong part of the passage—it's from paragraph 2.

58. C
Difficulty: Medium
Strategic Advice: With Function questions, be sure to answer, "Why?"
Getting to the Answer: The author mentions photography in paragraph 2. She says that photography took over some of painting's traditional documentary role, so painters began to think about painting in a new way.

(A) Opposite; photography filled some of the same needs as traditional painting, but the author is not contrasting the two media.
(B) Extreme; it is an influencing factor but not necessarily the most important one.
(C) This matches your prediction.
(D) Out-of-Scope; the description of the critical and public reception of Impressionism occurs in paragraph 3, whereas the discussion of photography takes place in paragraph 2.
(E) Out-of-Scope; the author does mention that photography and painting can fill some of the same roles (documentation), but a comparison of the two media is not the author's purpose.

59. B
Difficulty: Low
Strategic Advice: Even though the author uses several adjectives to describe photography, you need only one.
Getting to the Answer: According to the author, photographs took over much of the documentary role that paintings held previously because photography is faster, more accurate, and less expensive. So, you need a word that means either faster, more accurate or less expensive.
(A) Opposite; the author says that photography is less expensive than painting.
(B) *Precise* is a pretty close synonym for accurate, so this is a good fit.
(C) Opposite; the author says that photography is accurate, so this doesn't fit.
(D) Out-of-Scope; there's nothing in the passage to indicate that photography is particularly *consistent* (or inconsistent, for that matter).
(E) Out-of-Scope; the author never addresses the prestige of photography.

60. A
Difficulty: High
Strategic Advice: Complex Inference questions ask you to distinguish between the opinions of the author and other parties.
Getting to the Answer: The author writes that *such a critic would be in the minority today*. What does she mean by *such a critic*? The previous sentence says that a critic considered the Impressionist painting to be incomplete, so look for an opinion that fits with this outlook.
(A) This fits well with the critic described in the passage.

(B) Distortion; this is the opinion of the author, not the critic.

(C) Out-of-Scope; the critic described didn't much like the painting and might or might not describe it as influential.

(D) Distortion; although the author would certainly agree with this, you don't know the critic's opinion on the subject.

(E) Opposite; the critic doesn't like the paintings, so the word *rightly* makes this a statement that the critic would disagree with.

61. **C**

Difficulty: Low

Strategic Advice: Avoid common meanings in Vocab-in-Context questions.

Getting to the Answer: Critics and the public are now very fond of the Impressionists, so the word *prized* here means *valued*.

(A) This might be tempting, since prizes are awarded, but the passage doesn't indicate that awards are given to the paintings.

(B) The paintings are well-known, so it doesn't make sense to say they are *discovered*.

(C) Perfect.

(D) Like (A), this is related to the sense of giving out prizes or awards and doesn't fit here.

(E) The paintings are highly sought after, but this isn't conveyed by the word *prized*.

Math Questions

Information

$A = \frac{1}{2}bh$ $c^2 = a^2 + b^2$ Special Right Triangles $A = \pi r^2$ $C = 2\pi r$ $V = \ell wh$ $V = \pi r^2 h$ $A = \ell w$

The sum of the degree measures of the angles in a triangle is 180.
The number of degrees of arc in a circle is 360.
A straight angle has a degree measure of 180.

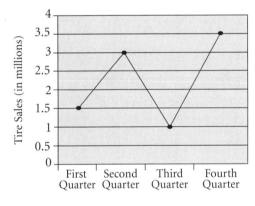

1 What is the percent increase from the third quarter to the fourth quarter for the tire sales represented in the chart above?

(A)   2.5%
(B)   40%
(C)   71.5%
(D)   100%
(E)   250%

2 Jeweler A can set an average round-cut diamond in 20 minutes. Jeweler B requires 15 minutes to set the same type of diamond. In 8 hours, how many more diamonds can be set by Jeweler B than by Jeweler A?

(A) 40
(B) 24
(C) 16
(D)   8
(E)   1

Figure 1   Figure 2

3 Based on the information in Figure 1 above, what is the value of y in Figure 2?

(A) 10
(B) 20
(C) 30
(D) 40
(E) 120

4 The force needed to stretch a spring varies directly with the distance the spring is stretched from its equilibrium position. If 50 pounds of force stretch a spring 8 inches from equilibrium, how much, in inches, will the spring be stretched by a force of 75 pounds?

(A) 10
(B) 12
(C) 33
(D) 248
(E) 468.75

5 If $x^{\frac{y}{2}} = 64$, where x and y are positive integers and $x > y$, what is the value of $x + y$?

(A) 4
(B) 7
(C) 8
(D) 10
(E) 12

6 If $n > 0$, what is the value of $3^{\frac{n}{2}} + 3^{\frac{n}{2}} + 3^{\frac{n}{2}}$?

(A) $\frac{3}{2}(3^{\frac{n}{2}})$

(B) $3^{\frac{n}{6}}$

(C) $3^{\frac{n}{2}+1}$

(D) $3^{\frac{3n}{2}}$

(E) $9^{\frac{n}{2}}$

7 If $f(x) = 3x - 8$ and $g(x) = \sqrt{2x^2 + 7}$, what is the value of $f(g(3))$?

(A) 1
(B) 3
(C) 5
(D) 7
(E) 9

9 If $-1 < N < 1$ and $N \neq 0$, which of the following statements is always true?

$$\text{I} \quad N < 2N$$

$$\text{II} \quad N^2 > N$$

$$\text{III} \quad N^2 < \frac{1}{N^2}$$

(A) I only
(B) II only
(C) III only
(D) I and III
(E) II and III

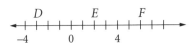

8 On the number line above, each of the letters D, E, and F corresponds to a different number. Which of those letters could correspond to the value of x if $|3 - x| > 5$?

(A) D only
(B) E only
(C) F only
(D) D or F
(E) D, E, F

10 If X is the set of positive multiples of 2, and Y is the set of positive multiples of 3, then the intersection of X and Y is:

(A) the set of all positive integers
(B) the set of all positive real numbers
(C) the set of positive multiples of 3
(D) the set of positive multiples of 5
(E) the set of positive multiples of 6

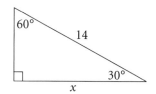

11 What is the value of x in the figure above?

(A) 7
(B) $7\sqrt{3}$
(C) $14\sqrt{3}$
(D) 28
(E) $28\sqrt{3}$

13 The sum of two consecutive positive integers is never divisible by

(A) 2
(B) 3
(C) 5
(D) 7
(E) 211

12 On a certain test, a class of 12 students has an average (arithmetic mean) score of 80. A second class of 18 students has an average score of 85. What is the average score of the combined classes?

(A) 82
(B) 82.5
(C) 83
(D) 84
(E) 84.5

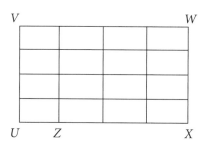

14 In the figure above, rectangle $UVWX$ is divided into sixteen identical rectangles, four to a column and four to a row, as shown above. The ratio of the length to the width of each rectangle is 2 to 1. If rectangle $UVWX$ has an area of 72 square units, what is the length of $\overline{UZ}$?

(A) 1.5
(B) 2
(C) 3
(D) 4
(E) 12

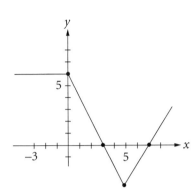

15 The graph of $f(x)$ is shown above. For what values of x does $f(x)$ have a negative slope?

(A) $x > 0$
(B) $x > 3$
(C) $x > 5$
(D) $0 < x < 5$
(E) $3 < x\ 7$

17 a, b, and x are positive integers, and $\begin{array}{c} x \\ a \diagdown b \end{array}$ is defined as the number of different triangles with sides of lengths a, b, and x.

Given $\begin{array}{c} x \\ 2 \diagdown 7 \end{array}$, which is a possible value of x?

(A) 2
(B) 3
(C) 4
(D) 5
(E) 6

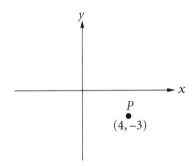

16 In the figure above, a line is to be drawn through point P so that it has a slope of 0. Through which of the following points must the line pass?

(A) $(0, 0)$
(B) $(-4, 3)$
(C) $(-4, -3)$
(D) $(-3, 4)$
(E) $(4, 3)$

18 In the standard x,y-coordinate plane, the center of circle O is the origin. If circle O has an area of 25π, which of the following points CANNOT lie on the circumference of the circle?

(A) $(5, 0)$
(B) $(4, -4)$
(C) $(3, 4)$
(D) $(-3, 4)$
(E) $(-4, 3)$

19 If m and n are positive integers and $2m + 3n = 15$, what is the sum of all possible values of m?

(A) 2
(B) 3
(C) 5
(D) 6
(E) 9

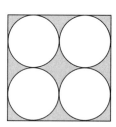

21 Each of the circles in the figure above has a radius of 2. If a point on the figure is chosen at random, what is the probability that point is in the shaded area?

(A) $\dfrac{1}{16\pi}$

(B) $\dfrac{1}{4\pi}$

(C) $\dfrac{\pi - 1}{4}$

(D) $\dfrac{4 - \pi}{4}$

(E) $\dfrac{1}{64 - 16\pi}$

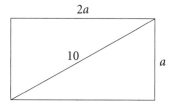

20 The figure above is a rectangle. What is the value of a?

(A) $\sqrt{5}$

(B) $\dfrac{10}{3}$

(C) $\dfrac{10\sqrt{3}}{3}$

(D) $2\sqrt{5}$

(E) $10\sqrt{5}$

22 If $\dfrac{2x}{3} = \dfrac{4}{5}$, then $x =$?

(A) $\dfrac{2}{5}$

(B) $\dfrac{5}{12}$

(C) $\dfrac{5}{6}$

(D) $\dfrac{6}{5}$

(E) $\dfrac{12}{5}$

23 On a certain test, if a student answers 80 to 90 percent of the questions correctly, he will receive a letter grade of *B*. If there are 40 questions on the test, what is the minimum number of questions the student can answer correctly to receive a grade of *B*?

(A) 24
(B) 28
(C) 32
(D) 33
(E) 36

25 Which of the following groups contains three fractions that are equal?

(A) $\dfrac{1}{3}, \dfrac{1}{6}, \dfrac{1}{9}$

(B) $\dfrac{2}{5}, \dfrac{10}{25}, \dfrac{12}{30}$

(C) $\dfrac{1}{2}, \dfrac{2}{4}, \dfrac{4}{6}$

(D) $\dfrac{2}{3}, \dfrac{2}{6}, \dfrac{2}{9}$

(E) $\dfrac{3}{4}, \dfrac{10}{12}, \dfrac{75}{100}$

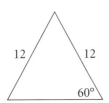

24 What is the perimeter of the triangle above?

(A) 24
(B) 28
(C) 30
(D) 36
(E) 40

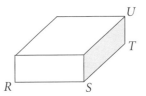

26 In the rectangular solid above, $RS = 8$, $ST = 12$, and $UT = \dfrac{1}{3} ST$. What is the volume of the solid?

(A) 384
(B) 240
(C) 96
(D) 32
(E) 24

27 If $m^2 + 7 = 29$, then $m^2 - 7 =$

(A) 15
(B) 22
(C) 71
(D) 78
(E) 484

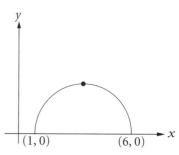

29 In the figure above, what is the x-coordinate of the point on the semicircle that is the farthest from the x-axis?

(A) 2.5
(B) 3.5
(C) 4
(D) 4.25
(E) 4.5

28 If 125 percent of x is 150, what is x percent of 75?

(A) 70
(B) 90
(C) 120
(D) 150
(E) 185

30 If a, b, and c are all integers greater than 1, and $ab = 14$ and $bc = 21$, which of the following must be true?

(A) $c > a > b$
(B) $b > c > a$
(C) $b > a > c$
(D) $a > c > b$
(E) $a > b > c$

31 There are a total of 20 marbles in a bag containing only red marbles, blue marbles, and yellow marbles. If a marble is selected at random, the probability of getting a red marble is $\frac{2}{5}$, and the probability of getting a blue marble is $\frac{1}{2}$. How many yellow marbles are in the bag?

(A) 1
(B) 2
(C) 4
(D) 8
(E) 10

33 If the sum of 4 numbers is between 53 and 57, then the average (arithmetic mean) of the 4 numbers could be which of the following?

(A) $11\frac{1}{2}$

(B) 12

(C) $12\frac{1}{2}$

(D) 13

(E) 14

32 What are all the values of x for which $(x - 2)(x + 5) = 0$?

(A) −5
(B) −2
(C) 2 and −5
(D) −2 and 5
(E) 2 and 5

34 If the lengths of the sides of a certain triangle are a, b, and c, which of the following statements could be true?

(A) $c = b + a$
(B) $c = b - a$
(C) $c = 2a + b$
(D) $c + 2 = a + b + 3$
(E) $c + 3 = a + b + 2$

35 If the sum of 5 different positive integers is 100, what is greatest possible value for the median of the 5 integers?

(A) 31
(B) 32
(C) 33
(D) 34
(E) 50

Each of the remaining 10 questions requires you to solve the problem and enter your answer by marking the ovals in the special grid, as shown in the example below. You may use any available space for scratch work.

Answer: 1.25 or $\frac{5}{4}$

Write answer in boxes.

Grid in result

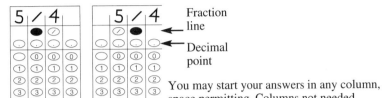

Fraction line

Decimal point

You may start your answers in any column, space permitting. Columns not needed should be left blank.

Either position is correct.

- It is recommended, though not required, that you write your answer in the boxes at the top of the columns. However, **you will receive credit only for darkening the ovals correctly**.

- Grid only one answer to a question, even though some problems have more than one correct answer.

- Darken no more than one oval in a column.

- No answers are negative.

- **Mixed numbers** cannot be gridded. For example: the number $1\frac{1}{4}$ must be gridded as 1.25 or 5/4.

(If 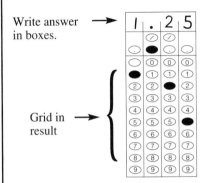 is gridded, it will be interpreted as $\frac{11}{4}$ not $1\frac{1}{4}$.)

- Decimal Accuracy: Decimal answers must be entered as accurately as possible. For example, if you obtain an answer such as 0.1666. . ., you should record the result as .166 or .167. **Less accurate values such as .16 or .17 are not acceptable.**

Acceptable ways to grid $\frac{1}{6}$ = .1666. . .

 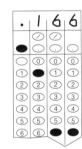 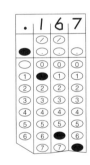

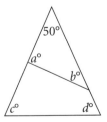

36 In the figure above, what is the value of $a + b + c + d$?

37 If an object travels at a speed of 3 feet per second, how many feet does it travel in half an hour?

38 How many square units is the area of an isosceles right triangle whose hypotenuse has a length of $8\sqrt{2}$ units?

39 The ratio of 1.5 to 18 is the same as the ratio of x to 2.4. What is the value of x?

40 If $a > 0$ and $a^b \, a^3 = a^{\frac{10}{3}}$ what is the value of b?

41 What is the least possible integer value for which 40 percent of that integer is greater than 2.8?

42
$$-2, -1, 0, 1, 2, 1, 0, -1, -2, -1, \ldots\ldots$$

The first ten terms of a sequence are shown above. What is the sum of the first 88 terms?

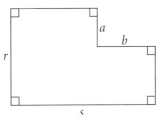

44 If $r + s$ in the figure above is 13, what is the perimeter of the figure?

43 If $x > 5$ and $\dfrac{14}{\sqrt{x-5}} = 7$, what is the value of x?

45 If $x > 0$ and $y > 0$, x^3 is half of x^2, and y^3 is one-third of y^2, what is the value of $x + y$?

46 If $d + 2h = 8$ and $4d = 10$, what is the value of h?

48 A restaurant has 25 entrées and 40 side dishes. If Mary wants to order one entrée and one side dish, how many different combinations of entrée and side dish could she order?

47 Points A, B, C, and D lie on a line in that order. B is the midpoint of segment AC, and C is the midpoint of segment AD. If the length of segment AD is 16 centimeters, what is the length of segment BD in centimeters?

49 For every positive integer n, $n! = n \times (n - 1) \times (n - 2) \times ... \times 1$. For example, $4! = 4 \times 3 \times 2 \times 1 = 24$.

What is the value of $\dfrac{29!}{27!}$?

50 If the median of the values of $3x$, $5x$, and $\frac{1}{2}x$ is 18, then what is the value of x?

Answers and Explanations

1. **E**
Difficulty: Low
Strategic Advice: Questions like this one ask you to interpret information in a graph. First, make sure you know what quantities are plotted on each axis. Then, review the question. This question asks you to find a percent increase, not simply an increase.
Getting to the Answer: Subtract the fourth quarter sales from the third quarter and divide by the third quarter sales.

$$\frac{3.5 - 1}{1} = 2.5 = 250\%$$

2. **D**
Difficulty: Low
Strategic Advice: Don't jump ahead of yourself on questions like these. Use ratios to analyze Jeweler A and Jeweler B separately. Then, compare the two.
Getting to the Answer: Be careful with units here. Twenty minutes equals one third of an hour. Fifteen minutes equals one quarter of an hour.
Jeweler A:

$$\frac{3}{hr} \times 8 \text{ hr} = 24$$

Jeweler B:

$$\frac{4}{hr} \times 8 \text{ hr} = 32$$

$$32 - 24 = 8$$

3. **A**
Difficulty: Medium
Strategic Advice: Questions with more than one figure require you to transfer information from one figure to the next. Analyze Figure 1 alone to solve for x. Then insert the value of x into Figure 2.
Getting to the Answer:
Figure 1:
$180° - 60° = 3x$ Angles of a triangle sum to 180°.
$40° = x$
Figure 2:
$4y = x$ Vertical angles.
$4y = 40°$
$y = 10°$

4. **B**
Difficulty: Low
Strategic Advice: The phrase, "varies directly," means that this problem can be solved by setting up a ratio. When dealing with a ratio question, be sure to compare like quantities. For example, set up a proportion with the number of pounds in the numerator of each fraction and the number of inches in the denominator of each fraction. That way you will solve for the correct values on Test Day.
Getting to the Answer:

$$\frac{50}{8} = \frac{75}{x}$$
$$50x = 600$$
$$x = 12$$

5. **E**
Difficulty: Medium
Strategic Advice: Don't be intimidated when exponents are fractions. Think about how you can make the equation true. Work backwards to solve for the missing variables.
Getting to the Answer:
$8^2 = 64$, so $x = 8$.

So $\frac{y}{2} = 2$, $y = 4$.

$8 + 4 = 12$

6. **C**
Difficulty: Medium
Strategic Advice: Questions such as this will be your pay off on Test Day for having absorbed certain facts during your preparation—such as how to add terms with like exponents. (This question is also a great one for Picking Numbers. The easiest number to try is $n = 2$, which narrows the choices down to (C) and (E). Choosing $n = 4$ gets you to (C) right away.)
Getting to the Answer:

$$3^{\frac{n}{2}} + 3^{\frac{n}{2}} + 3^{\frac{n}{2}} = 3\left(3^{\frac{n}{2}}\right)$$
$$= 3^1 \cdot 3^{\frac{n}{2}}$$
$$= 3^{\frac{n}{2} + 1}$$

7. D
Difficulty: Medium
Strategic Advice: Many test takers are intimidated by functions such as this one. The trick is to take your time and fill in the variables as you can. In this case, start inside the parentheses and find $g(x)$ when x is 3. Then use this value to solve for $f(x)$ when $x = g(3)$.
Getting to the Answer:
$g(3) = \sqrt{2(3)^2 + 7}$
$= \sqrt{18 + 7} = \sqrt{25} = 5$
$f(5) = 3(5) - 8 = 15 - 8 = 7$

8. A
Difficulty: Medium
Strategic Advice: On Test Day, be sure to analyze the information in any number lines, graphs, or diagrams before you begin. In this question, you can figure out the values of the letters. Then, try each value in the inequality described in the question.
Getting to the Answer:
D = −3 |3 − (−3)| = 6 > 5 Yes
E = 2 |3 − 2| = 1 > 5 No
F = 6 |3 − 6| = 3 > 5 No

9. C
Difficulty: Medium
Strategic Advice: This question raises two important insights for Test Day. One is the value of Picking Numbers. The other is to pay attention to qualifying words such as always and never.
Getting to the Answer:
Try −0.5 for N:

    I. $N < 2N$
        $-0.5 < 2(-0.5)$
        $-0.5 < -1$
        No

    II. $N^2 < N$
        $(-0.5)^2 < -0.5$
        $0.25 < -0.5$
        No

    III. $N^2 < \dfrac{1}{N^2}$

        $(-0.5)^2 < \dfrac{1}{(-0.5)^2}$

        $.25 < 4$
        Yes

10. E
Difficulty: Medium
Strategic Advice: It's always a great idea to read a question and then ask yourself, "OK, what essentially is being asked of me here?" In this case, the issue boils down to realizing that the only numbers that are multiples of both 2 and 3 are multiples of 6—the product of 2 and 3.
Getting to the Answer:
$X = \{2, 4, 6, 8, 10, 12, 14, 16, 18,...\}$
$Y = \{3, 6, 9, 12, 15, 18,....\}$
$X \cap Y = \{6, 12, 18,...\}$

11. B
Difficulty: Medium
Strategic Advice: This type of question will earn you quick points on Test Day if you can work nimbly with the rules of right triangles during your preparation. (Those rules, by the way, will be provided to you on Test Day.) The ratio of side lengths for a 30-60-90 triangle is $1 : \sqrt{3} : 2$.
Getting to the Answer:
The measure of the side opposite 30 is 7—half the hypotenuse. The measure of the side opposite 60 is therefore $7\sqrt{3}$.

12. C
Difficulty: Medium
Strategic Advice: Some questions seem tough on the first read but are easier than you think. This one, for example, really just tests whether you know the average formula:

$$\frac{\text{sum of terms}}{\text{number of terms}}$$

Getting to the Answer:
$$? = \frac{12(80) + 18(85)}{30}$$
$$? = \frac{960 + 1530}{30} = \frac{2490}{30} = 83$$

13. A
Difficulty: Medium
Strategic Advice: The trick to questions such as this one is to recognize the relationship between the terms. If one integer is even, the next consecutive integer must be odd (and vice versa).
Getting to the Answer:
Odd + even = odd
Even + odd = odd
An odd number is not divisible by 2.

14. **C**

Difficulty: Medium

Strategic Advice: The wording of the question makes the content sound more complex than it really is. Take your time and label the figure with the information you know. Once you do so, you will find the question boils down to simple algebra. (This is also an excellent candidate for backsolving.)

Getting to the Answer:

Call the width of *UVWX* w and the length 2w:

$2w(w) = 72$

$2w^2 = 72$

$w^2 = 36$

$w = 6 = UV$

If 2w is length, then the length is 2(6) = 12.

$UX = \dfrac{12}{4} = 3$

$\overline{UZ} = 3$

15. **D**

Difficulty: Medium

Strategic Advice: The problem almost solves itself if you recall that a slope is negative when it slants downward.

Getting to the Answer:

The slope is negative when the height of the line is decreasing, between the *y* axis and *x* = 5. Thus, all values from the point where the descension begins, *x* = 0, to where it ends, *x* = 5, would have a negative slope. Your answer is 0 < *x* < 5.

16. **C**

Difficulty: Medium

Strategic Advice: Perhaps the best beginning you can make with a question is to sharply define its key issue or issues. In this case, that issue is the properties of a line whose slope is zero.

Getting to the Answer:

A line with a slope of zero is horizontal. A horizontal line that passes through (4, –3) has infinitely many points, every one of which has a *y*-coordinate of –3.

17. **E**

Difficulty: High

Strategic Advice: Don't let complex-looking symbol questions fool you. They merely give you some rule that you'll be asked to work with later in the question. In this case, the symbol should make you think, "How many triangles could exist with integer side measures a, b, and x?" This

question, in turn, should get you thinking about the Triangle Inequality Theorem, which requires that in any triangle, the measure of any side be less than the sum of, and greater than the difference between, the two other sides.

Getting to the Answer:

$7–2 < x < 7 + 2$

$5 < x < 9$

x = 6, 7, 8 Only (E) fits.

18. **B**

Difficulty: High

Strategic Advice: How could the facts that a circle is centered at the origin and has area 25π relate to the identification of points on the circumference of the circle? If its area is 25π, its radius is 5, which is also the hypotenuse of an infinite number of right triangles whose side lengths are the absolute values of the *x*- and *y*-coordinates of the points named in the choices. Once you realize this—and you might realize it more easily if you draw out the situation described here—answering the question is as easy as applying the Pythagorean Theorem to the choices.

Getting to the Answer:

(A) $5^2 + 0^2 = 25$? Yes.

(B) $4^2 + (–4)^2 = 25$? No.

(C) $3^2 + 4^2 = 25$? Yes.

(D) $(–3)^2 + 4^2 = 25$. Yes.

(E) $(–4)^2 + 3^2 = 25$? Yes.

19. **E**

Difficulty: High

Strategic Advice: The question stem mentions that *m* and *n* are positive and that they're integers. These data limit the possible values of *m* and *n* more severely than you might have imagined.

Getting to the Answer:

If *m* is 1, 3*n* is not an integer.

If *m* is 2, 3*n* is not an integer.

If *m* is 3, 3*n* is an integer—*n* is 3.

If *m* is 4, 3*n* is not an integer.

If *m* is 5, 3*n* is not an integer.

If *m* is 6, 3*n* is an integer—*n* is 1.

If *m* is 7, 3*n* is not an integer.

If *m* is 8, you've exceeded a sum of 15.

So *m* can be 3 or 6, and the sum of 3 and 6 is 9.

20. D
Difficulty: High
Strategic Advice: Identifying *how* a question is hard can help you by focusing on the skills needed to tackle it successfully. In this case, nothing conceptually advanced is happening; you're just called upon to use the Pythagorean Theorem using some variables instead of numbers only.
Getting to the Answer:
$a^2 + (2a)^2 = 100$
$a^2 + 4a^2 = 100$
$5a^2 = 100$
$a^2 = 20$
$a = \sqrt{20} = 2\sqrt{5}$

21. D
Difficulty: High
Strategic Advice: A great beginning to a question like this one is to map out a path that will get you to the answer. By comparing the area of the entire square to the areas of the circles inside, you can find the requested probability. (Since the figure is drawn to scale, you could also eyeball to eliminate (A) and (B), which are too small.)
Getting to the Answer:
$$\text{probability} = \frac{\text{desired outcomes}}{\text{possible outcomes}}$$
$$= \frac{\text{area}_{\text{square minus circles}}}{\text{area}_{\text{square}}}$$
$$= \frac{8^2 - 4(\pi[2]^2)}{8^2} = \frac{64 - 16\pi}{64}$$
$$= \frac{16(4 - \pi)}{64} = \frac{4 - \pi}{4}$$

22. D
Difficulty: Low
Strategic Advice: This type of question simply tests your ability to be careful in your calculations.
Getting to the Answer:
Cross multiply:
$10x = 12$
$x = \frac{12}{10}$
$x = \frac{6}{5}$

23. C
Difficulty: Low
Strategic Advice: Remember that questions involving ranges of possible values often require you to use either or both extreme values—a minimum or maximum to answer correctly. Here, for example, you need only 80% of 40.
Getting to the Answer:
$.80(40) = 32$

24. D
Difficulty: Low
Strategic Advice: Focus how one piece of data leads to another. If two sides are equal, the two angles opposite are equal. Then only 60 degrees remains for the top angle—which means that the triangle is equilateral: all three sides and all three angles are equal.
Getting to the Answer:
$12 + 12 + 12 = 36$

25. B
Difficulty: Low
Strategic Advice: Define an issue in its simplest terms. Here, for example, ask yourself, "In which choice does every fraction reduce to the same thing?"
Getting to the Answer:
Once you see that every fraction in (B) equals $\frac{2}{5}$, there's no need to check the remaining choices—but you can do so quickly to be sure.

26. A
Difficulty: Medium
Strategic Advice: Many test takers are intimidated by three-dimensional shapes. But in many cases, these questions break down to simple arithmetic once you label all of the information you know.
Getting to the Answer:
$\overline{UT} = \frac{1}{3}(\overline{ST}) = \frac{1}{3}(12) = 4$
$V = lwh = 8 \cdot 12 \cdot 4 = 384$

27. A
Difficulty: Low
Strategic Advice: On Test Day, you can save time and stress if you avoid unnecessary calculations. In this question, for example, you don't need to calculate a square root. You can also save time if you review the answer choices.

The difference $m^2 - 7$ must be less than $m^2 + 7$, so you can quickly eliminate (C), (D), and (E).
Getting to the Answer:
$m^2 + 7 = 29$
$m^2 = 22$
$m^2 - 7 = 22 - 7 = 15$

28. **B**
Difficulty: Medium
Strategic Advice: Like many questions on the SAT, this one requires you to translate from English into math. Once translated, this question becomes straightforward arithmetic.
Getting to the Answer:
$1.25x = 150$
$x = 120$
Expressed as a percent, 120 is 1.2.
$1.2(75) = 90$

29. **B**
Difficulty: Medium
Strategic Advice: Questions such as this involve mechanical calculation based on abstract reasoning. Do the latter first and then the mechanical calculation quickly but carefully.
Getting to the Answer:
The point on the semicircle farthest from the x-axis is the topmost point of the semicircle—the point directly above the center of the semicircle. We can see that the diameter of the circle is the difference between (1, 0) and (6, 0), which is 5. If the diameter of the circle is 5, it's radius is 2.5. So 1 (the point on the x-axis at which the semicircle starts) plus 2.5 is 3.5. Don't just find the radius and quit. The question asks for the x-coordinate.

30. **B**
Difficulty: Medium

Strategic Advice: If time is short, some very quick and simple algebraic manipulation can bring you down to a 50-50 guess on this question. If $ab = 14$ and $bc = 21$, then $b = \dfrac{14}{a} = \dfrac{21}{c}$. If $\dfrac{14}{a} = \dfrac{21}{c}$, $\dfrac{a}{c} = \dfrac{14}{21} = \dfrac{2}{3}$, so c must be more than a, leaving only (A) and (B) as possibilities.

Getting to the Answer:
Given that your range is integers greater than one, if ab is 14, either a is 2 and b is 7, or vice versa. And if bc is 21, either c is 3 and b is 7, or vice versa. Because b and 7 are the only common elements in both equations, b must be 7. Because a and c are in the ratio of 2 to 3, a must be 2 itself, and c must be 3 itself.

31. **B**
Difficulty: Medium
Strategic Advice: As you read a question, ask yourself, "What could I do with this piece of data?" In this case, if you know that 20 is the total number of marbles, then when you read that "the probability of getting a red marble is $\dfrac{2}{5}$," you should think,

"From this I could figure out the quantity of red," and so on with blue. Once you've done this, what your left with will be the number of yellows—the answer.

Getting to the Answer:
$\dfrac{2}{5}(20) = 8$ red

$\dfrac{1}{2}(20) = 10$ blue

$8 + 10 = 18$ red marbles and blue marbles

20 total marbles $- 18$ red and blue marbles

$= 2$ yellow marbles

32. **C**
Difficulty: Low
Strategic Advice: For the given equation to equal 0, either $(x - 2)$ or $(x + 5)$ equals 0.
Getting to the Answer:
$x - 2 = 0$
$x = 2$
or
$x + 5 = 0$
$x = -5$
Choice (C) is correct.

33. **E**

Difficulty: Medium

Strategic Advice: The average is the sum of the terms divided by the number of terms. The question stem gives you a range for the sum of the terms, so all you need to do is divide the smallest and the greatest by the number of terms (4) to determine the range of the average.

Getting to the Answer:

$$\frac{53}{4} = 13\frac{1}{4}$$

$$\frac{57}{4} = 14\frac{1}{4}$$

The average is between $13\frac{1}{4}$ and $14\frac{1}{4}$.

Only (E) works.

34. **E**

Difficulty: High

Strategic Advice: The sum of the lengths of any two sides of a triangle is greater than the length of the third side. Therefore $a + b > c$, $a + c > b$, and $c + b > a$. Look through the answer choices to determine which is possible, keeping these inequalities in mind.

Getting to the Answer:

(A) $c = b + a$ Incorrect. $c < a + b$.

(B) $c = b - a$

$c + a = b$ Incorrect. $c + a > b$

(C) $c = 2a + b$

If this was true, then $c > a + b$ Incorrect. $c < a + b$

(D) $c + 2 = a + b + 3$

This could be not true because in this equation, c is greater than $a + b$.

(E) $c + 3 = a + b + 2$

This could be true because c is less than $a + b$.

35. **A**

Difficulty: High

Strategic Advice: The median is the middle term in a group of terms that are arranged in numerical order. Try the terms in the answer choices to see if they could be the median.

Getting to the Answer:

(A) 31

Two terms could be any different positive integers <31, and two terms could be any positive integers >31.

Try the smallest possible values:

1, 2, 31, 32, 33

$1 + 2 + 31 + 32 + 33 = 99$. This is less than 100. Try the next answer choice.

(B) 32

Try:

1, 2, 32, 33, 34

$1 + 2 + 32 + 33 + 34 = 102$. This is greater than 100. (A) must be correct.

36. **260**

Difficulty: Low

Strategic Advice: Expect the first Grid-In, like the first few multiple-choice questions, to test your mechanical ability or your understanding of basic facts. One such fact is that the sum of the angles of a triangle must be 180 degrees.

Getting to the Answer:

Small triangle:

$a + b = 180° - 50°$

$a + b = 130°$

Large triangle:

$c + d = 180° - 50°$

$c + d = 130°$

$130° + 130° = 260°$

37. **5400**

Difficulty: Low

Strategic Advice: Sometimes part of the challenge of questions involving units of measurement is making such units—in this case, seconds and hours—consistent.

Getting to the Answer:

$$\frac{3 \text{ ft}}{\text{s}} \times \frac{60 \text{ s}}{1 \text{ min}} \times \frac{30 \text{ min}}{1 \text{ half hour}} = \frac{5{,}400 \text{ ft}}{\text{half hour}}$$

38. **32**
Difficulty: Low
Strategic Advice: Hone your skills with 45-45-90 right triangles (and 30-60-90s, as well). Even though the ratios of the sides are provided on Test Day, you'll move more quickly through questions if you've practiced beforehand.
Getting to the Answer:

Leg : leg : hypotenuse in a 45-45-90 is $x : x : x\sqrt{2}$. If the hypotenuse is $8\sqrt{2}$, each leg is 8. Because the legs are also the base and height, the area of the triangle in question is $\left(\frac{1}{2}\right)(8)(8) = 32$

39. $\frac{1}{5}$ **or .2**
Difficulty: Medium
Strategic Advice: Don't let the decimals throw you. Proportions always work the same way, without respect to the kinds of numbers they relate.
Getting to the Answer:
$$\frac{1.5}{18} = \frac{x}{2.4}$$
$$18x = (1.5)(2.4)$$
$$x = 0.2$$

40. $\frac{1}{3}$ **or .333**
Difficulty: Medium
Strategic Advice: Fractional exponents are subject to the same rules as any other kind of exponent, so if you know those rules—and you should make knowing them a priority—you'll slice through questions like this one quickly and efficiently.
Getting to the Answer:
$$a^b a^3 = a^{b+3}$$
$$b + 3 = \frac{10}{3}$$
$$b = \frac{10}{3} - 3 = \frac{1}{3}$$

41. **8**
Difficulty: Medium
Strategic Advice: On Test Day, look for clues that tell you how to solve the problem. The words *greater than* in this question suggest that you are solving an inequality.
Getting to the Answer:
$$0.40x > 2.8$$
$$x > \frac{2.8}{0.40}$$
$$x > 7$$

The question asks for the least possible integer value, which is 8.

42. **0**
Difficulty: High
Strategic Advice: Look for a pattern.
Getting to the Answer:
The terms repeat in groups of 8, and the sum of every such group is zero. The eighty-eighth term will be the last of eleven repetitions of this cycle. So the sum is zero.

43. **9**
Difficulty: High
Strategic Advice: Questions with square roots can be intimidating. However, they are solved like any other type of algebra question. Treat the square root as a single quantity until you isolate it on one side of the equation. Then square both sides to get rid of the square root.
Getting to the Answer:
$$\frac{14}{\sqrt{x-5}} = 7$$
$$\frac{14}{7} = \sqrt{x-5}$$
$$(2)^2 = (\sqrt{x-5})^2$$
$$4 = x - 5$$
$$9 = x$$

44. **26**

Difficulty: High

Strategic Advice: This question challenges you to rearrange in clever and creative ways the information you are given in the question stem. Also, remember that you're solving for perimeter, not area.

Getting to the Answer:

$P = 2r + 2s$
$\quad = 2(r + s)$
$\quad = 2(13) = 26$

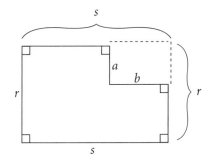

45. $\dfrac{5}{6}$ **or .833**

Difficulty: High

Strategic Advice: One way to make a question very daunting to most test takers is to present data in a relatively complex form. Use algebra to manipulate the situation by rendering complicated-looking relationships into simple terms.

Getting to the Answer:

$x^3 = \dfrac{1}{2}x^2$

Divide both sides by x^2:

$x = \dfrac{1}{2}$

$y^3 = \dfrac{1}{3}y^2$

Divide both sides by y^2:

$y = \dfrac{1}{3}$

$x + y = \dfrac{1}{2} + \dfrac{1}{3} = \dfrac{3+2}{6} = \dfrac{5}{6}$

46. **2.75 or $\dfrac{11}{4}$**

Difficulty: Medium

Strategic Advice: Many SAT questions require multiple steps. In this case, first find the value of d from the second equation; then use that in the first equation to find the value of h.

Getting to the Answer:

$4d = 10$

$d = \dfrac{10}{4} = \dfrac{5}{2}$

$d + 2h = 8$

$\dfrac{5}{2} + 2h = 8$

$2h = \dfrac{16}{2} - \dfrac{5}{2} = \dfrac{11}{2}$

$h = \dfrac{11}{4}$

47. **12**

Difficulty: Medium

Strategic Advice: Sketching a diagram will often help you visualize geometry problems. Think about the relationship between the lengths of the different line segments in this problem.

Getting to the Answer:

Since C is the midpoint of segment AD, which is 16 cm long, segments AC and CD must each be 8 cm long. B is the midpoint of AC, so AB and BC are each 4 cm long. Segment BD is $4 + 8 = 12$ cm long.

48. **1000**

Difficulty: Medium

Strategic Advice: This question deals with finding the number of possible combinations of two objects. No matter which entrée Mary selects, she could order any of the 40 side dishes.

Getting to the Answer:

$25 \times 40 = 1,000$

49. **812**

Difficulty: Medium

Strategic Advice: Although you could find the value of 29! and the value of 27!, this would be extremely time-consuming. Many SAT problems can be done in both a time-consuming manner and a faster way. Try to find parts of the problem that cancel out to save yourself time and effort.

Getting to the Answer:

$$\frac{29!}{27!} = \frac{29 \times 28 \times 27!}{27!} = 29 \times 28 = 812$$

50. **6**

Difficulty: High

Strategic Advice: The median of a set of numbers is the number in the middle when the numbers are arranged in increasing order.

Getting to the Answer:

These numbers should be in the order $\frac{1}{2}x$, $3x$, and $5x$. The median is $3x$.

$3x = 18$

$x = 6$

CHAPTER EIGHT

Writing: Multiple-Choice Questions

The following sentences test correctness and effectiveness of expression. Part of each sentence or the entire sentence is underlined; beneath each sentence are five ways of phrasing the underlined material. Choice A repeats the original phrasing; the other four choices are different. If you think the original phrasing produces a better sentence than any of the alternatives, select choice A; if not, select one of the other choices.

In making your selection, follow the requirements of standard written English; that is, pay attention to grammar, choice of words, sentence construction, and punctuation. Your selection should result in the most effective sentence—clear and precise, without awkwardness or ambiguity.

EXAMPLE: ANSWER:

Every apple in the baskets <u>are ripe and labeled according to the date it was picked</u>.   Ⓐ ● Ⓒ Ⓓ Ⓔ

(A) are ripe and labeled according to the date it was picked.
(B) is ripe and labeled according to the date it was picked.
(C) are ripe and labeled according to the date they were picked.
(D) is ripe and labeled according to the date they were picked.
(E) are ripe and labeled as to the date it was picked.

1 Community meetings <u>were most effectively at eradicating crime</u> in our neighborhood because the adults and young people learned to trust one another.

(A)   most effectively at eradicating crime
(B)   effectively at eradicating crime
(C)   most effective at eradicating crime
(D)   most effectively eradicating crime
(E)   most effective eradicated crime

2 First, the spark plugs fire in the automobile engine, igniting a series of gasoline explosions, <u>and after that there are these pistons that are driven up and down inside the engine</u>.

(A)   and after that there are these pistons that are driven up and down inside the engine
(B)   and then pistons drive the engine up and down
(C)   and then there are pistons who are driven up and down inside the engine
(D)   which causes pistons to be driven up and down inside the engine
(E)   which after that there are these pistons that are driven up and down inside the engine

3 Mahatma Gandhi, one of India's most highly respected leaders, <u>were convinced that the practice</u> of peaceful resistance, or Satyagraha, was the only viable means of protest.

(A)   were convinced that the practice
(B)   were convicted whenever the practice
(C)   were practically convinced that the idea
(D)   was convinced that the practice
(E)   was convinced by the practice

4 The Baja peninsula is a stretch of barren desert <u>in my Mexican guidebook</u> bordered on both sides by stunning beaches.

(A)   in my Mexican guidebook
(B)   from my Mexican guidebook
(C)   that, according to my guidebook about Mexico, is
(D)   that I read about in my guidebook about Mexico
(E)   in our enormous guidebook about Mexico

5 Five-year-old <u>Maria shaked her head vigorously from side to side</u>, indicating emphatically that she did not want to go to the dentist.

(A)   Maria shaked her head vigorously from side to side
(B)   Maria shaked her head vigorously sideways
(C)   Maria shook her head vigorously from side to side
(D)   Maria shook her head vigorously on both sides
(E)   Maria vigorously shook around her head

6 Government agencies have developed an early warning system <u>which system also warns people about the strength of the storm that the warning is about</u> so that residents know how to prepare.

(A) which system also warns people about the strength of the storm that the warning is about

(B) that also rates the strength of the approaching storm

(C) that is a system that also warns people about the strength of the storm that is approaching

(D) which is a system that also rates the approaching storm that the warning is about

(E) which is a system that also warns people about the strength of the storm that is being warned about

7 <u>Poetry throughout the ages have always been</u> a spoken art form, and many poets are celebrating the current resurgence of community poetry slams.

(A) Poetry throughout the ages have always been

(B) Poetry throughout the ages has always been

(C) Poetry throughout the ages always having been

(D) Poems throughout the ages has always been

(E) Poems throughout the ages will have been

8 The weather along the Irish coast broke clear and unusually calm on Saturday, so we were astonished to observe, as we walked several miles along the shore, that <u>there was not a single ship on site</u>.

(A) there was not a single ship on site

(B) there was not a single ship in sight

(C) there is not a single ship on site

(D) the single ship was on the site

(E) there was not a solitary ship on site

9 <u>Julia felt well when she remembered</u> the thrill of defeating her traditional tennis rival Katie O'Mara in the annual Lakeview summer tournament.

(A) Julia felt well when she remembered

(B) Julia felt more well when she remembered

(C) Julia felt good when she remembered

(D) Julia remembered feeling good at

(E) Julia felt well because she remembered

10 That night, <u>one of the keynote speakers argue persuasively</u> that the growing influence of exit polls on public opinion and politics was inherently dangerous.

(A) one of the keynote speakers argue persuasively

(B) the keynote speakers argue persuasively

(C) one of the keynote speakers argues persuasively

(D) one of the keynote speakers persuaded

(E) one of the keynote speakers argued persuasively

11 Among the accomplishments of President James Knox Polk are <u>the creation of an independent treasury, establishing lower tariffs, and purchasing</u> the Oregon territory.

(A) the creation of an independent treasury, establishing lower tariffs, and purchasing

(B) the creating of an independent treasury, the establishment lower tariffs, and purchasing

(C) the creation of an independent treasury, the establishment of lower tariffs, and the purchase of

(D) creating an independent treasury, establishing lower tariffs, and the purchase of

(E) creation of an independent treasury, establishing lower tariffs, and purchasing

12 In order to convict a suspect of a crime, <u>guilt beyond a reasonable doubt must be proven to the jury by the prosecutor</u>.

(A) guilt beyond a reasonable doubt must be proven to the jury by the prosecutor

(B) guilt must be proven to the jury by the prosecutor beyond a reasonable doubt

(C) guilt beyond a reasonable doubt must be proven to the jury by the prosecutor

(D) the prosecutor must prove guilt beyond a reasonable doubt to the jury

(E) the prosecutor must, to the jury, prove guilt beyond a reasonable doubt

13 One of the first signs of spring is the budding of plants, another sign is the lengthening of the days.

(A) plants, another sign is
(B) plants; another sign is
(C) plants, another sign would be
(D) plants, also that
(E) plants and another sign is

14 Despite the seriousness of the accident, the driver refused to let the paramedics examine him nor going to the hospital for treatment.

(A) examine him nor going to the hospital for treatment
(B) examine him nor went to the hospital for treatment
(C) examine him nor had he gone to the hospital for treatment
(D) examine him or going to the hospital for treatment
(E) examine him or go to the hospital for treatment

15 The editor-in-chief has written about New York for almost as long as he has lived there.

(A) written about New York for almost as long as he has lived there
(B) written about New York for almost equally as long as it has been that he has lived there
(C) been writing about New York for as long as he has lived there
(D) written about New York, while living there for almost as long
(E) written about New York for almost so long as he has lived there.

16 Looking through my high school yearbook, the pictures reminded me how much fun we had during our senior year.

(A) Looking through my high school yearbook
(B) As I looked through my high school yearbook
(C) Having looked through my high school yearbook
(D) I looked through my high school yearbook,
(E) While looked through my high school yearbook

17 The math department has arranged free tutoring for those of us which had problems on the midterm and want to bring our grades up.

(A) for those of us which had problems on the midterm and want to bring our grades up
(B) for those of us which had problems on the midterm and want bringing our grades up
(C) for those of us who have had problems on the midterm and are wanting to bring our grades up
(D) for those of us who had problems on the midterm and want to bring our grades up
(E) for those of us who had problems on the midterm; and want to bring our grades up

18 Underestimating the demand, tickets were in short supply at the broker's office.

(A) Underestimating the demand, tickets were in short supply at the broker's office.
(B) Tickets were in short supply at the broker's office because of underestimating the demand.
(C) The demand having been underestimated, tickets were in short supply at the broker's office.
(D) Because the broker underestimated the demand, tickets were in short supply at his office.
(E) Because of underestimating the demand, the broker's office found tickets to be in short supply.

The following sentences test your ability to recognize grammar and usage errors. Each sentence contains either a single error or no error at all. No sentence contains more than one error. The error, if there is one, is underlined and lettered. If the sentence contains an error, select the one underlined part that must be changed to make the sentence correct. If the sentence is correct, select choice E. In choosing answers, follow the requirements of standard written English.

EXAMPLE: ANSWER:

<u>Whenever</u> one is driving late at night, <u>you</u> must take extra precautions <u>against</u>
    A   B   C

  (A) ● (C) (D) (E)

falling asleep <u>at</u> the wheel. <u>No error.</u>
          D   E

---

19 <u>Because</u> the previous night's storm <u>had downed</u>
     A   B
several trees along the road, it <u>appeared unlikely</u>
                                    C
that many students <u>would</u> arrive on time for the
                    D
assembly. <u>No error</u>
         E

20 As the curtain rose <u>to reveal</u> the <u>darkened</u> stage,
                A   B
the audience could <u>distinguished</u> the
                 C
<u>shadowy movements</u> of seven dancers. <u>No error</u>
     D   E

21 <u>Filing</u> bankruptcy, while <u>it may ultimately</u> be the
     A   B
only solution <u>for some failing</u> businesses,
              C
<u>is hardly never</u> the first choice. <u>No error</u>
     D   E

22 In Jungian analysis, dreams are <u>thought to be</u>
                               A
<u>windows into</u> the <u>unconscious</u> desires and
     B   C
conflicts of <u>the person which</u> undergoes analysis.
               D
<u>No error</u>
  E

23 Although during the past year many parents
<u>have asked about</u> our reasons for including a
     A
writing sample on the test, <u>never before has</u> the
                         B   C
qualifications of the test makers been <u>so widely</u>
                                  D
challenged. <u>No error</u>
         E

24 If one <u>is interested</u> <u>in understanding</u> <u>even more</u>
           A   B   C
about the history of democracy in the ancient
world, <u>they should</u> consider taking our course in
         D
Ancient Civilizations. <u>No error</u>
                  E

25 It is hilarious <u>when</u> my sister pulls on
                        A
<u>her black wig</u> and <u>performs</u> her
        B   C
<u>imitation of Elvis Presley</u> singing
                D
"Blue Suede Shoes." <u>No error</u>
                              E

26 Shakespeare's tragedy *Richard II* <u>about a king</u> who
                                                A
<u>was</u> an <u>ineffectual ruler</u> <u>because he had</u> the
 B   C   D
temperament of a poet. <u>No error</u>
                              E

27 The spokesman for the university <u>indicated that</u>
                                              A
this year a <u>significantly lower</u> percentage <u>of their</u>
                  B   C
student enrollment resulted directly <u>from</u> its mass
                                          D
mailings sponsored annually by the alumni

association. <u>No error</u>
                    E

28 Unlike Florence, <u>which lays</u> in the northern
                            A
regions of the Italian peninsula, Sicily <u>was once</u>
                                              B
settled by the Greeks, and <u>therefore</u> <u>boasts</u> many
                                C   D
ancient Greek temples and theaters. <u>No error</u>
                                            E

The following passage is an early draft of an essay. Some parts of the passage need to be rewritten.

Read the passage and select the best answers for the questions that follow. Some questions are about particular sentences or parts of sentences and ask you to improve sentence structure or word choice. Other questions ask you to consider organization and development. In choosing answers, follow the requirements of standard written English.

Questions 29–34 are based on the following passage.

(1) I recently read a great book by Dava Sobel, called "Longitude." **(2)** I don't usually enjoy books about science. **(3)** I couldn't put this one down. **(4)** Sobel has written this book for the general public, not for scientists, and I found it lively and engrossing.

(5) The process for measuring latitude had been figured out in the 16th Century, the problem of measuring longitude was proving to be insurmountable. **(6)** They didn't know where their ships were in relation to land. **(7)** This meant that ships' captains had no way to accurately determine longitude, and they often ran aground. **(8)** In October, 1707, for instance, over 1,600 sailors lost their lives when the ships they were sailing in were wrecked off the Isles of Scilly during a storm. **(9)** These ships were under the leadership of Sir Cloudesley Shovell, the Admiral of the Fleet.

(10) "Longitude" is the story of a clockmaker, John Harrison, who displayed a chronometer in 1735 that was so accurate that captains could rely on it to determine the longitude of their ships. **(11)** Prior to Harrison's chronometer, the timepieces on board ships lost several minutes a day, making the accurate calculation of longitude impossible.

(12) To solve this problem, the British Parliament had passed The Longitude Act of 1714, which offered a reward of £20,000 to anyone who could come up with a way to accurately measure longitude. **(13)** Harrison's creation was accurate enough to do this, but the judging committee reneged on its promise and didn't pay him. **(14)** Finally, when Harrison was eighty-three years old, the King and Parliament intervened and he gets his reward.

29 What's the best way to deal with sentence 3?

(A) Leave it as it is.
(B) Replace the period with a comma and use the word "but" to connect it to sentence 2
(C) Place it after sentence 4.
(D) Change "one" to "book."
(E) Omit it.

30 Which word, if inserted at the beginning of sentence 5 (reproduced below) best fits the context?

The process for measuring latitude had been figured out in the 16th Century, the problem of measuring longitude was proving to be insurmountable.

(A) Although
(B) Because
(C) And
(D) Since
(E) Fortunately,

31 In context, what's the best way to deal with sentence 6?

(A) Leave it as it is.
(B) Change "They" to "Scientists."
(C) Start a new paragraph after "insurmountable," and begin sentence 6 with the word "Because."
(D) Move it to the end of sentence 7 and connect it with the word "since."
(E) Place the word "Unfortunately" at the beginning of the sentence.

32 In context, what's the best way to deal with sentence 9?

(A)   Leave it as it is.
(B)   Connect it to sentence 8 with a comma.
(C)   Change "under the leadership" to "were being led by."
(D)   Place "Admiral of the Fleet," before "Sir Cloudesley Shovell."
(E)   Omit it.

33 In context, what's the best version of "and he gets his reward" in sentence 14?

(A)   so he gets his reward
(B)   and he gets rewarded
(C)   and, thankfully, he gets his reward
(D)   therefore he got rewarded
(E)   and he got his reward

34 Which of the following sentences, if placed after sentence 14, would be the best concluding sentence for the essay?

(A)   Harrison felt vindicated after all his years of struggle.
(B)   In the end, Parliament repealed The Longitude Act of 1714.
(C)   At long last, Harrison received what was due to him.
(D)   Ultimately, Harrison died a happy man.
(E)   When all is said and done, his chronometers always kept accurate time.

Answers and Explanations

1.   C
Difficulty: Low
Strategic Advice: The error here is the misuse of an adverb *effectively* instead of the adjective *effective*.
Getting to the Answer: (C) corrects the error without introducing a new one. (B) drops the superlative for no reason. (D) doesn't have a verb in the main clause. (E) doesn't correct the error and doesn't have a verb in the main clause.

2.   D
Difficulty: High
Strategic Advice: The underlined segment is unnecessarily wordy.
Getting to the Answer: (D) succinctly and clearly expresses the action. (B) is tempting because it is so short, but while the shortest answer is frequently correct, this one has the pistons driving the engine. (C) incorrectly uses *who* in reference to an object. (E) is also unnecessarily wordy.

3.   D
Difficulty: Medium
Strategic Advice: When a subject and verb are separated by a phrase, it may be more difficult to recognize a subject-verb agreement problem.
Getting to the Answer: (D) is the correct answer, as the singular verb form *was* agrees with the singular subject *Mahatma Gandhi*. (B) changes the meaning of the sentence, confusing *convicted* with *convinced*. (C) doesn't correct the error, and changes the meaning by introducing the word *practically*. (E) uses the wrong preposition, changing the meaning of the phrase.

4.   C
Difficulty: Medium
Strategic Advice: The problem is that the underlined prepositional phrase implies that the stretch of desert is actually inside the book.
Getting to the Answer: First, determine what was meant, then decide what words will convey the meaning. (B) and (E) do not address the problem. (D) changes the problem; now beaches border the guidebook.

5.   C
Difficulty: Low
Strategic Advice: Make sure you know the forms of commonly tested irregular verbs.
Getting to the Answer: This sentence contains an irregular verb *shake*; its past tense is *shook* not *shaked*. (B) doesn't correct the error, and changes the meaning of the sentence. (D) and (E) are idiomatically incorrect.

6.   B
Difficulty: High
Strategic Advice: The meaning of the sentence is confused by the clumsiness of the modifying phrase.
Getting to the Answer: (B) clarifies the meaning. (C) rearranges a few words but is also wordy (for example repeating the verb *warn* unnecessarily). (D) reduces some, but not all, of the wordiness. (E) is even wordier than the original.

7.   B
Difficulty: Medium
Strategic Advice: Subject and verb should always agree in number, and verbs should be in the simplest tense that conveys the intended meaning.
Getting to the Answer: The plural verb *have been* does not agree with the singular subject, *poetry*. (C) makes the first clause, which was independent, a fragment without a verb. (D) uses an acceptable alternative subject, but there is no need for this change, and with a new plural subject we still have a problem with subject-verb agreement. (E) illogically uses a future perfect form.

8.   B
Difficulty: Medium
Strategic Advice: The writer used the phrase *on site* when what is meant is *in sight*.
Getting to the Answer: Since the speaker walks several miles along the shore, it is clear that no particular site is intended. (B) contains the correct idiomatic expression. The verb change in (C) adds another problem. (D) changes the meaning of the phrase. (E) changes the adjective, for no reason.

9. C
Difficulty: High
Strategic Advice: Some adjectives and adverbs are easy to confuse.
Getting to the Answer: The underlined phrase uses the adverb *well* in place of the adjective *good* to describe how Julia felt. As an adjective, *well* relates to health, not happiness. Therefore, (C) is the best revision. (B) and (E), while adding an adjective and changing the preposition respectively, do not revise the original mistake. (D) incorrectly changes the meaning of the sentence.

10. E
Difficulty: High
Strategic Advice: In the underlined text the subject and verb do not agree, and the words *That night* tell us that the verb should be in the past tense.
Getting to the Answer: (E) corrects both errors. (B) changes the meaning of the phrase. (C) corrects the agreement problem, but not the tense. (D) does not work with the rest of the sentence.

11. C
Difficulty: High
Strategic Advice: Here you encounter a case of similar elements not being expressed in similar form.
Getting to the Answer: The sentence talks about *the creation ... establishing ... and purchasing*. In order to make this list parallel you need to replace the two gerunds with nouns, or the noun with a gerund. Look among the choices for either of these two options. Choice (C) changes everything to nouns—*the creation ... the establishment ... and the purchase*. All the other choices maintain the incorrect mix of nouns and gerunds.

12. D
Difficulty: Medium
Strategic Advice: Although there are some constructions that require the passive voice, it is generally preferable to use active verbs whenever possible.
Getting to the Answer: (A), (B), and (C) all use the passive voice. (D) and (E) make the prosecutor the subject and change the passive verb phrase "must be proven" to the active "must prove." However, (E) is awkwardly constructed and unclear, so (D) is the best choice.

13. B
Difficulty: Low
Strategic Advice: As written, this is a run-on sentence.
Getting to the Answer: Combining the two sentences by the use of a semicolon, as (B) does, corrects the error. (C) and (E) are both run-ons; (C) introduces an inconsistent verb tense as well. (D) is not idiomatic English.

14. E
Difficulty: Medium
Strategic Advice: When a sentence has more than one error, make sure your answer choice corrects all of them, without introducing any additional problems.
Getting to the Answer: This sentence has two errors. The verbs in the parallel structure are not in consistent form, and *nor* is used without *neither*. Since the first verb is the infinitive *to let*, the second should be *to go*. Only (E) reflects this; it also changes *nor* to the correct *or*. (B) and (C) do not change *nor* and each introduces a new, but still incorrect, verb form. (D) correctly replaces *nor* with *or*, but does not change the verb.

15. A
Difficulty: Medium
Strategic Advice: Expect sentences that have no errors.
Getting to the Answer: (B) is overly long and awkwardly constructed. In (C), the editor has lived in and written about New York for the same amount of time, which changes the meaning of the original sentence. (D) also changes the sentence's meaning, stating that the editor has written about New York for longer than he's lived there. (E) is incorrect grammatical structure.

16. B
Difficulty: Medium
Strategic Advice: Make sure descriptive words and phrases are used logically.
Getting to the Answer: As written, this sentence has pictures looking through a yearbook. (B) corrects the error without introducing a new problem. (C) changes the verb tense, but does not correct the problem. (D) creates a run-on sentence. (E) doesn't include a subject in the first clause.

17. D
Difficulty: Medium
Strategic Advice: The relative pronoun *which* is not correct when referring to people; *who* is the proper pronoun in this case.
Getting to the Answer: (C), (D), and (E) all correctly change *which* to *who*, but (C) introduces an incorrect verb tense, and (E) misuses the semicolon, because *those of us* is the subject of the verb *want*.

18. D
Difficulty: Medium
Strategic Advice: As written, *underestimating the demand* modifies *tickets* and not *broker*.
Getting to the Answer: The sentence needs to be reworded. (D) makes the broker the subject of the dependent clause, thus eliminating the passive voice and making it clear who did the underestimating. (B) and (C) reword the sentence, but neither makes clear who or what underestimated the demand. (E) indicates that the office, not the broker, underestimated the demand.

19. E
Difficulty: High
Strategic Advice: Don't forget that (E) is the correct answer choice as many times as the other choices are.
Getting to the Answer: In the opening clause, the underlined word *because* is used correctly, and the verb tense *had downed* is also correct. The phrase *it appeared unlikely* (C) shows correct subject-verb agreement, and it also makes sense within the context of the sentence. (D) also shows the correct usage of the verb *would*, so there is no error in the sentence.

20. C
Difficulty: Medium
Strategic Advice: Be sure that all parts of the sentence are in the same tense.
Getting to the Answer: (C) is the past tense form of the verb *distinguish* which cannot be used with *could*, and therefore (C) is the correct answer. (A) is a prepositional phrase in which both the preposition and the verb tense are correct. (B) is the adjective *darkened*, an appropriate descriptive word for a stage.

(D) includes an adjective and a noun which are both correct in relation to each other and within the sentence.

21. D
Difficulty: Medium
Strategic Advice: Double negatives are not allowed in Standard English grammar.
Getting to the Answer: (A) is in correct form for the subject of the sentence. (B) is idiomatically correct, with an adverb modifying the verb. In (C) *for* is the correct preposition, and two appropriate adjectives describe *business*. In (D) *hardly never* is incorrect diction. Some people may speak this way, but it is an error in diction, or choice of language.

22. D
Difficulty: High
Strategic Advice: This is a tricky question. Be sure the pronoun use is logical.
Getting to the Answer: (D) incorrectly uses the relative pronoun *which* instead of *who* when referring to *the person*. (A) is the correct verb tense and number, and *thought to be* is the correct idiom. (B) is the correct number, matching *dreams*. (C) is an adjective modifying the noun *desires*.

23. C
Difficulty: Medium
Strategic Advice: A good rule of thumb is to always check that the subject agrees with the verb.
Getting to the Answer: The error in this sentence is the singular verb *has* in (C), because the subject *qualifications* is plural. Since *qualifications* is not underlined, the only way to correct this error is by changing the verb: *have the qualifications*. The perfect verb form is correct in (A) because it refers to actions the happened over the past year. (B) and (C) are idiomatically correct word choices. (D) is correctly an adverb, modifying the verb *challenged*.

24. D
Difficulty: Low
Strategic Advice: When more than one pronoun occurs in a sentence, both pronouns must be parallel.
Getting to the Answer: The pronoun *they* does not agree with the pronoun *one* already used in

the sentence. Since *one* is not underlined, this can be corrected only by replacing *they should* with *one should*. (A) is correctly in the present tense, (B) and (C) are idiomatically correct word choices.

25. E
Difficulty: Medium
Strategic Advice: Trust your ear. If all parts of the sentence sound correct, choose (E) and move on.
Getting to the Answer: (A) is a correct use of *when* to indicate time. (B) contains a possessive pronoun and adjective that appropriately describe the noun *wig*. The verb *performs* in (C) agrees with the subject *sister* and also with the previous present tense verbs (*is* and *pulls*). (D) is idiomatically correct.

26. A
Difficulty: Medium
Strategic Advice: A complete sentence requires both a subject and a verb.
Getting to the Answer: (A) is missing the crucial verb *is*, which should be placed between Richard II and the word *about*. Therefore (A) is the right answer. (B) is a verb in agreement with its subject *who*. (C) contains an adjective correctly modifying the noun *ruler*. (D) is introduced by an appropriate transition word, uses the pronoun *he* correctly to refer to Richard, and uses a verb with the correct tense and number.

27. C
Difficulty: Medium
Strategic Advice: Identify the subject of the sentence first, and then check that the rest of the parts agree.
Getting to the Answer: There is a problem with the plural pronoun *their* being used to refer to a particular university. If you were uncertain about whether using *their* to refer to the university was an error, seeing the singular *its* later in the sentence should have helped you decide.

28. A
Difficulty: Medium
Strategic Advice: Writers may confuse words that are similar in spelling, such as the verbs *raise* and *rise* and *lay* and *lie*. Make sure you understand the differences.

Getting to the Answer: In (A), though *which* is correctly used, the word *lays* is the wrong word. The writer should have used *lies*, which refers to the location of Florence. (B) is the correct verb tense and number. (C) correctly uses the transition word *therefore*. (D) is the correct verb tense and agrees with the subject, *Sicily*.

29. B
Difficulty: Medium
Strategic Advice: Look at the context and know what kind of change is needed before checking the answer choices.
Getting to the Answer: You probably recognized that sentence 2 and sentence 3 are very closely connected. So close, in fact, that they should be joined into one sentence. Look for the choice that does this. (A) Since you already determined that you need to do something, you can omit this choice. But don't forget to read choice (A) in Paragraph Corrections—it may not be the same as the original. (B) Here's a choice that does exactly what you want—it connects sentences 2 and 3. (C) If you place sentence 2 after sentence 4 you've removed it even further from sentence 2; that's the opposite of what you want to do. (D) The pronoun "one" is used correctly here. In this context, it's clear that it refers to a book about science. (E) There's no reason from a grammatical or stylistic point of view to omit sentence 3.

30. A
Difficulty: Low
Strategic Advice: You have to know the relationship between this sentence and the one before it (and perhaps the following one) before you consider the choices.
Getting to the Answer: As it stands now, this sentence is a run-on. It has two independent clauses. One way to correct that is to turn one of the clauses into a dependent clause by adding a conjunction and making one clause dependent. Four of the five choices (A through D) are conjunctions, so you need to choose the one that makes the most sense in context. It's clear that you need a contrast word because the sentence in contrasting the measurement latitude with that of longitude. (A) This is the contrast word you need. (B) This is a cause/effect word. (C) This is an addition word. (D) This is a cause/effect word. (E) This isn't a conjunction.

31. D
Difficulty: High
Strategic Advice: You don't know who *They* are at the beginning of this sentence.
Getting to the Answer: You need to find a place for this sentence that will clear this up. (A) You already determined that you need to do something with this sentence, so you can't leave it alone. (B) While changing a pronoun to a noun will often make a sentence clearer, in this case, "Scientists" is not the correct noun. (C) There's no need to start a new paragraph with this sentence. Remember, you need a new paragraph when you start a new idea to develop your essay. Furthermore, you still have the original problem of who "they" are. (D) This choice makes it clear that "They" are the ships' captains. It also provides the correct cause/effect conjunction "since." (E) By placing "Unfortunately" at the beginning of the sentence, you haven't corrected the problem of the antecedent for "They."

32. E
Difficulty: High
Strategic Advice: Whenever a question asks how to deal with a sentence, first determine its relationship to the sentences surrounding it and the passage as a whole.
Getting to the Answer: While the information provided in sentence 9 is interesting, and the Admiral's name is even more so, the sentence is unnecessary to the essay. You should omit choice (E). (A) If you leave it alone you haven't corrected the problem. (B) This would create a run-on sentence. (C) This change puts the sentence into passive voice, which is to be avoided when possible. In addition, the verb tense is incorrect. (D) The placement of these two parts of the sentence is fine; it's the sentence itself that needs to go.

33. E
Difficulty: Medium
Strategic Advice: Look at the sentence in context to determine why we might want to change the underlined portion.
Getting to the Answer: Since the events that the essay recounts took place in the 18th century, you need to put this verb into the past tense. (A) leaves the verb problem and replaces the correct conjunction *and* with the incorrect one *so.* (B) The

gets problem remains. (C) *Gets* is still there. (D) *Therefore* indicates a cause and effect that's not present in the sentence. (E) correctly changes gets to *got.* This is it.

34. C
Difficulty: Medium
Strategic Advice: The best concluding sentence will capture either the purpose of that paragraph or the purpose of the passage as a whole.
Getting to the Answer: Look for a choice that is consistent with sentence 14. (*Finally, when Harrison was eighty-three years old, the King and Parliament intervened and he gets his reward.*) (C) refers back to sentence 14 and is consistent with the information found there. (A) You can't tell from the essay what Harrison's feelings were when he got his reward. (B) This has nothing to do with Harrison finally getting the money that was promised to him. (D) This choice is incorrect for the same reason that (A) is—you can't know what Harrison's feelings from the information given to you in the essay. (E) While sentence 14 is talking about Harrison's reward, this sentence is talking about his chronometers.

CHAPTER NINE

Writing: Essays

Essay One

The essay gives you an opportunity to show how effectively you can develop and express ideas. You should, therefore, take care to develop your point of view, present your ideas logically and clearly, and use language precisely.

Your essay must be written on the lines provided on the following pages—you will receive no other paper on which to write. You will have enough space if you write on every line, avoid wide margins, and keep your handwriting to a reasonable size. Remember that people who are not familiar with your handwriting will read what you write. Try to write or print so that what you are writing is legible to those readers.

You have twenty-five minutes to write an essay on the topic assigned below. DO NOT WRITE ON ANOTHER TOPIC. AN OFF-TOPIC ESSAY WILL RECEIVE A SCORE OF ZERO.

Think carefully about the issue presented in the following excerpt and the assignment below.

Consider carefully the following excerpt and the assignment below it.

1. "When I examine myself and my methods of thought, I come close to the conclusion that the gift of fantasy has meant more to me than my talent for absorbing positive knowledge."
   Albert Einstein

2. "There is nothing more dreadful than imagination without taste."
   Johann Wolfgang von Goethe

Assignment: Do you believe that fantasy or imagination is more important than knowledge? Plan and write an essay in which you develop your point of view on this issue. Support your position with reasoning and examples taken from your reading, studies, experience, or observations.

DO NOT WRITE YOUR ESSAY IN YOUR TEST BOOK.
You will receive credit only for what you write on your answer sheet.

Essay Two

The essay gives you an opportunity to show how effectively you can develop and express ideas. You should, therefore, take care to develop your point of view, present your ideas logically and clearly, and use language precisely.

Your essay must be written on the lines provided on the following pages—you will receive no other paper on which to write. You will have enough space if you write on every line, avoid wide margins, and keep your handwriting to a reasonable size. Remember that people who are not familiar with your handwriting will read what you write. Try to write or print so that what you are writing is legible to those readers.

You have twenty-five minutes to write an essay on the topic assigned below. DO NOT WRITE ON ANOTHER TOPIC. AN OFF-TOPIC ESSAY WILL RECEIVE A SCORE OF ZERO.

Think carefully about the issue presented in the following excerpt and the assignment below.

"Courage is doing what you're afraid to do. There can be no courage unless you're scared."

Eddie Rickenbacker, *Fighting the Flying Circus*

Assignment: Does having courage mean that we have no fear, or that we act despite being afraid? Plan and write an essay that states an opinion on this question. Supply evidence for your opinion using examples from your observations, studies, or your own life.

DO NOT WRITE YOUR ESSAY IN YOUR TEST BOOK.
You will receive credit only for what you write on your answer sheet.

ESSAY ONE: EXPLANATIONS

Sample Grade 6 Essay

In my opinion, it may be hard to know whether the imagination or facts are most important, because we need them both. Without facts, scientists and inventors would have nothing to think about. But then again, being able to see things in your mind seems crucial to making new discoveries and inventing new products.

To conduct even a basic experiment requires an imagination. Scientists begin with what they know. Then they have to imagine a result so they can state a hypothesis or theory. Then, if experimenting can't prove the theory, the scientist has to combine the same facts or new ones and use his or her imagination again to make another educated guess.

In 2003, a robot was invented that could be controlled by a monkey's mind. Someone had to imagine the robot and to believe it was possible to build it. I believe that many people must have also been imagining this machine for a long time. For example, paraplegics might have dreamt of a useful invention like this. Some lazy people who have no handicaps might also fantasize about a machine that makes it so they never have to lift a finger.

Most inventive people are always using their imaginations. The man who invented the microwave oven was doing radar research, testing a new vacuum tube and noticed that the candy bar in his pocket melted. So he put a few popcorn kernels near the tube and they popped. Art Fry invented the post-it because he was irritated when his bookmark kept falling out of his hymnal at church. He worked with adhesives, and suddenly realized one of them would make a removable but secure bookmark.

I think most inventions result from combining facts and imagination. Perhaps that's what an imagination is, to combine facts in a unique and surprising way. In this way the imagination and information are partners in discovery.

Grader's Comments: This essay does well on all criteria, so it has earned a 6.

This essay demonstrates an especially strong grasp of the writing assignment, earning high points for topic, support, and organization. The author states a thesis in paragraph 1, and then provides several specific, relevant examples of how the imagination and facts are used together by both scientists and inventors.

The essay stays on track, using the writer's previous knowledge to discuss the topic comfortably. The writer uses key phrases such as "in my opinion," "but then again," "I believe that," and "for example," to link connected ideas. Vocabulary is strong (crucial, hypothesis and fantasize, for example). The closing paragraph sums up the writer's opinion.

Sample Grade 4 Essay

I think that for most people imagination is the most important thing. We all love superheroes, because they have superhuman traits that we can imagine ourselves having as well. In novels, normal people solve problems by using their imaginations. And the ideas a person thinks of that no one else thinks of, is what makes them the person that they are.

And anyway, people are always using their imaginations. Politicians need to have a vision for a better future. Then, advertisers try to get us to use our imaginations so we buy products we didn't even want. Then, this morning in geometry, our teacher asks us to use our imaginations to see the shapes of an equation. Then, in science, I always have to imagine black holes in outer space. In history, I have to imagine important places and things that happened. If I didn't use my imagination, I couldn't understand these facts.

The more I think about it, the more I realize that imagination is much more important to me than facts and information and anyway I like to use my imagination to reach my goals. When I have a problem, I usually solve it by imagining my way out. When I have a goal, such as winning the track competition, I always begin training by imagining myself winning. Then I can do the work I need to do. And anyway, if I was thinking only about facts, I would never even try.

Grader's Comments: This author attempted, with some success, to fulfill the assignment, but several of the references to literature and to the author's own experience are undeveloped and confused. Although you can guess what the author meant, there is not a clear explanation of why superheroes are interesting. In the final paragraph, the author begins to explain an example from his or her own life, but doesn't fully develop it with convincing details.

The essay has a moderately strong beginning, but the ending introduces new ideas rather than summing up the main ideas, so the reader does not have a good sense of completion.

The language and vocabulary in the essay could be improved. Phrases like "and anyway" distract the reader from meaning. In the second paragraph, the verb "asks" is the wrong tense, and the use of "then" is repetitive.

Overall, the essay looks like the writer began seriously thinking about the idea in the final paragraph. It would have been a better essay if the writer had spent a few minutes thinking and outlining ideas before beginning to write. Then one or two main ideas could have been better developed.

Sample Grade 2 Essay

My neighbor did something different that nobody did before and it was the start of a new idea. He learned to be a cook at a restaurant but in the town where we lived, nobody cooked anything but regular American food. He was from India. They are from India so my neighbor got this new idea to cook Indian food. So the first thing he did was make some stuff at home and we are his neighbors. We got to eat lots of new kinds of food. Some of it was not so good and we didn't like it and so, he wouldn't make it no more. And my sister came home late that night because she had missed the bus.

But some was good and then, he started a catering business. He would go to people's houses and make them the food. Everybody started to like it more and he got bigger and bigger and then he had more money and he opened up a restaurant of his own.

Our neighbor got a lot happier after he thought of his new idea and then he wanted to move back to India for awhile so he could learn more, but his family didn't really want to go. His daughter is in my class and she is good at math.

Grader's Comments: In this essay, the author addresses the general idea of using the imagination but does not present a point of view and tells a story that has very little logical organization. Many of the sentences are too long and have grammatical problems (like "he wouldn't make it no more" and "Some was good". The essay lacks a thesis statement and a closing summary and in general does not answer the assignment. The writer could use this story to write an acceptable essay, if each paragraph expressed ideas related to one another and related to the comparative importance of imagination and fact.

ESSAY TWO: EXPLANATIONS

Sample Grade 6 Essay

There are some very courageous people in this world. They are the ones who do things that the rest of us would be afraid to do. I never realized what it meant to be brave until read about the actions of the firefighters on September 11th. After that I formed my own definition of courage. It means to be without fear.

Firefighters are trained to do things that regular people would be horrified to even think of. When everyone is running away from smoke and flames, firefighters are running right into the heat. I imagine they go through rigorous training, learning to use their ropes and axes, learning what to do when there's not enough air to breathe, and learning to maneuver in dark, tight places. They can be trained to know what to do in a burning building. But there's no training that can teach someone to suppress all their natural instincts to run for safety. That is based on one thing: courage.

I think I used to take firefighters for granted. I would read newspaper articles about them rescuing a family from a third floor bedroom, for example, and not really think anything about it. That was just what firefighters were supposed to do. But when I read accounts of 9/11 it suddenly struck me how phenomenal their performance was. When I think back even now, I can recall the feeling of that day. Nobody knew what was going on or whether there would be more attacks. Everyone I talked to all across the country was scared. New Yorkers, of course, were especially frightened. And in the midst of that, these firefighters were climbing into their trucks and speeding toward ground zero. They were running through ash clouds into the buildings. And instead of just helping people come down the stairs, the firefighters charged up the stairs toward the flames. Loaded down with all their heavy equipment and clothes, they hauled themselves up thousands of steps, without stopping to wonder what lay ahead or what dangers there might be.

If these firefighters faced each new challenge with fear, and then had to stop and conquer their fear, they would never be able to take quick, forceful, incredible actions like these. Because of the tragedy of September 11th, I am convinced that some people truly do have courage, and that courage means to have no fear.

Grader's Comments: Although the ideas presented aren't particularly scholarly or startling, this author has done quite well. The essay uses a single, well-developed example to support the author's clearly stated opinion—sharply disagreeing with the quotation.

Descriptive, active phrases such as "climbing into trucks," "running from smoke and flames," and "hauled themselves up thousands of steps" make the essay more interesting than most. It sounds spontaneous and convincing.

This essay is well planned and organized, with an engaging introduction, three tightly-structured paragraphs of evidence, and a conclusion that follows from the evidence. The author uses keywords well to link sentences or ideas, such as "when," "but," "suddenly," and "of course." The author never digresses.

Although the whole essay deals with firefighters, the author's varied vocabulary avoids sounding repetitive. The writing and proofreading were done carefully: the spelling, grammar and diction are consistently correct.

Sample Grade 4 Essay

I used to think I was braver than my brother. That's because I thought that courage meant being wild and dangerous. But my brother changed my mind. Now I know bravery happens after you get scared and go do something anyhow.

My friends and I would set up skateboarding ramps, or ride our bikes full speed down the sand piles on the construction sites where they were building new houses.

I didn't think about falling at all. Helmets were a pain but my mom made me promise. My brother Stan would be reading books or building forts or something.

One day we were down there swimming in the quarry. There was a rock hanging over way up high. It was scary because if you didn't push out away from the cliff then you could hit the rocks when you jumped. I jumped off and even learned to dive.

Stan was too scared. So I thought that I was braver than he was.

It was late afternoon and most of the grown ups went home. I looked over and there was five big guys standing around Stan. They were teasing him and shoving a little.

I looked. I thought Stan would cry or beg or something. He said: "You think I'm a baby? Do you want to see me jump off?"

He climbed up the path and onto the rock. He looked down at the water.

I didn't think he could do it. But he did it. He jumped off and swam to shore and didn't get hurt.

Then I thought different. Stan was scared to jump. He jumped. I was wild but what Stan was was brave. Stan had real courage.

Grader's comments: The purpose of the essay is clear, and it accomplishes it with a compelling, well-developed anecdote. It stays on topic throughout and is organized in a logical, chronological fashion. The introduction is strong. The conclusion is weaker, because it does not directly revisit the opinion stated in the introduction.

The lack of keyword transitions makes this essay difficult to understand in several parts. For example, between the first and second paragraphs, the author jumps backward several years in time. An opening clause such as "when I was twelve…" would clarify that for the reader.

The author breaks his writing into new paragraphs where none are necessary. The third paragraph, for example, is a continuation of the second. This hinders comprehension as readers begin a new paragraph expecting a new idea.

Spelling and diction are generally good. The grammar is adequate, but there are a few examples of the wrong verb tense being used, such as "there was five guys standing around Stan."

Sample Grade 1 Essay

What is courage? I have wondered this for myself many times. Does having courage mean you have to climb Mt Everst? Does it mean that you need to go fight in a way? Or can you have corage if you just stay home and lead a kind of quiet life?

I think I'm a pretty brave person. I'm not a race car driver or something like that. But I don't run away from fights. I stick up for what I believe in. When I think I'm right I'm not afraid to tell other people what I feel even if they have the opposite opinion or something. I'm chosing my own course in life not letting other people tell me what to do. I'm going to chose the career I want and not the one my parents want me to. They want me to be an engineer because I like drawing. I don't want to be an engineer. I would consider being an architect but right now I still want to be an artist. I think I'm pretty brave in my own way.

Grader's comments: This author didn't read the assignment completely: The essay deals with the first part of the assignment, "what is a courageous person," but leaves out the crux of the question, the relationship between fear and courage. That makes this essay off topic. It digresses further toward the end, when the author begins to discuss his own personal predicament and fails to bring the discussion back to the general topic.

The language is adequate, with vocabulary that's easy to understand. But the author adds words and phrases that slow the reader down without adding meaning, such as: "or something," "in a way," and "kind of." There are several errors that may have been corrected after careful proofreading.